Brian Barder's
Diplomatic
Diary

Edited by
Louise Barder

Library of Congress Cataloging-in-Publication Data

Barder, Brian.

Paperback ISBN 978-1-944066-29-1

1 2 3 4 5 6 7 8 9 10

FOR JANE

CONTENTS

Introduction   7

Editor's Note   12

U.S.S.R., Early 1970s   15

Australia, Mid-1970s   107

Canada, and Around the World, Late 1970s   147

Ethiopia, Mid-1980s   171

Poland, Late 1980s   245

Nigeria, Late 1980s   269

Looking Back, Christmas 1992   299

Acknowledgements   306

INTRODUCTION

Sir Brian Barder, born on 20 June 1934, was one of the most prominent, dedicated, and influential British diplomats of the late 20th century. His *Diplomatic Diary* offers an insightful and entertaining glimpse of British foreign service life. Spanning two decades from the early 1970s, the diary takes us behind the scenes of Barder's career, from his first overseas posting in Moscow to his head-of-mission posts as ambassador to Ethiopia and Poland and high commissioner to Nigeria. We find him on the spot at moments of historical significance, whether playing cat-and-mouse with the KGB in Cold War Moscow, during the wave of tit-for-tat diplomatic expulsions that anticipated those taking place today, or being a driving force behind the realisation of British relief efforts to Ethiopia during the nation's devastating mid-1980s famine. Along the way, he rubbed shoulders with some of the most iconic political and cultural figures of the day, including Richard Nixon, Margaret Thatcher, and Muammar Qadhafi; Labour politicians Neil Kinnock and Tony Benn; novelist Chinua Achebe; classical musicians Benjamin Britten, Yehudi Menuhin, Witold Lutoslawski and Dmitri Shostakovich; pop star activist Bob Geldof; media baron Robert Maxwell; and double agent Kim Philby, among many others. An accomplished writer, Barder authored a popular blog, and his 2014 book, *What Diplomats Do*, was warmly received.

Jonathan Steele described Barder's life and career in an obituary in *The Guardian* a few weeks after his death on 17 September 2017. Steele's eloquent essay follows below.

Brian Barder, who has died aged 83, was one of the most energetic and politically committed diplomats of his generation. In retirement, he campaigned against injustices in the British legal system. From a range of postings from New York to Australia, the Soviet Union, Canada,

Brian in his retirement

Poland and Nigeria, his most gruelling but rewarding service came as Britain's ambassador in Addis Ababa during the great Ethiopian famine of 1984-85. As the crisis developed, he waited with trepidation at an airfield in the capital with his wife, Jane. Media barons such as Robert Maxwell and rock stars including Bob Geldof were helping to fuel massive media and parliamentary pressure for Britain to help to feed the millions of starving people.

The UK government decided to send three RAF Hercules freight planes with aid. But after constant effort Barder had still not managed to get official clearance for them to land. Ethiopia's socialist leadership was split, with hardliners arguing that no planes from a NATO air force should be allowed inside their country. Their main weapons supplier, the Soviet Union, took a similar line.

All that Barder could rely on was an unofficial last-minute telephone call from a senior member of the Ethiopian leadership, explaining that no agreement would be announced but the RAF planes would not be stopped from landing and could tacitly operate further flights.

It was a tenuous and easily deniable promise. As the Barders anxiously watched, the Hercules appeared in the African sky. There were no oil drums on the runway and no fighter planes ready to shoot them down. They landed safely and for the next 14 months regularly brought supplies for air drops to the famine-ridden highlands without ever getting official permission.

Beside the tension over the RAF's role, Barder had to cater for "famine tourists" or "grandstanders on ego trips" who, he later recalled, usually expected meals at the residence. He and Jane were happier to give hospitality to genuine relief workers when they came out of the highlands for a rare break.

Born in Bristol into relatively well-off circumstances, Brian was the son of Vivien (nee Young) and Harry, a descendant of Polish Jewish immigrants and a successful furrier. His parents separated when Brian was four, and he was sent to a boarding preparatory school and then Sherborne school, Dorset.

At St Catharine's College, Cambridge, where he gained a degree in classics, Barder was active in student politics and became chairman of the Labour Club. In 1956 he met Jane Cornwell when both were canvassing, and they married two years later. He remained a party member until his death, standing down for a few years towards the end of his diplomatic service only because he felt it was appropriate to be non-partisan while serving as an ambassador or high commissioner.

After taking the civil service exam he started in the Colonial Office in 1957, and in 1964 was sent to the UK desk at the UN on four-year secondment to what in 1967 became the Foreign and Commonwealth Office. It was the peak of decolonisation, and Barder met most of the leaders of the African independence movements, sparking his lifelong interest in the continent.

Back in London during the Biafra crisis in Nigeria, he made daily visits to Downing Street to brief Harold Wilson. During a stint in Moscow (1971-73) he was subjected to intimidation by KGB thugs who frequently jostled him and

Barder seated next to Lord
Caradon at the UN,
New York 1967

his wife in the lift going up to their flat in retaliation for the Heath government's astonishing decision to expel 105 Soviet diplomats as alleged spies.

As ambassador in Poland (1986-88) when the Solidarity trade union movement was still banned, Barder frequently met its leader Lech Wałęsa in the Gdansk shipyards. Other Solidarity activists were invited to the Warsaw embassy. These encounters were designed to offer them protection.

Barder was knighted in 1992, during his final diplomatic posting, as high commissioner to Australia (1991-94).

Barder awarded the KCMG in 1992 with his wife, Jane.

In 1997 he was invited to join the newly created Special Immigration Appeals Commission as its lay member, sitting alongside two judges. The layperson was required to have security clearance and experience in assessing secret intelligence, as the SIAC's job was to adjudicate cases of people whom the government wished to deport without giving defence lawyers the chance to know or challenge the reasons.

In 2004, when the home secretary, David Blunkett, gave the SIAC the additional job of examining the cases of people who were to be detained without trial because they were allegedly threats to Britain's security, Barder resigned. His opinion, later endorsed by the law lords, was that sending people to prison without charge or trial breached the UK's obligations under the European Convention on Human Rights.

Barder moved on to the issue of indeterminate sentences, a procedure also promoted by Blunkett whereby people could be sentenced on conviction to a "tariff" of a fixed number of years but then be held indefinitely in prison after serving the "tariff" if the authorities felt they would pose a threat to society on release. Barder considered it a Kafka-like system, since people had to refute subjective assessments about their future behaviour and there was almost no funding for them to make their case from behind bars or with adequate legal assistance.

Barder blogged and regularly had letters printed in *The Guardian* and other newspapers on issues including indeterminate sentences. Always convivial, he was a man of great generosity who was often contacted by partners or relatives of people given these unfair sentences, and he corresponded with many of them.

Barder with Australian Prime Minister Bob Hawke, early 1990s

When the Conservatives took power in 2010 Barder started informal contacts with the Ministry of Justice under Ken Clarke, who also deplored the system and was battling against Theresa May as home secretary to have it abolished. Though it was finally stopped in 2012, some 2,200 prisoners who had been given these sentences before abolition and have served their tariff are still in custody today.

In 2014 Barder published *What Diplomats Do*, an imaginary account of the typical duties and challenges faced by a diplomat as he or she progresses up the career ladder, interspersed by reminiscences of key events in his own life. The book is probably the most useful introduction currently available for anyone thinking of diplomacy as a career.

He is survived by Jane and their children, Virginia, Louise and Owen.

• Brian Leon Barder, diplomat and civil rights campaigner, born 20 June 1934; died 19 September 2017

The Guardian, 3 October 2017. *(Reprinted with permission.)*

Editor's Note

In July 2017, just a few months before my father's death, I was with both my parents when they stumbled on my dad's "diplomatic" diary: a full binder of A4 sheets that he had typed up regularly during his overseas postings, writing down his experiences living and working abroad during his 20+ years as a career diplomat. I read a few passages from the binder aloud to my parents – some were fascinating, some laugh-out-loud funny, and some poignant. I suggested that the diary was eminently publishable, and my father laughed and gave his hearty permission for me to pursue this possibility. He seemed tickled pink by the idea.

My father started the diary when he took up his first overseas posting at the British Embassy in Moscow (U.S.S.R.) in 1971, and stopped writing it during his stint as High Commissioner in Lagos in 1990 – just a few years before his retirement in 1994. The diary covers episodes from his daily life as a diplomat, including notable events, journeys, meetings, visits (both to and from friends, colleagues, dignitaries and celebrities), incidents, holidays, and parties, etc., as well as describing the details and challenges of daily life as a diplomat abroad with a young family in tow. The episodes vary in frequency and length/time-span, depending apparently on how often and how much time he was able to devote to writing. He didn't write about his postings in London or his mid-post "home leaves" (with one exception). There are several letters – addressed to specific people – in among the diary entries, a couple of them written by my mother, Jane

Barder. I have included these letters (with some private material redacted) because they were included in among my father's diary pages, and they read very much like the diary entries; I believe my father intended for them to be read as part of his diary. Similarly, a few "round-robin" letters sent to friends around Christmas and the New Year (again, a couple of them written by my mother) are included for the same reasons. In the diary itself, my father occasionally writes in the second person – to an unspecified "you". It's my understanding that he wrote the diaries with a particular close friend (or friends) in mind.

My father typed his diary entries on any typewriter he could find during his postings abroad; then, periodically, he would Xerox* several pages and send copies to his friends and family back home and around the world. He was a proficient and accurate typist, and – perhaps more importantly – an eloquent and florid writer who was creative and playful with his words, often deliberately breaking rules of grammar, punctuation or spelling to witty, emphatic or descriptive effect.

In re-typing and then copy-editing my father's prose I have done my best to reproduce his texts faithfully and verbatim. What you read is for the most part exactly what he wrote and how he wrote it. On the rare occasions that I believe my father made a genuine typo, I've corrected it. Similarly I've corrected any rare but obvious spelling mistakes. I've left all the spelling inconsistencies and quirks as is, since my father was writing over a period of more than 20 years, during which time there were plenty of variations and changes in spelling norms, both in his own writing and in standard English. Some of the spellings are mighty old-fashioned.

Please remember that my father was writing his thoughts and observations at the time of the events he was describing – in the '70s and '80s when we were all far less sensitive and politically correct than we are today. Like many others of his age and generation, and especially given some of the challenging places, situations and people he encountered during his career, he could be guilty of being a bit snarky and sexist – but even then his observations were invariably softened by affectionate irony and humor. I haven't edited these 'dodgy' words or passages, with only one or two exceptions where I felt a word might cause real offence today. In those cases I've replaced the offending words or phrases with ellipses.

In a few cases, when I felt it was appropriate or necessary, I have replaced full names with initials to protect the privacy and identity of certain individuals.

— Louise Barder, May 2019

Xerox: probably what he would have called photocopying back in the '70s and '80s

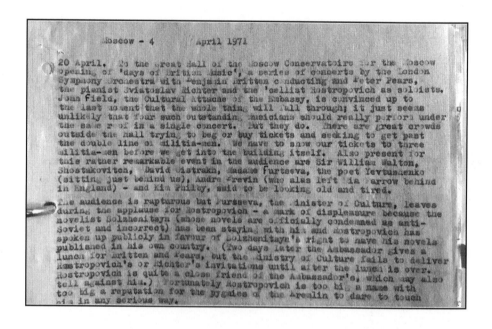

PART I

U.S.S.R.,
EARLY 1970S

CHAPTER 1

FEB–MARCH 1971: MOSCOW

16 February.   Arrive at Sheremetievo Airport. Everyone on the aircraft wraps up in layer upon layer of clothes, scarves, hats, fur gloves, etc. The air as we step out is crisp but doesn't strike particularly cold. Snow everywhere. The Scotts (Ken and Gay) are there behind the barrier as we queue to have our passports inspected: reassuring to see familiar faces immediately, even if not all that familiar. A certain amount of amiable muddle over customs clearance for our baggage, but not on the scale of (say) Cairo or Istanbul. We are through all the formalities in about 15 minutes which compares favourably with Heathrow. Into Moscow (about 40 minutes) by two Embassy cars: Jane and Gay with the girls in the first, Ken, Patricia and I with Owen in the second. On the way Ken gives me a daunting programme for the first few days: this evening (it is already five o'clock) a cock-tail party, tomorrow a press conference at the cultural department of the Soviet Foreign Ministry, a lunch with Western press correspondents, another cocktail party, two dinners ….

Wide two-lane highway, clear of snow, into Moscow, with flat featureless fields on each side and occasional clusters of dilapidated wooden huts and houses. Occasional small shops. Gradually we come on clusters of large off-white apart-ment blocks: functional, even ugly, but not strikingly offensive. Then the density rises and we are in Moscow. Some pale green and brick brown buildings, a few quite ornate, some with character and attractively quirky. Thick crowds in all the streets doing nothing discernible except trudge along, stand in vast queues at bus stops, crowd round unremarkable shop windows. Everyone in big dark hats, dark coats, heavy shoes or boots. But not badly or poorly dressed: just not very colourful. What are they all doing out in the streets on a week-day afternoon?

Past Lenin Stadium, the Moscow Dynamo ground, some ornate late-Victorian skyscraper blocks fantastically decorated, one of two snow-laden squares and small parks. Suddenly we are at the apartment block where our flat is: Kutuzovsky Prospekt, all occupied by foreign diplomats or newspaper correspondents, cut off from the nearby Russian residents by high wire netting fences. High (ten or eleven storey) buildings in grey-brown brick: no architectural or aesthetic pretensions, functional, heavy. Up in an apparently antiquated little lift (notice on the gates of which says: "Before opening the door, be sure that the lift is present, so as not to fall down the shaft") to the fifth floor and flat 9/10 (it used to be two, 9 and 10, and they were knocked into one). Inside the front door is our air freight, sent off from Chelsea only last Friday, all apparently intact. Splendid.

The flat is better than we expected. Rooms smaller than ours in Beckenham and much smaller than in New York, but adequate (or so we think at first glance). Bathrooms (two) pretty ropey. Kitchen note over-large but with a good fridge and quite a lot of cupboard space. Fridge turns out to be well stocked with food, tea, bread, milk, meat, etc.; and a bottle of whisky and a bottle of gin in the dining room, along with enough beer for a few days. A good welcome.

17 February.   It turns out that there are many others from the British Embassy in the same building: some we met at the Doyne-Ditmases' cocktail party last night. One gives me a lift into the Embassy in the morning. First glimpse of the Kremlin: high fortress walls, and the familiar golden onion-shaped domes glittering in the thin snowy sunlight. Am a little alarmed to see the car-starting ritual as we leave Kutuzovsky: long whinnying attempts to get the engine turning over, choke full out: finally a reluctant cough and the engine fires, and starts; then five full minutes of warming up while we attack the overnight ice and snow on the windows with scrapers, brushes and sprays. The windows have to be kept open all night to stop the condensation inside freezing on the interior glass as well as the external snow and ice formed during the night. "This has been a very mild winter, of course," says Nick Livingston. "Usually it's quite difficult to start – when the temperature gets down to about minus 30. Last night it was only about minus 20."

The Embassy is just across the river from the Kremlin with a splendid view of it. Am introduced to about forty people in ten minutes and end up not remembering who any of them are or what they do. Everyone very friendly and encouraging.

Press conference at the cultural department of the Foreign Ministry. Confirmation that my Russian isn't up to it. Peer over Ken Scott's shoulder and try to read his notes: "USSR has cultural links with 78 (178?) states .... Student exchanges ... priority for other socialist countries.... Africa... Asia.... Shakespeare...." David Bonavia of 'The Times' asks a pointed question afterwards about Solzhenitsyn and the ban on foreign tours by the cellist Rostropovitch. Lunkov, big and square in double breasted suit and wide trousers, is not embarrassed. "Rostropovitch owes a duty to the Soviet people as well as to people overseas. It has been decided that for a while he will play to Soviet audiences. His foreign tour has been postponed, not cancelled." He repeats the last phrase in English.

Meet various journalists and other press attaches. Sit next to another large square Russian (also from cultural department of the Ministry). He gives me an enormous boiled sweet when I start coughing. Kindness, no doubt. Also to prevent his boss's press conference being drowned out by my coughing.

18 February.   The heavy luggage arrives. Flat full to the ceilings in every room with huge cardboard boxes full of everything we possess. It's wonderful to have it so soon but where is everything to go? Spend half the night wading about in seas of wrapping paper, fixing electric plugs to things, gingerly unwrapping our two or three hundred glasses, each individually wrapped.... Jane exhausted.

19 February.   Begin the routine of trying to read Pravda (in the morning) and Izvestya (in the evening). Have to be ready to hold forth at the morning Embassy meeting (presided over by the Ambassador) on anything of interest in these newspapers on "my" areas of the world: Europe, Africa, North America.

Both papers seem to be devoted exclusively to very long boring articles about these areas. Further confirmation that my Russian isn't good enough. Extreme difficulty of discovering what each article is about without reading the whole of it first. Headlines say only such things as "Struggle of the people" or "Further Imperialist Provocation" – which could be anything from the new 5-year plan to a commentary on the latest Warsaw Pact Meeting in Bucharest. Seem to be up until 1.30 a.m. trying to decipher Izvestya.

20 February. Go in the evening to an American party to see a film. Turn up one hour early owing to misunderstanding of (telephone) invitation. Much embarrassment. Eventually others arrive (all American). Drink a good deal of Bourbon to cover embarrassment. Watch film ("A Lion in Winter") – projected in full Cinemascope wide screen on the living room wall, long and thin like a strip cartoon. Sound very loud and blurred. Film very long. Quite good, but very long. Long pauses between reels for more Bourbon, ham sandwiches, etc. Eventually leave in driving snow at about one a.m. Get hopelessly lost on the way home. Back at about two. Settle down to read Izvestya. Bed at 3.30. How long can this go on?

This morning the car arrived. Went out in an Embassy car with (non-English-speaking) Embassy driver to collect it. Interminable form-filling before we go round to a sort of snow-covered railway goods yard. There is the car in a long line of vehicles, delivered by rail from Helsinki. It's covered in a thick layer of grey ice, with icicles as thick as a man's arm suspended from it. Discover that the front door window is missing and has a piece of cardboard wired crudely across the gap. The windscreen has been crushed and cracked across one corner. But miraculously it starts after only a couple of attempts. Scrape off some ice, disconsolate about damage. Find glove compartment door has been broken, one seat belt cut off and removed, general air of some maniac having been loose in the car at some stage of its journey. But it goes. Arrive back at the Embassy in it, very late for the Ambassador's lunch for the Maltese Ambassador.

21 February. Finding one's way around in the car is a nightmare. Each road junction has its own rules. Sometimes these can be deduced from the lines on the road (unless these are covered up with snow) or from signs suspended high above the traffic; more often they can't. You just get to know them. You can hardly ever turn left; sometimes you can do a U-turn, usually not; often you can't turn right, for no perceptible reason. A militiaman stands at almost every junction blowing his whistle at those whose behavior displeases him, and inspecting the documents of serious offenders. An intricate system of underpasses (especially at the numerous bridges and at the junctions of the various ring roads) adds to the confusion. Hardly any of the streets have signs up showing what they are called, but this makes no difference because there is no street map of Moscow anyway. It must all be for abstruse reasons of security.

22 February.   Everyone says that Moscow is drab, and so it is, but there is a good sprinkling of modern buildings and some splashes of colour. No advertisement hoardings, of course. But instead there are gigantic red and white banners with slogans, yards high, proclaiming "Glory to the great Soviet People" or "The Communist Party has achieved fresh successes".

We try the metro (tube trains) and get lost. But we admire the incredibly ornate and lavish metro stations, all marble, statues and chandeliers. Our colourful Anglo-American clothes attract much rather dour attention. Also the car. There's little traffic for a major city, and, except for the diplomats and occasional ministers in vast black monsters with curtains drawn across the back windows, the bulk of the cars are little chugging "Moskvitch" efforts which cost a fortune. When a Ministerial car appears the militiamen clear the fast lane of the road to let them whizz by. Not very democratic.

25 February.   The incessant round of lunches, cocktail parties, dinners, continues. Am becoming accustomed to returning, dazed with beer on Courvoisier on claret on Chablis on Scotch, to tramp through Izvestya in the small hours. Cocktail party with the Head of Chancery (and my predecessor) Ken Scott tonight, one of three he is giving for the entire Embassy staff down to the humblest Chancery guard: the first for names beginning with A to H, the second for I to P, the third for Q to Z. Meet about forty new people including assorted wives. Realise afterwards that I have no idea what any one of them is called, whereas all of them will now know me and expect me to know them.

4 March. Go to a "kino-coktel" (cocktail party with film show) at the Chinese Embassy. It is a vast, imposing structure, lavishly ornate, with gigantic rooms and lofty ceilings. Shake hands with two Mao-suited anonymous Chinese on entry, return their ferocious smiles, and see no other Chinese until we leave. Served with very small glasses of pink sweet wine and are ushered almost immediately into a vast cinema, passing on the way a huge room done up as a grotto, with lake, fountains, nymphs, etc. Sit in large arm chairs covered with grey dust-covers. Film begins. Colour, very loud sound-track of singing, martial orders, martial music, all fortissimo. A sort of stylized folk opera depicting adventures of Communist guerrillas fighting in Northern China against Kuo Mintang in 1946. Much dancing, rushing forward of soldiers, striking of militant poses, speeches about Mao leadership. Story unintelligible but goodies easily distinguishable from baddies. (Latter have greenish make-up.) All performed on wooden stage with billowing painted backdrop of mountains, trees, snow, etc. Fall asleep after first hour and a half despite competition with soundtrack from another loud-speaker at the back of the hall over which someone is thoughtfully interpreting the Chinese into Russian, also fortissimo. Finally it finishes and we are ushered into yet another huge room, this time with long tables laid with delicious Chinese food and bottles of less delicious Chinese wine. On a dais at the far end, looking weirdly over the proceedings as we fight each other to get at the chicken and bamboo shoots, stands a twice-life-size statue of Mao, done in what appears to be white plastic. Chat desultorily with a Pakistan Airlines official and a Zambian second secretary. All agree that the film set new records for earsplitting tedium.

5 March. Jane's driving instructor appears. Very friendly, cheerful, much heel-clicking, bowing, shaking hands. He is called Alexandrovich. He does not speak English. Communication seems likely to be difficult but in fact he seems able to signal his meaning in some strange sub-linguistic – or perhaps supra-linguistic – manner. He forecasts that with about 25 lessons of theory "za stol" (at the table) and 10 of practice in the car, there will be no problem about passing the test. It seems typical of the Soviet approach that the test consists mainly of a prolonged theoretical examination about the fantastically convoluted Soviet traffic laws and only about ten minutes perfunctory driving in a car to see if the candidate can actually drive.

7 March (Sunday).　　We drive out to the Embassy dacha to spend the day, and have lunch, with the other first secretaries and their families – the Ratfords (commercial) and the Nicholsons (Soviet internal affairs). The dacha is only 40 minutes away, still in the outskirts of Moscow, but on an island musically called Serebryanny Bor (silver pine forest). There are a number of dachas quite to-gether, crumbling villas with a vaguely Victorian air and an agreeable surrounding of pine forest and snow-covered fields. Round the back there is an open area with an inlet of the river curving in to form a sort of lake, with bridges and banks. The water is frozen and covered with snow, but on one stretch of it about twenty men and a few women are busy cutting the ice into large squares and hauling them up onto the bank, revealing blackish stagnant water beneath. Up a little path is a car-avan converted into a sort of sauna bath with a smoking chimney. They actually plunge into these icy waters from the sauna when they have cooked themselves for a while in the caravan. No wonder they put up with Mr Brezhnev.

On the fields and slopes around people in relatively brightly coloured clothes are ski-ing, Russian/Finnish fashion – not much like the Alpine or Swiss variety, with slaloms and swoops down steep hills, but done mainly on the flat, briskly, and covering considerable mileages in quite a short time. The skis, so we are told, are different, with different edges and boot fastenings which allow the heel to come up off the ski. We are already beginning to accumulate second-hand skis from people who will have left by next winter and hope to embark on this strange and bracing occupation next autumn.

10 March.　　Much colder. It has been about -20° centigrade in the night. When I try to start the car in the vast ice and snow-covered car parking area outside the Kutuzovsky diplomatic compound it turns the engine over quite nicely but there is no sign of a spark. I squirt special aerosol cold-starting fluid up the air cleaner intake and try again but by now the carburetor seems to be flooded. I leave it for five minutes while I attempt to scrape off the night's ice from the windows, and try again. Still no sign of firing. By now I am afraid of running down the battery. Some other British Embassy people come out and, seeing a comrade in difficulty, come over to offer help. They take it in turns to try starting the Cortina. Each has his own theory about how this should be done. Some advocate pumping the accelerator, others warn not to touch it until the engine is running. No-one can start it. We fix jump-leads to the battery of another British car and try again. Not a cough. More squirts from the aerosol. By now a crowd has collected, mainly British. All are full of tips and suggestions. Two produce tow-ropes and offer a tow to get the thing started – or alternatively to get it to the Embassy and the Embassy mechanics. I accept one. The rest scrape off their cars and vanish in clouds of exhaust down Kutuzovsky Prospekt and Kalinina towards the Embassy. The other, Mike Hewitt, the assistant administration officer, and I wrestle for half an hour with the tow rope and eventually after much manhandling get both cars lined up and roped together. But the weight of the Cortina proves too much and the Hewitt car's wheels spin helplessly on the ice. We unhook the rope and I get a lift into the Embassy with Mike. An Embassy driver goes out later in the morning for the Cortina, and starts it on the first touch of the button, drives it in to the Embassy for me, and explains that I should not have touched the accelerator before trying to start the car. Later the head driver expresses sympathy and explains that the trick is to pump the accelerator five times before switching on. The Embassy accountant, an attractive girl in a shiny black maxi-coat, says the thing to do in cold weather is to pump the *clutch* pedal four times.

17 March.   Cocktail party at the American Embassy to meet some visiting State Department bigwigs. Chat to various American press correspondents. These are the main victims of KGB harassment: if they write unfavourable pieces they get waylaid outside their apartments or on their way out of restaurants by KGB thugs in square coats, and jostled or pushed around or even in one or two cases quite badly beaten up – sometimes while their small children look on. Breaking the windows of their cars is another favourite method of expressing differences of view. Part of the object of all this is to discourage them from having contact with dissidents in Moscow – especially Jews who want to emigrate but can't get permission. Diplomats on the whole are spared this treatment because of (a) the Soviet fear of retaliation against their diplomats overseas, (b) their immunity, and (c) their general lack of contact with dissidents.

Talk to the doyen of the Moscow press corps, Henry Shapiro of United Press International, who has been here off and on since the Thirties. He is mortally offended at having been asked for means of identification by the militiaman outside the French Embassy the other day. Shapiro, a little fellow about five feet tall, pushed the militiaman aside and stalked into the Embassy. "He should know my face by now."

19 March. Our first dinner party. Almost everyone rings up during the 72 hours beforehand and explains that although they had accepted, they now find that to their immense regret they can't come after all. We spend the day frantically ringing round the few people we know trying to find someone free to come and fill the gaps. A few agree reluctantly although several say they can't arrive until after nine p.m. A French woman talks from the moment of her arrival until she leaves at 1.30 a.m., without pausing for breath. When she finally submits to being dragged away, everyone else is more than half asleep. Our Russian maid, Zena, performs just adequately, her face pink with effort and embarrassment. She's a nice friendly girl who probably doesn't fully realise the real purpose of the reports she has to make every week on us.

30 March. Suddenly the weather is much warmer and there is a golden sun in a pale blue sky. The snow begins to melt into huge pools and muddy puddles. The car is covered in a thick film of mud as soon as I take it out. Everyone says it is too early to be spring.

1 April. Snowing. Ice on the windscreen.

2 April. Sunny and warm again. Our wedding anniversary. We celebrate by going to one of the best recommended restaurants in Moscow, the Uzbekistan (with Uzbek food). We have to use my diplomatic identity card to get in past the throng of people outside the door struggling to get in. (Only senior party members and diplomats are allowed to book tables in advance.) An enormous meal – cabbage and fried onion salad, sundry coleslaws, various cold meats, and then an individual portable barbecue of savoury hamburger, beef and lamb with potatoes and sauce. Much Moldavian white wine. A band plays deafening Glenn Miller type dance music and an improbable blonde sings very loudly into a distorting microphone. People dance in 1955 style. There seem to be Uzbeks here and there. How did they get in?

The impossibility of finding one's way around Moscow in a car, already virtually absolute because of the capricious system of traffic rules and the mad road network, is now compounded by the presence of 5000 delegates to the 24th Party Congress. Bridges, roads, etc. closed. Find our way back to Kutuzovsky by inspired guesswork.

CHAPTER 2

APRIL-MAY 1971: MOSCOW

9 April. Good Friday – not a Soviet feast, naturally. Beautiful crisp sunny weather, like an ideal English spring day. Tempted by the description in our (Soviet) guide book of a little old street in the centre of Moscow, Kuznetsky Most, as a quaint and unspoiled example of an old Moscow shopping street, we all go off there. It is very ordinary. The quaintness has to be taken on trust. We stop at every little kiosk and at Moscow's sole map shop, which happens to be in Kuznetsky Most, to ask for a metro (tube stations) and bus lines map: but the answer everywhere is 'Nyet'. This must be the only major capital in the world where there is no telephone directory, no street map (except a fanciful thing for tourists which bears not the smallest resemblance to the streets on the ground) and no transport map of any kind. Luckily a military attaché from the American Embassy whom we met at a party has sent us the only good map of Moscow which exists. It is printed in Washington D.C. and is very hard to get.

11 April. We go to the Moscow circus. Excellent. A small, cosy building next to the very picturesque, multi-storey Central Market. (They have almost finished a new circus building which will seat thousands and, no doubt, have no character at all.) The performance begins with all the lights being turned out, and a large tin rocket, belching flames and smoke, being hauled up into the roof, clanging loudly as it hits the pulley at the top; and then two acrobats in luminous costumes swing about high above our heads on invisible trapezes. All this terrifies Owen and Louise who hide their heads in our rib-cages. Later the lights go up and they venture out of our rib-cages and enjoy the rest of the show greatly. All the traditional acts are there, with clowns, jugglers, people doing things on grimly circulating horses, animals performing tricks for the benefit of ladies in black tights with whips (very kinky, this), tight-rope walkers and a gigantic band which plays with passive disinterest very loudly, and includes (rather less usually) massed strings. One animal act boasts three bears, a wart-hog, five rats, assorted birds, a porcupine and a pig. The girls vary in age from about 20 to 50 but all have in common the fatal Russian tendency to stoutness – all too visible in circus costumes of leotards, bikinis and so forth. So this unique example of Soviet permissiveness turns out to be quite untitillating because of all those rolls of fat. This has to be the least sexy society in the world. No wonder they have so few children.

12 April. Easter Monday. The weather has been fine and sunny for two weeks so we set off with a picnic lunch for what is about the only tourist spot worth seeing which is outside Moscow, but inside the 40-kilometer limit (beyond which diplomats may not venture unless they have obtained permission from the Soviet Government 48 hours in advance) – namely Archangelskoye, formerly the country residence of Prince Yussupov and now a museum, in beautiful rolling wooded country to the north-west of the city, about 20 miles away. As we turn out of the diplomatic ghetto past the militia boxes which "guard" us, it begins to rain. It rains more and more heavily until by the time we get to Archangelskoye it is coming down in torrents. We park at the vast empty car-park and toil, sopping, up the hill to the house, which is shut. We toil back down the hill and return to the car, steaming. Eat lunch beside the road with the rain pattering on the roof. Later, on the way back into Moscow, we stop at a red traffic light, until it turns green, when we turn right. As we do so, a militiaman blowing his whistle rushes out from his little box at the crossroads and motions me in to the side. He comes over to my window and says in Russian something to the effect that I have committed an offence. I say that I stopped at the red light and proceeded only when it changed. He beckons me to get out. We walk in the rain together back to where I stopped. He points to a small wooden sign on the side of the road about two cars' lengths before the traffic lights. It says 'STOP' – and apparently means that if you have to stop at all for the traffic lights, you should stop there and not at the lights themselves. I find tiny traces of white paint on the road and point out to the militiaman that there was once a line there which is now worn right away. He agrees but again points to the little sign. He orders me to accompany him to his little box. "Documents." I produce my Russian driving licence and my diplomatic identity card. He writes my name and Embassy laboriously in an enormous ledger, then demands my 'talon' – the card issued to all drivers in which militiamen punch holes when a "gross offence" is committed: three holes punched and you lose your licence, and no right of appeal at any point. All diplomats keep their 'talons' safely in their Embassies so as not to be subjected to this arbitrary justice. I explain that my talon is in the Embassy. Militiaman becomes apoplectic and says he will insist on its production from the Embassy. I invite him to address himself to the Ministry of Foreign Affairs – the prescribed drill. Eventually he reluctantly returns my licence and we move off. All very tiresome and rather distressing, but it turns out that this sort of minor persecution happens to everyone all the time. Unfortunately our diplomatic licence plate numbers identify our country of origin – all the British cars are '01' – so it is easy to single out the imperialists, westerners and capitalists for petty harassment.

In the afternoon Ken Scott, my head of chancery, rings up to see whether we are free to go with him and Gay that evening to the Bolshoy to see Mussorgsky's opera Boris Godunov. We jump at this. The Bolshoy is extremely impressive – all imperial gold leaf, chandeliers and huge framed mirrors, like a sort of Palladium in good taste. The only sign of Sovietisation of this Csarist magnificence is the hammer and sickle motif worked unobtrusively into the enormous red velvet curtains. The stage is unquestionably the hugest I have ever seen, stretching back almost as far as the eye can see – and revolving, so that there is as much again behind what can be seen. The sets are of an almost unimaginable lavishness: this is real spectacle on a Cecil B de Mille scale but, again, in superb taste. The coronation scene outside St Basil's cathedral in what is now Red Square, with a colossal set and a coronation parade of hundreds of magnificently costumed people, Orthodox priests in gorgeous robes with huge banners and ikons, noblemen in equally splendid costumes, and finally the Csar himself, preceded by a Boyar throwing handfuls of silver coins at his feet, while the gigantic choir sings massive music and the big Bolshoy orchestra thunders out the Mussorgsky with uninhibited relish, is unforgettable.

Afterwards back to the Scotts' capacious flat for steak and (Russian) champagne, the champagne having been contributed by ourselves.

13 April. Lunch at the Residence (on the floor above the Embassy offices) given by the Ambassador for a visiting delegation from the Greater London Council, led by its Chairman, Peter Black, and Leader, Desmond Plummer. The Mayor of Moscow attends – a real burly party boss in the style of Mayor Daley of Chicago. He tells the Ambassador that he prefers summer to winter because in summer he can go to his dacha in the country where reception of the BBC is so much better than in Moscow.

16 April. Brezhnev's nightmare, according to the more irreverent young Muscovites: Czechoslovakian soldiers in Red Square, eating matzos – with chopsticks....

17 April. Our deep freeze arrives from Copenhagen. Now at last we can buy up and store for weeks or months if necessary the excellent meat which appears at the diplomatic gastronom for a day or two and then vanishes again just when one has a dinner party coming up. Also J. will be able if she wants to prepare some of the more tedious dishes for our dinner parties a few days in advance, cook them and freeze them – thus avoiding a terrible rush on the day of the party itself. In the winter too it should be possible to continue to have some fresh vegetables which we'll buy and freeze in the summer. Handy too for storing milk: supplies come from Helsinki only once a week and the six of us crammed into the little flat – plus the maid, Zena, for lunch and tea five days a week – get through a fair amount. It keeps surprisingly well frozen.

We have booked a summer holiday at a cottage in Finland, on the west coast – not ideal, but all the lakeside cottages in central Finland which we have tried are fully booked by now. Tonight we have a Finnish couple to dinner and also the (Indian) correspondent of the 'Observer', Dev Murarka, and his (Dutch) wife. Dev and the Finn urge us to scrap the booking on the coast and continue the search for a lakeside place, even if we have to pay half as much again. Dev tells the correspondent of the Baltimore Sun (who has a Beatles-type moustache and is J's favourite person in Moscow for reasons which I don't entirely follow, although he's nice enough) that the United States is the source of all evil in the world; and me that the BBC should be called 'The Voice of Pakistan'. A second secretary from the Indian Embassy spends most of the evening trying to persuade Dev and myself to help him to get up a cricket team so that he can indulge his sole and consuming passion by playing cricket throughout the Moscow summer (heaven knows where or with what).

Jane, having been taking grueling and almost wholly theoretical driving lessons with a view to taking the bizarre Soviet driving test, has followed a casual tip and applied for a Soviet licence on the basis of her UK provisional (learner's) licence. Today the Soviet licence duly appears. This is really the higher lunacy of bureaucracy: the applicant produces a foreign licence (never mind whether it is a learner's or a qualified driver's) so she is entitled to a Soviet licence. So at last Jane can – legally – drive. What's more it is valid until 1966 – and she can legally use it for a whole year in the UK.... Being conscientious she decides to continue with driving lessons, but practical ones only. We are greatly concerned about how to explain to the Russian driving instructor the fact that she no longer needs to take the test, but he turns out to be tickled pink by the sight of the new licence and wants no explanation at all.

No sooner were we back from Archangelskoye last weekend than the rain dried up and the sun came out again for more idyllic, sunny weather, with blue cloudless skies. Today it's snowing hard, and freezing thickly on the windscreen.

20 April. To the Great Hall of the Moscow Conservatoire for the Moscow opening of 'days of British Music', a series of concerts by the London Symphony Orchestra with Benjamin Britten conducting and Peter Pears, the pianist Sviatoslav Richter and the 'cellist Rostropovich as soloists. John Field, the Cultural Attaché of the Embassy, is convinced up to the last moment that the whole thing will fall through; it just seems unlikely that four such outstanding musicians should really perform under the same roof in a single concert. But they do. There are great crowds outside the hall trying to beg or buy tickets and seeking to get past the double line of militia-men. We have to show our tickets to three militia-men before we get into the building itself. Also present for this rather remarkable event in the audience are Sir William Walton, Shostakovitch, David Oistrakh, Madame Furtseva, the poet Yevtushenko (sitting just behind us), Andre Previn (who alas left Mia Farrow behind in England) – and Kim Philby, said to be looking old and tired.

The audience is rapturous but Furseva, the Minister of Culture, leaves during the applause for Rostropovich – a mark of displeasure because the novelist Solzhenitsyn (whose novels are officially condemned as anti-Soviet and incorrect) has been staying with him and Rostropovich has spoken up publicly in favour of Solzhenitsyn's right to have his novels published in his own country. (Two days later the Ambassador gives a lunch for Britten and Pears, but the Ministry of Culture fails to deliver Rostropovich's or Richter's invitations until after the lunch is over. Rostropovich is quite a close friend of the Ambassador's, which may also tell against him.) Fortunately Rostropovich is too big a name with too big a reputation for the pygmies of the Kremlin to dare to touch him in any serious way.

21 April. I go to see the head of the British section of the press department of the Soviet Foreign Ministry to discuss press matters. The deputy head of the department, Fedorenko, joins us. After polite chat about nothing much, I mention that the Soviet press coverage of the Ulster situation seems to be disproportionate and excessively slanted. There are other stories about life in Britain besides Ulster but one never reads of them. Fedorenko growls that the British press never reports anything about the Soviet Union except praise of Solzhenitsyn – a very poor and unimportant writer whose work gives a bad smell. I point out that the British press has reported nothing of Solzhenitsyn for many months; that the press have shown interest in him not because of his excellence or lack of it as a writer but because people in the West feel that he should be allowed to publish what he writes in his own country; and that a very widely-held view in the West holds that he is an outstanding writer who brings much honour to the Soviet Union. At this Fedorenko gets up, goes over to the corner of the room and spits in the waste-paper basket.

22 April. After a week of summery, sunny days, the temperature is back to freezing and it is snowing quite hard.

In the evening we go to the flat of an American Military Attache to see the film 'Patton'. Patton, beautifully acted by George C. Scott, is portrayed as a mindless hoodlum with an obsessive blood-lust – and as a wholly admirable character. If there's a case for censorship this sort of perverted values surely ought to be banned. But the general view of those present seems to be that it's "a great movie".

24 April. Still icy cold with intermittent snow. I am to attend a ceremony at the BEA Office in the National Hotel, just opposite Red Square, at which some cricket equipment – bats, balls, stumps, coconut matting and so forth – is to be presented on behalf of the MCC, the Daily Express and BEA to an Indian student at Moscow's Lumumba University and a group of his friends who want to start up a cricket team at the University. The equipment has been brought out by a girl called Grace Mills of BEA, free of charge. Unfortunately the Soviet customs authorities impound the equipment at the airport and say that they cannot contemplate releasing it until next week. Grace Mills has to return to London today. Nevertheless we all assemble, with an Associate Press photographer (a Russian) in the BEA office. The Indian brings a Pakistani student, a Nepalese and a Nigerian – all keen would-be cricketers. They seem quite unsurprised that the equipment is not available. However Grace Mills turns out to be a splendid chick with very long legs in minuscule suede hot-pants and a see-through blouse. BEA public relations department obviously know their stuff. I am there as press attache – a rare perk, seeing to the photographing of Grace Mills. We troop out into Red Square which is closed for a parade of the Pioneers (boy scouts and guides, rehearsing for the 1st of May celebrations) and for an enormous queue waiting to visit Lenin's tomb. The photographer persuades the militia-men to let us in on the grounds that we are on important British Embassy and University business. He takes about a hundred photographs of Grace Mills and her hot-pants with a background of Indian, etc. students, the press attache, and Lenin's tomb with queue (also the Kremlin and St Basil's cathedral with its sugar-candy, multi-coloured twirling striped onion domes). Grace's hot-pants have a sensational effect on the Lenin queue, which becomes highly agitated. The militia seem about to intervene but apparently think better of it. Grace turns slowly blue with the intense cold. Eventually we run out of film, wrap Grace in a large coat and restore her to BEA. The Daily Express may possibly be publishing pictures of Miss Hot-pants and the Kremlin, but I doubt whether the cricket equipment or the press attache will get a mention.

The USSR announces to the foreign press through Tass that it has launched a 3-man space-craft to join the unmanned space station – but not a word of this appears on the Soviet radio, TV or press for a further 24 hours!

Britten and Pears are giving a private recital in the Embassy tonight for the Ambassador and his friends – including most of the other Ambassadors in Moscow, various eminent Soviet musicians and so forth. We are to attend as ushers, with two pages of instructions as to when the chairs are to be stacked away in the Blue room and when to put them out in the White room, who is to eat caviar in the Red room and who is to be content with sausage rolls in the dining room. It promises to be an almighty muddle.

*   *   *

24 April. Private recital by Britten and Pears in the Ambassador's residence on the first floor of the Embassy. The ornate nineteenth century rooms have been elaborately rearranged so that everyone can either see or hear. A favoured few – namely the other Ambassadors who are out in force – can see <u>and</u> hear. The rest are way behind in corridors and doorways on rows of canvas chairs. Before the performance we are all allocated jobs – welcoming guests on arrival, showing them where to put their coats, escorting them up the stairs, ascertaining their names, announcing them loud and clear to the Ambassador and Ambassadress at the head of the staircase, giving them programme and showing them to a seat appropriate to their importance, or lack of it. I am a greeter, coat-divester, shower-upstairs, identifier and announcer. I manage to select reasonably easy clients: the American Ambassador, Jake Beam; Gunnar Jarring, the Middle East mediator who is also Swedish Ambassador in Moscow in his spare time and who is easily recognizable; and, rather excitingly, no less a person than Dmitri Shostakovich, arguably the greatest living composer (come to hear the next greatest, Benjamin Britten, at the piano). Shostakovich shakes hands warmly, says "Zaravstsvuyte", has to be assisted up the stairs because he is so ill and frail. Other greeters are less fortunate, picking prima donnas who expect to be recognized and display considerable spite when they are not – Plisetskaya, the ballet dancer, some of the lesser musicians and most of the Ambassadors of medium and small powers are in this category. Richter and Oistrakh are of course recognized, as is Kyril Kondrashin, so that's all right. A group of wives stand in rows behind the Ambassador and Lady W., dispensing (duplicated) programmes, looking, as J. says, like ageing debutantes.

The concert goes on a very long time. Britten plays at a piano set up just outside the main bedroom door, Pears standing just behind it. Between groups of songs Britten and Pears disappear into the bedroom together in the approved manner.

28 April. I am giving a lunch for the British newspaper correspondents to meet the new Minister at the Embassy, Joe Dobbs. It proves to be an awkward day to have chosen because at the end of last week the Russians told us that David Miller, the second secretary in the internal affairs section of the Embassy, was to be expelled and he is actually leaving today. As is usual on these occasions we have not told the press and we are anxious that if possible David and Caroline and their baby should get home without publicity; but the Russians leak the story to Reuters shortly beforehand. Rumours are beginning to circulate although Reuters have agreed to freeze the story until David is safely home, unless of course it breaks elsewhere. We are doubtful of the chances of getting through lunch without at least one correspondent asking point-blank whether the rumours have any truth in them. Eventually we decide that as Reuters have it we may as well tell all, but embargo the story until the evening to enable David to get back first. We do so. Half-way through lunch however the Head of Chancery rings me up: a telegram has just arrived from London to say that the story has broken there and News Department in the Office are announcing it at 2 p.m. Moscow time. I return to the lunch table and announce this. People rush off to telephone to the UK (not, happily, at our expense) but they all conscientiously return to finish their coq-au-vin, so the occasion is not a total disaster. Never a dull moment in a press attaché's life. Even a part-time press attaché.

1 May. May-day – one of the two big Soviet holidays (the other is the anniversary of the October Revolution). It is raining intermittently and a bitterly cold wind is blowing. Nevertheless the parade straggles along Kutuzovsky Prospekt, where our diplomatic ghetto is, on its way to Red Square and the saluting base (where Ambassadors, Ministers and Counsellors are gathered, but not First

Secretaries – just as well in weather like this). I take the children out to see the procession. The banners and posters of Lenin are sodden, but the Party faithful don't seem bothered.

In the evening the usual firework display from various points of the city – almost all spectacular rockets, beginning precisely at 9.00 p.m. and stopping precisely at 9.10.

9 May.   Temperature about 88° and a blazing sun. We set off for the main diplomatic beach, at Uspenskoye – just inside the 40-kilometer limits and almost wholly confined to diplomats. It is of course a river-side beach, quite pretty, on a long bend in the river with open fields, gentle hills and some pine forests around. The place is stiff with East Germans, Bulgarians, Hungarians and Yugoslavs, mostly mountainously fat, playing obscure ball games and Russian transistor radios. Luckily we find a sort of Western enclave with only a few Americans and some other British, separated from the fat Bulgars by a small wood. There is sand here and the children look as if this is the first good thing that has happened to them since we left swinging Beckenham and the excitements of Lakeside.

11 May.   I discover that the Daily Express has (on about 29 April) printed quite a sizeable story about the non-arrival of the cricket gear for the Lumumba University students, and its non-handover in Red Square by the BEA girl in hot pants. There is a large picture of the girl, the students, and me, with a background of Kremlin and gaping Soviet populace. I am even correctly identified. Compensations for the rigours of (part time) press attaché life. It is anyway more palatable publicity than that accorded to poor David Miller, who had done nothing remotely wrong to deserve it except being a second secretary – and therefore the right grade for retaliation since we expelled a Soviet second secretary from London.

16 May.   We set off for an apparently interesting and attractive park and old pre-revolutionary country house on the outskirts of Moscow, Kuskovo. We follow the rather involved directions which we have had from one of the Embassy experts and find ourselves after several involuntary diversions driving alongside a railway line over which there appears to be no bridge. Kuskovo is just the other side. The map shows a bridge and our Embassy adviser said that he actually found, and used it; but we can't find it anywhere, amid a maze of minor roads. We ask three passing Russians – one of them obviously a local since he is filling his bucket at the communal water-pump – where the bridge over the railway is. One says he thinks there is a bridge but he can't remember where it is. The others both say that there is no bridge, that it is necessary to do a six or seven mile detour via the main outer ring road and that no other way exists. As we have insufficient petrol for this, we give up.

CHAPTER 3

MAY 1971:
LENINGRAD

20 May.   Leave at 11 p.m. from the Embassy for Leningradsky Station and the night train to Leningrad. I am accompanying Shura and Muriel Elkin: he a Leningrader by birth, age about six at the time of the Great October Revolution in Leningrad (then of course St Petersburg) in 1917, now legal adviser to the Foreign Office negotiating team at the Common Market talks. He is an old friend of the Ambassador. As he is of Russian origin and a fluent Russian speaker he is regarded by the Soviet authorities with special interest and so it is thought to be prudent to have him accompanied by someone from the Embassy in case the attentions of the KGB become too insistent. It is clearly a chance in a lifetime to be introduced to this famous city by someone who knows it well and has memories of the earth-shaking events there of 1917.

Moreover the ever-grateful taxpayer will foot the bill, or most of it. We decide reluctantly that we cannot afford to pay for Jane to come too but we agree to regard the trip as a reconnaissance for our own visit later.

The all-night train is a bulky, iron thing reminiscent of scenes in "Anna Karenina" (although disappointingly this one is electric!). The compartments are all four-bunk, without curtains or segregation by sex; so the possibilities are intriguing. Muriel Elkin, a woman with an Irish flash of fire in her, in her fifties, is sufficiently well-travelled not to appear unduly embarrassed at undressing for bed in front of me, and then watching while I do the same. Alas, the fourth occupant of our compartment turns out to be a cheerful but uninteresting man of forty-odd, returning to Leningrad with a huge electric type-writer of which he is extremely proud. It transpires that his father was in the Ministry of Foreign Trade and visited England a couple of times. No doubt our companion has been fairly carefully selected. He changes into a clinging sky-blue track-suit for sleep.

21 May. Glasses of hot, sweet black tea greet us: the first drinkable early-morning tea I have ever had. We steam into Leningrad Station punctually to the minute at 7.25 a.m. The Oktyabrskaya Hotel is just across the square: our rooms are ready (a privilege for which we shall have to pay as if we had spent the night there; fair enough, I suppose) and we separate to bath and shave, etc. The hotel is like most Soviet public places, rather cheerless and dull, paint peeling and carpets worn, with faded décor reminiscent of the Queen Elizabeth I.

The morning turns out warm and sunny. We walk down Nevsky Prospekt, one of the most celebrated streets in the world, which begins at the square outside the hotel. At the end is the golden spire of the old Admiralty building. It is a wide, fine thoroughfare, better than anything in Moscow, better kept and with brighter shops. We turn off and walk down Liteiny Prospekt to the Liteiny Bridge over the Neva, a magnificent broad sweeping river with noble buildings along both banks. Just beyond the fork in the river to our left lies the "Aurora", the cruiser whose shots fired in support of the Bolsheviks in 1917 began the modern era. I leave the Elkins to visit the Leningrad office of the Ministry of Foreign Affairs, mainly to deliver the Embassy's invitations to prominent Leningraders for the Queen's Birthday Party but also to pay a courtesy call on the head of the Office, Mme. Semenyonovna. This lady is away sick and the deputy with whom I had arranged an appointment by telephone from the hotel has, I am informed on arrival, "just left". However I am greeted by a friendly plump lady who accepts the invitations and gives me a good deal of advice on what to see in Leningrad.

Leaving the Foreign Ministry office I walk along the Neva and then cut in to the Fontanka, one of the very attractive tree-lined canals which run parallel with the river. Here is the modern steel-and-glass building which houses "Leningradskaya Pravda", the main Leningradskaya newspaper and organ of the Leningrad Communist Party. As I am the Embassy Press Attache I have asked the Press Department of the Foreign Ministry in Moscow to arrange an appointment for me with Leningradskaya Pravda; they have promised to do so but (of course) failed to give me a time or a name, so I have to play the visit off the cuff. Sure enough no-one has ever heard of me and there has been no message from Moscow. By making lavish use of my diplomatic identity card I bulldoze my way, in improvised Russian, to the office of a bewildered official who turns out to be the man in charge of typography, past numerous door-keepers, guards and cleaners, each of whom takes five or ten minutes to scrutinize my card with an uncertain mixture of curiosity, courtesy, and suspicion. The typographer makes a distinctly deferential telephone call and then ushers me into the presence of the Editor, a burly beetle-browed character who turns out to be called Mikhail Stepanovich Kurtynin. To begin with the Editor obviously supposes that I have come for some dark ulterior purpose, probably indistinguishable from espionage. Eventually he realizes that I have merely come to pay him a courtesy call and he relaxes. We have as friendly and informative a conversation as is possible in view of the fact that neither the Editor nor any member of his staff speaks English. Eventually I am ushered out amid mutual promises of extreme eagerness to give any possible help to the other in any possible way on any possible occasion – safe enough undertakings, as we both no doubt think to ourselves.

Duty done, we spend the afternoon sight-seeing. Shura Elkin skillfully leads us to the crowning view by the route which will reveal it most spectacularly: past St Isaac's Cathedral, round the back of the Admiralty building, a quick beer in the garden by the Neva behind the statue of Peter the Great (the subject of the famous Pushkin poem), along to the Winter Palace, now the hermitage Museum, but in 1917 the seat of the Provisional Government which was successfully stormed by the Bolsheviks, and before that the winter home of the Czars – and so out into the most beautiful and noble setting of any city I have ever seen, a broad spacious square with the front of the Hermitage forming one side, and the curving "General Staff Headquarters" opposite, a superb civilised building by Rossi. In the centre of it is Red Army Arch surmounted by a flying equestrian group, and there are fine, varied but beautifully blending classical buildings forming the other sides of the square. The buildings are all Italian-classical, mostly in a pale gold or yellow with white pillars and pediments, but some in a pale green wash and just a few in a dark magenta. There is hardly any traffic in the square, whose centre has a huge column topped by a statue of Alexander holding a cross (how surprising that this has not been replaced by Lenin, and what a relief). The whole effect is breathtaking. It is utterly Western and European, with no trace of the oriental influences, the Mongol and Tartar strain with the brilliantly coloured onion-shaped domes which give Moscow its special flavor.

22 May.　　Grey and chilly. Good for sight-seeing but bad for photography. Much of the day in the Hermitage: a fabulous collection of splendid paintings housed in a fantastic building. The marble staircases and gilt chandeliers are on such a scale that one wonders why the Russians waited until 1917. Marvellous Rembrandts, Cezannes, Picassos.

We visit the street where Shura lived as a child. It stimulates a flood of fascinating reminiscence of the stormy days of 1917 and 1918. I photograph him, with Muriel, standing at the entrance to the very flats where they lived. His mother, still alive and now in London, will (Shura is certain) be enormously moved if the picture comes out. I wish the light was better.

In the evening to the Gorky Theatre for (appropriately) a Gorky play, "Meshchane" ("Petit Bourgeois"). Although the language is difficult and I can follow very little of it, the whole thing is very contemporary in feel and splendidly performed, with much realism and spirit. A very successful bit of staging: there is a huge Victorian picture frame covering the front curtain before the play begins, with the space for the picture left blank. When the lights go down, a Victorian-style photograph of a family group is projected into the space in the frame. This is faded and the frame rises. The Curtain goes up to show the same picture in the same frame, this time ordinary picture size, standing on a piano and picked out by a white spotlight. The rest of the lights come up and the characters turn out to be the same as those in the photograph. At the end of each act the light on the photograph on the piano is the last to fade, so we are reminded of it each time. At the final curtain, the huge frame again descends in front of the stage and the photograph is once more projected onto it for the first few minutes of the applause. Then the frame rises to reveal the whole cast on stage assembled for their first curtain-call, arranged in an exact replica of the family group. Very nicely done.

23 May.   Snow. This seems hardly credible after the summer sun of two days ago. It's not settling but it is certainly cold. More sight-seeing. It is a superlative city. We visit Pushkin's house and the Russian Museum, another splendid classical building by Rossi, once the palace of the Grand Duke Michael Pavlovich. It houses the most gorgeous glowing icons, many by the master of icons, Rublev. I attempt to photograph one or two (having discovered to my amazement that photography of the exhibits is permitted) but the light is so poor and I have to allow such a slow shutter speed that the results are not likely to be up to much.

A good and cheerful dinner at the Chaika Restaurant by the Moika canal, and back to the station to catch the train at five minutes to midnight back to Moscow. This time our night companion is a Czechoslovakian administrator of surgical appliances, who speaks only Slovak. I give him a glass of whisky in return for which he gives me a rather pretty liquor glass in the shape of a hookah pipe. I spend the early part of the night drinking Scotch out of this, sucking the whisky up the stem of the glass hookah, to the accompaniment of mutual protestations of friendship delivered in our respective languages. Another train leaves just before ours from the adjoining platform: it is bound for Baku, the capital of Soviet Azerbaijan, hundreds of miles away on the Caspian, and light-years from the Western classicism of Leningrad.

CHAPTER 4

JUNE 1971:
KIEV, BRYANSK,
OREL, MOSCOW

1 June.   Fly soon after lunch (comprising on this occasion a bottle of kefir, or sour milk, and a slab of dry bread with a curling strip of salami on it, at the Vnukovo Airport buffet) to Kiev, with Martin Nicholson of the Embassy. We board our Il-134 as one might board a bus, giving up our tickets only at the foot of the steps up to the aircraft. All very casual. On the flight they sell tiny very expensive plastic Aeroflot badges and small bottles of vodka. Our landing at Kiev is one of the worst I've ever experienced: a virtual nose-dive to the run-way, a stomach-wrenching levelling out just as the wheels hit the tarmac with the aircraft travelling much too fast, and a hectic career at about 150 m.p.h. along the length of the runway with the engines flat out in reverse thrust and the wing-tips swaying wildly from one side to the other.

Kiev makes a marvellous impression: trees everywhere, broad streets, fine squares and solid buildings, some of them in the odd neo-baroque decorated style of the more bizarre apartment blocks on the West side of central park in New York (except that the New York ones were built in the twenties and Kiev's in the late fifties!). Picturesque trams and trolleybuses, not too much traffic, and fewer nagging militiamen than in Moscow. It is hot and sunny. Our hotel is not at all bad: no plug in the basin (but then the cognoscenti say that the Russians wash in running water as being more hygienic), but a nice view across a busy square to the hills and, through a gap in the trees, the Dnieper.

2 June. We call on the Chief of Protocol at the Ukrainian Ministry of Foreign Affairs (since Kiev is the capital of the Ukraine and the Ukraine, like all the other autonomous republics of the USSR, has its own Foreign Ministry, we start there). To our surprise Mr Tsyba has heard all about us from Moscow and even knows what other calls we wish to make. We go on from him to the Secretary of the Gorispolkom (the Executive Committee of the Kiev City Soviet) who supplies us with glasses of mineral water and an animated account of his duties. He gets so carried away at one point in his explanation of how it falls to him to explain to applicants for permission to build a house somewhere why this is quite impossible that he begins to shout quite fiercely at us as if it was <u>we</u> who were wanting to build a house in his city. He talks quite unstoppably with a mass of detail about everything from the committee structure of the Kiev Soviet to the roster that he and some of his colleagues have organized to enable each of them to have Saturday off every other week. We explain that we are late for our next appointment but he nevertheless gives us a 20-minute parting lecture on the symbolism and origins of the Kiev coat of arms. We finally escape to interview the International Editor of <u>Radianska Ukraina</u> (the Ukrainian equivalent of <u>Pravda</u>) and (very late indeed by now) the Director of the Kiev Film Studios, who gives us Russian cognac (very good it is, too) but fails to show us round his studios.

In the evening we meet the one British student at Kiev University and take her out to dinner at a charming restaurant built on an island in the Dnieper river. We eat at a table on the terrace overlooking the river, opposite a pleasant sandy beach where people are still sitting in the evening sun and swimming. Canoes, large steamers, dinghies and motor boats pass by. We eat Ukrainian food (barely tepid, but otherwise very palatable) and drink Ukrainian wine (less good) and Russian cognac (still good). The student is a pretty, self-possessed girl from Belfast who speaks Ukrainian almost as well as Russian. We give her our second bottle of Scotch which seems to go down well, as it were.

3 June. A pleasant lazy morning, after a 5.30 a.m. start, in the train to Bryansk (back in Russia, and about half-way between Moscow and Kiev). Divide the time between dozing on my (upper-berth) bunk and reading "War and Peace". At Bryansk station we get an ancient taxi with a radio-telephone which emits strange hollow noises and shrill cries. We ask to be taken to the "Gorispolkom Hotel", having been told by Intourist in Moscow that this is where we have been booked. It seems quite likely that this will be the place because often the Gorispolkom has its own hotel and since we are official visitors we might well be booked in there. But the taxi-driver has never heard of it. We set off at a hair-raising pace for the centre of town while the driver consults his office on the antique radio-telephone about the whereabouts of our hotel. After much deliberation he takes us to what appears to be a smallish private house with a flowery garden, assuring us that this is indeed the Gorispolkom. We get our cases out and pay him, and he drives off muttering. In the house is a little old white-haired lady who greets us affably enough with the information that this is the guest-house run by the Central Committee of the local Communist Party.

We wind up eventually in the Central Hotel just off the main square, and are ushered into the office of the Administrator who struggles hastily into his jacket and elaborately combs his hair as soon as we appear. He has been entrusted by the Gorispolkom with the organization of our programme. Besides the calls on the Chairman of the Gorispolkom (a businesslike man who presents us solemnly with boxes of totally unsmokeable locally-made cigars at the conclusion of his lecture on the history, amenities and successes of Bryansk) and the editor of Bryansky Rabochy (who receives us flanked by his entire editorial board and assures us proudly that the purpose of his newspaper is party propaganda – and gives us more unsmokeable cigars), our arrangements include attendance at a concert in the local music school by the Soviet State choir. A vast body of stout matrons in long white satin dresses and male eccentrics in dinner-jackets who look like something out of a Hogarth cartoon, they sing an assortment of fifth-rate Russian music with magnificent energy and precision. Eventually they get on to a little judicious non-Russian music ("Santa Lucia" and Brahms's Cradle Song) but this is so arranged and sung as to sound just like all the Russian rubbish that has gone before. The Administrator is there in the audience too, applauding fanatically, still in his jacket, the sweat running down his face.

BRIAN BARDER'S DIPLOMATIC DIARY

4 June.   A tour of Bryansk in the Gorispolkom car with a very svelte English-speaking Russian girl as our running commentator. The tour concentrates almost exclusively on the war memorials, of which the town possesses an extraordinary number. During the German occupation the partisans kept the fight going in the forests around the town, supplied and sheltered by the townsfolk. This traumatic event in the lives of everyone over the age of about 30 or 35 seems to dominate the place still. In one rayon (ward or district) of Bryansk over 90 per cent of the buildings of all descriptions were destroyed during the war and in the main rayon containing the centre of the town and the main municipal offices, theatre, etc., over 70 per cent. So the whole place has been totally rebuilt since 1944, although you would never guess this to look at it. The theatre for example – a fine classical pile with columns, gracious steps, pediments and porticoes, frieze of Muses, the lot – despite its blistered stucco, was built in 1953.

Evening on the train to Orel (pronounced "Arry-OL". I can explain this but not just now, dear) with more "War and Peace" and the usual unlimited quantities of delicious not tea (in glasses, sugar but no milk) from the dejurnaya or "duty-girl" who officiates with her big iron samovar at the end of each coach of the train.

5 June.   Orel. As it is Saturday we do not attempt to pay any official calls but take a taxi out to Spasskoye Lutovinovo where Turgenev lived for most of his life. The main house on the estate was burned down early in this century but the smaller house survives and has been turned, inevitably, into a pleasant museum. Among the items on display – placed unobtrusively in a corner and not singled out by the guide – is a photograph of the group of Red Army Officers who commanded the unit which liberated Spasskoye from the Germans in 1944. One of the boyish faces looks vaguely familiar. There is a faded type-written slip with the names of the officers underneath the photograph: the familiar face belongs to Boris Pasternak.

Back in Orel we visit the other, bigger Turgenev Museum and then wander round the town, along the river and through the gardens and park to the shops, down to a fine shady beach and back through another park to the hotel. Throughout the day we are followed by a troop of KGB goons who behave like agents from a low-budget Hollywood thriller of about 1949. Whenever we look round they dodge into doorways and peep surreptitiously at us; when we join a tram queue they come and stand in it too; when (just to tease) we change our minds and walk, they change their minds too and walk. We sit in the park and they actually hide in the bushes. The final farce is enacted at dinner-time when we sit at an empty table and the duty goon hastens in, takes a seat at the next table (ostentatiously avoiding our eyes) and instructs the waitress in a stage whisper to take away the two unoccupied chairs at our table lest an innocent pair of Soviet citizens should come in all unsuspecting and expose themselves to our contaminating presence. Presumably the Orel KGB has little enough to do on an average day and today has been a field-day for them. They certainly need some practice.

6 June.   After five days of cloudless blue skies and warm sunshine we arrive back at Kursky Station Moscow at 6.30 a.m. on a Sunday morning in a grey drizzle of rain and an unmistakeable symbolic chill in the air. Outside Moscow in these pleasant provincial towns it is possible to believe that some of the spirit of the revolution has survived and that the men and women in charge of affairs are, some of them, ordinary unpretentious people genuinely trying to do the job as best they can, with some feeling at the back of their minds that they are the workers' representatives governing for and through the workers. But Moscow is something else.

13 June.   We spend the day at the tiny dacha of the Professor of English at Moscow University, Olga Sergeyevna Akhmanova. (This arises because Lady Wilson, the Ambassadress, and another of the Embassy wives have been holding weekly seminars in the English language and in the etymology of English words at the University English department; and now that Lady Wilson and the other wife are shortly to leave Moscow, Jane and one of the other wives are being groomed to succeed them.) Olga Sergeyevna, a weighty blonde who claims to be nearly 70 and has the vitality, if not dominating personality, of a woman half her age, presides over a sizeable crowd of assorted characters (she keeps open house on Sundays and no-one knows who else might turn up): her sister, a delightful little white-haired lady as unassuming as Olga Sergeyevna is the grande dame; indistinguishable English lecturers with pink shirts and beards, from Exeter and Bristol Universities respectively; a melancholy Russian girl with beautiful eyes and a plain face who is

Moscow University's phonetics expert and yearns to speak idiomatic English with a Yorkshire accent; Olga Sergeyevna's son, a greying physicist with a Lenin prize, and his very distinguished week-end house guest, a Dutch physicist from Harvard University, and his plump Dutch-American wife; an unidentified old woman who came and went, leaving behind her escort of three silent men, two of them silent in this Anglophone gathering because their only language other than Russian is German, the other a Red Army Colonel in uniform with an American accent to his (very fluent) English, who turns out to have been at school at Lytham St. Anne's; a pretty Finnish girl; an English lady lexicographer, presented to the company as the greatest since Saml. Johnson (no doubt accurately); and a supporting cast of bit players (wives, husbands etc. of the leading players; two small boys; the landlady, doubling as maid and cook; Virginia, Louise, Owen and self; onlookers, serfs, kulaks, agents provocateurs, proctors, praelectors, etc.).

After lunch – kidney and sauerkraut, chopped spring onions with sour cream, beef pilaf, black bread, cod baked in onion, the whole washed down with *kvass* (a drink which varies from the delicious to the undrinkable, made from black bread, sugar and yeast, lightly fermented) – the Exeter University lecturer produces a guitar and sings a large number of Russian, English and American folk-songs quite loudly in a light tenor voice. The assembled company joins in the better-known numbers (notably "Old Macdonald Had a Collective Farm" and "On Ilkley Moor Bar Tat"), several of the performers achieving a close approximation to the melody, others to the words.

The Red Army Colonel offers advice on brands of vodka and explains the efforts of Soviet technology to construct artificial caviar. When cups (not glasses; this is the English department) of tea and six large cream and chocolate cakes are produced, Owen gets a laugh by uttering an admiring whistle and announcing loudly that he thinks he will try all of those.

Upon our departure we are awarded the ultimate accolade of an invitation to return on any dry Sunday when the spirit moves us. As we depart the Exeter man is singing a mournful song about how much the soldiers in the land of the endless treeless steppes miss the sun rising over the pine trees and their babushkas back in the land of their childhood.

CHAPTER 5

July 1971:
Moscow, Helsinki

3 July. More expulsions: this time Martin Nicholson (my travelling companion in Kiev) and Patrick Jackson, the Cultural Attache seconded from the British Council, and their wives (Finnish and Dutch respectively). Once again it's straight retaliation against expulsions of Russians from London. Martin and Patrick are both fluent Russian speakers and both were students at Moscow University – hence no doubt in part their selection as counter-victims. But it's not a fair swap: we caught the Russians misbehaving, MN and PJ have done nothing whatever wrong. It's a special blow for Martin who's a Soviet specialist and would have expected to come back regularly throughout his service to Moscow: now there's a question mark over whether he can ever return at all. If he can't, his whole career is dislocated.

In the morning we see off the Jacksons at the airport, along with a good turnout of other well-wishers (British and other) showing sympathy and solidarity. Everyone brings bottles of champagne according to tradition, and we all sip it out of plastic beakers. They are going to Vienna for a holiday in Austria en route for home and the Austrian Airlines flight is one of those used for the periodic groups of Soviet Jews who are able to get exit visas to allow them to go to live in Israel (some are tried and sent to labour camps, some are let out; the stick and carrot technique, not ineffective). There are terrible tragic scenes of weeping women kissing men goodbye as the arbitrary selection procedures separate people from each other – in most cases, certainly, for ever. On a less tragic level the Jacksons' departure is made more fraught by the fact, remembered at the last moment, that their Dutch nanny has no exit visa (the Jacksons as diplomats don't need exit visas, but their nanny has no diplomatic status and does). Much frantic telephoning to the Foreign Ministry by the duty officer at the Embassy and by Austrian Airlines and Embassy see-ers-off at the airport; but it is Saturday morning and difficult to get hold of anyone with authority to agree that the girl should be allowed to go. Eventually someone at the Foreign Ministry says that he has authorized the issue of a visa and instructed the airport authorities accordingly. Sighs of relief all round and the girl, in tears, is comforted. But no-one at the airport has heard anything about the matter from the Ministry and so the plane goes without the unfortunate girl, by now in tears again. The next flight to Vienna is not for three days.

In the evening Martin and Raili Nicholson leave by train for Helsinki for a holiday in Finland on their way home. More champagne and plastic beakers on the platform. An even bigger turn-out: numerous British, Americans, Dutch, Germans, French, some press correspondents, all in hilarious mood. The KGB, out in force to make sure that the Nicholsons are actually on the train, seem suitably amazed at the scenes. It is just on midnight when the train leaves, to a roar of goodbyes and a spirited rendering of the Internationale.

11 July. A farewell party for, and given by, a nice couple from the Netherlands Embassy, Count and Countess (and they use their titles!) Hendrik Bentinck. Everybody seems to be there. Plenty to drink, then vast quantities of excellent food. Then – a novel twist, even to the old Moscow hands – we are seated on the floor and around the walls to enjoy a cabaret turn by a group supplied, like everything that the diplomatic corps wants, by UPDK, the diplomatic service organization which serves the KGB and the Foreign Ministry rather than the diplomatic corps. On this occasion UPDK has come up trumps. The first turn is a female singer, an impressively bulky blonde lady with a maniacal smile who bellows gay uplifting songs at us for half an hour, accompanied by an impassive male group on drums, double bass and piano accordion (there are ironical cries from the audience of "Ura!", the approving noises which according to <u>Pravda</u>

punctuate the speeches of the more senior party functionaries on great occasions; these delight the blonde). Next there is a tiny grinning conjuror who produces coloured handkerchiefs from improbable places, summons members of the audience to hold his props and finally, to deafening applause, fishes their wrist-watches (removed without the victims or the audience noticing) from his pocket with a flourish and returns them. It is a bizarre occasion.

15 July. Off for our holidays in Finland. We drive the 350 or so miles to Novgorod (still in the Soviet Union) and stay the night there in the hotel booked in advance for us by UPDK. Our rooms are not adjoining: there is one room in between. The management are insistent that Jane and I sleep in 529 and Patricia and the girls in 531, not vice versa. We discover that a wire runs along the walls and floor from our telephone, out into the corridor and into the mysterious room in the middle – 530. All rather obvious. Also our door does not lock from inside, the lock having been manifestly doctored to stop this. As a result, Owen gets up at about 4 a.m., doesn't realise that we are in the same room, wanders out into the corridor and is rescued by the <u>dejurnaya</u> (the woman on duty on each floor in Soviet hotels) who puts him in the girls' room. This gives us a nasty fright when we wake next morning and find no-one in Owen's bed.

Lots of churches in Novgorod (once a great centre of Orthodox religion, icons and so on) and a rather run-down but quite picturesque Kremlin which we view in a steady drizzle. The museum custodian lets us in free because she's about to close, and then lectures us for hours in minute detail about some carved elephant tusk presented to the museum by some soldier who had fought on the Novgorod in the war. We are left with only a few minutes to see the icons which turn out to be fabulous.

Terrible dinner in the hotel restaurant. Food cold, brought after endless delays, and everything on the menu that looks at all tempting is off. We are pressed to accept "kebab" and do so because there is nothing else. Kebab in Novgorod turns out to be cigar-shaped hamburgers with a few of the inevitable, ubiquitous chopped spring onions. There is no wine and there are no desserts available.

16 July.   Out through Leningrad where we stop for an hour and look entranced at Palace Square, as noble as I had remembered it. Over the Neva and onto the Karelian Isthmus, formerly part of Finland but taken by the Russians after the Winter War and repopulated with Russians. Through Zelenograd and Viborg, former Finnish towns of note, and past a check-point for the last thirty or so kilometers before the border – the check-point because the Russians daren't let ordinary citizens live, or even go, that near the border, and they are stopped on the way out of Viborg and turned back unless they have documents permitting them to go nearer to the edge of their country. The border formalities are quite quick and easy, mainly because we are diplomats: a Dutch couple in the car in front who have been visiting Leningrad as tourists for [?] days are being kept back for thorough searches of all their possessions and have already been waiting for more than an hour and a half. We are there for only about 15 or 20 minutes and then we are waved through and drive the remaining half-mile to the border. We show our passports once again to the armed border guard there and he salutes and raises the barrier. Ten yards of no-man's land and the Finnish barrier goes up for us. Friendly Finnish border guards glance at our passports and our car insurance documents and then wave us through: two and a half minutes (and here we have no diplomatic status). The children cheer as we drive away towards Helsinki.

Spend the night at Hamina near the border. Beautiful comfortable hotel, more friendly Finns, an excellent although expensive meal in the restaurant. We had forgotten how civilised lavatories and bathrooms could be.

17 July.   Spend the day driving across Finland, skirting Helsinki and Turku, to Sieravuori Holiday Village, near Honkilahti – about 150 km. north of Turku and about 40 km away from the West coast. It pours with rain nearly all day and we branch off with some misgivings onto the rough mud and rock tracks for our last 15 miles or so. They are a quagmire and the car rattles and bounces around over the half-flooded boulders and potholes, the luggage on the roof-rack leaping and streaming. We have to ask the way about a dozen times and as no-one speaks anything but Finnish the results are not much use. We finally become convinced that we are totally lost but see nothing for it but to plough on. Louise begins to wail that she wants to go back. Finally we crash our way into a small clearing with a couple of huts in it. This proves to be the office and centre of the Holiday Village. No-one in the office speaks English. We have to wait for 45 minutes in the rain before our cabin is ready for us. It turns out to be a tiny shed with four bunkbeds (i.e. two pairs) and one other bed, a table and two benches and two small electric rings. No water, no lavatory, no oven. General dismay. We sit in the little shed and watch the rain pouring through the pine trees, eat what's left of our picnic lunch of cheese and spam (the Holiday Village has a shop which we assumed, wrongly, would be open mid-afternoon on a Saturday in the middle of nowhere; it won't in fact be open again until Monday mid-morning).

We are directed by a friendly Finn to the place in the woods where there is a tap fixed to a post in the ground. It's a short walk through thick undergrowth, easier with an empty bucket than with a full one.

To bed, amid universal gloom.

18 July.   Bright warm sunshine greets us. The pine trees are dry and sparkling. Discover that the lake is only about a hundred yards down the track. There is a sauna right by it. The water is clear and pure. Birds sing. We find rowing boats, two deserted sandy beaches and rocks in the woods where it's safe for the children to climb and play. Indeed everything about the place is superbly safe: the lake shelves so slowly and gently that even Owen could come to no harm.

We all cheer up and decide that the place is fine after all.

21 July.   Spend the day sightseeing in Turku, in fierce sun. A very pretty, flavoury place. Rapidly cover the main attractions: 15th-16th century castle of fairy-tale variety, Sibelius museum, cathedral (with dazzling blonde beauty selling postcards in foyer, or whatever a cathedral foyer is called), central market, Aaltonen museum, open-air handicrafts museum (reminiscent of Skansen in Stockholm and similar places in Bergen and Oslo) and of course the river, sparkling in the sun and colourful with little boats.

We wind up at tea-time calling on the Kallios, friends of GCS whom we never met but of whom we have heard a good deal since our Scandinavian holiday in 1969 when the S.'s stayed with them in Finland and we went back across Sweden to stay with the Ahmans, meeting up again later with the S.'s in Copenhagen. The Kallios give us a splendid warm and friendly welcome and although we have specifically disavowed in advance any thought of a meal (on the grounds that there were six of us; and anyway we didn't actually know the Kallios) they nevertheless produced a vast three-course dinner winding up with a mountain of strawberries and cream.

24 July.   To Helsinki, after an idyllic week by the lake in our cabin to which we have become really rather attached. Although there has been rain every day, it has always been short-lived (except on the disastrous day of our arrival) and the rest of the time has been hot and sunny. We have lounged on the little beaches, walked in the peaceful woods, drunk cold beer in the café and watched the Finns hopping happily about in the national dances, swum in the lake, rowed little boats along the lake shore, sweated in the sauna and then plunged into the clean cold water of the lake 15 yards from its door (sometimes emulating those of our Finnish fellow-sauna-users who wore swimming costumes for these activities, sometimes emulating those who did not). We have barbecued steaks and hamburgers (barbecue grill provided with the cabin) and crashed around in the car from boulder to boulder on the occasional expedition to the nearest village for money, food and provisions. It has been as refreshing a contrast to Moscow life as one could wish for.

Helsinki is also a sharp contrast with Moscow in a different way: modern buildings and crowded streets, shops everywhere bursting with every kind of good thing, hotels and restaurants, pedestrian precincts and twin-level shopping areas.

26 July.   Helsinki. It is Monday and time for the winter's shopping. We spend the day in Stockmann's, the big department store which supplies most of the needs of most of the diplomatic community in Moscow by its super-efficient telex, telephone and postal ordering service and its weekly truck run to Moscow. We wander from floor to floor signing pieces of paper for everything from ski-pants to kettles, pencils and paper to snow-tyres and ice scrapers. When all this treasure-trove is delivered to Moscow for us next week we shall wonder whether we were really of sound mind when we ordered it, and the bill will be a catastrophe. But it's our last chance for six months – of which four will be the kind of weather that defeated Napoleon.

Take the car to the garage next door to the hotel to have the wheels balanced but am told that what is needed is new shock absorbers. Not surprising after the bashing on Soviet corrugated roads and Finnish dirt-tracks, but we can ill afford the 260 Finnmarks (£26). Since we can't have the work done in Moscow we have no choice but to grin and bear it.

27 July.   A final sauna at the splendid Seurahuone Hotel in Hamina where we spend our last night in Finland. Fill up the car at a spotlessly clean Esso station where uniformed attendants rush around and check the oil, clean the windscreen <u>and</u> all the other windows and the headlamp lenses, sell excellent ice-cream and car accessories, and smile too.

28 July.   Last shopping in Hamina and then to the border. The children groan as the Soviet barrier comes down behind us. We're back behind the Curtain.

There's no sign of a petrol station until Viborg, but, full of Esso, we don't need one yet. Eventually we do, and as the petrol stations here are anything up to 150 miles apart, one can't afford to wait until one is nearly empty. Find a petrol station eventually. As usual it is about 500 yards away from the main road and it takes a divining rod to find it. When it appears it is the usual rusty iron shack, inhabited by a scowling old woman who pre-sets the pumps to deliver precisely the amount which the customer has ordered in advance. She won't (usually) accept money, only the special petrol coupons which have to be bought in advance. You work your own pump once your turn in the long queue of ancient lorries has arrived. Generally there is no air pump, no oil and no water. Just petrol. No-one cleans your windscreen. No-one smiles. We're back in Russia.

The Sadko Hotel in Novgorod puts us in the same rooms as before: surprise, surprise. Mindful of Owen's nocturnal wanderings, we swop rooms so that our room (also his) will lock from inside. The girls, in the room meant for us, make suitable conversation at the telephone which is wired up to the next room. Hope it gives them a lot of fun trying to transcribe it. Get on amiable terms with the fat <u>dejurnaya</u> on our floor and agree in execrable Russian with her that the

Russians and the English are the greatest tea-drinkers in the world and therefore natural allies. (Decide not to suggest China as candidate for great tea alliance.) Beautiful relationship ruined when dejurnaya provides sheets for the extra beds in each of our two rooms and these prove to be, not damp, but actually wet. Tell her to find dry ones. She protests that sheets are perfectly clean. Try to explain that we want clean <u>dry</u> sheets. <u>Dejurnaya</u> goes into monumental sulk. End of tea-drinkers' alliance.

Eat in hotel restaurant again, this time joining forces with Canadian military attache and his wife. Several dishes are shown on the menu as available. We select various of these but are told that all are off. Only steak available. Steak turns out not too bad. On the menu someone has written in ink "Struberris and Kreme", which we order. These too are off. There are in fact no desserts of any kind. No wine either. Drink quantities of undrinkable beer and lots of vodka to take the taste away.

29 July.   Last lap back to Moscow. Very hot and boring. Endless vistas of nothing in particular with our road visible right to the furthest horizon: most depressing. Soon after lunch have a puncture and get covered in wet tar while changing the wheel – which entails unloading virtually all our luggage to get at the jack, spare wheel, etc. Wonder whether it's all worth it.

Arrive at Kutuzovsky flat at 6.30. Usual squalor. Decide it <u>was</u> worth it.

CHAPTER 6

AUG-SEP 1971: MOSCOW, BECKENHAM, LONDON

2 August. Gromyko's farewell lunch for Sir Duncan Wilson, our Ambassador, who is due to depart on retirement in a few days' time. The lunch is given at the Foreign Ministry hospitality centre in Alexey Tolstoy Street, a resplendent former residence of Count Morozov (left-wing pre-revolutionary aristocrat and sugar millionaire, incarcerated as mad for, among other things, collecting French impressionist paintings). The usual Soviet multi-course meal, catering by the Praga Restaurant staff: lots of tasty zakuskie (hors d'oeuvres, more or less), caviar with little gherkins and cucumbers, carrots and tomatoes, with brown bread; sliced cold fish; soup; a conventional main course and dessert, fruit and coffee, all accompanied by a kaleidoscope of different Soviet wines, Soviet cognac and, throughout, a bottomless well of vodka which reappears in one's glass as fast as one drinks it. Beautiful Meissen china shepherdess salt and pepper cellars, exquisitely engraved silver. After the exchange of quite amiable but formal speeches (during which both the Ambassador and Gromyko scold their interpreters for minuscule omissions, to show that each knows the other's language quite as well as the interpreters do), Grom speaks in English about "that American film actor who was married to Rita Khay-voorth – what is his name?" "Orson Welles," we all supply. "Yes, Orson Ou-elles. It is said that he made a broadcast of the invasion of the earth by persons from Mars. The Americans were very frightened and came out into the streets shouting because they believed it all. That is …. very interesting."

Afterwards we tell our Russian maid, Zina, that we have had lunch with Gromyko and also with Mrs Gromyko. She is very interested and asks about Mrs Gromyko. We say that she is very friendly, very ordinary and unassuming, rather – <u>big</u> (with gestures indicating her bulk, typical of four out of five women in Moscow, most of whom are elephantine). "Ah," Zina says, "She is fat because they are Ukrainians and the Ukrainian women are very fat."

5 August.   We celebrate Jane's birthday at the Embassy dacha, a crumbling wooden building about 40 minutes' drive from the centre of Moscow in a pleasantly pastoral setting of pines, firs and birches, fields and rivers, and other similar dachas, where we are spending the week with the Ratford family (he is the First Secretary Commercial). There are four bedrooms and three or four sitting-cum-dining-rooms usable also as bars, dance floors, sites for children's races, or other indoor needs. The furniture is unmistakeably cast-offs but comfortable. There is a large log fire and central heating for winter. Often people give parties here, for anything up to 200 people. We have to bring out our own food and (especially) drink, glasses, linen, etc., and we pay a fee for each night spent there, although there is also a Government subsidy. It is an extremely agreeable haven from the rather rudimentary and drab life of Moscow.

11 August.   Departure of Sir Duncan and Lady Wilson, on his 60th birthday (and compulsory retirement from the public service). He is to be Master of Corpus Christi College Cambridge. I congratulate him (an Oxford man – Balliol, of course) on going to a college with such a good view of St Catherine's. He replies in his donnish way that he fears that St Catherine's cannot be seen from the Master's Lodge. At the airport a large part of the Embassy staff, including us, turn out to see the Wilsons off. J. and I are a little early and arrive in time to see and shake hands with Rostropovich, the cellist, and his equally eminent wife the singer Galina Vishnevskaya – both close friends of the Wilsons during their time in Moscow. The Rostropoviches embrace the Wilsons after being introduced to all the Embassy staff who have arrived so far, and depart, both in tears, to their splendidly incongruous Land Rover which Rostropovich drives off at high speed. We shall miss the Wilsons with their passionate devotion to music, their Scottish canniness and his dry, donnish sense of humour. One very senior official in the Foreign Office, whose duties include the circulation of round-robin letters to all Ambassadors overseas, is inclined to use a matey, hail-fellow-well-met mode of speech, designed to show that despite his seniority he is a warm human being at heart. Sir Duncan was apt to read out, at our daily Embassy meeting, the choicer passages from these communications – references to members of the Foreign Service as "Us lads and lasses", assertions that as the gentleman in question walks in St James's Park at lunch-time he is "scheming away to do his bit for you chaps overseas who are bearing the burden in the heat of the sun" and so forth – in a voice of comically fastidious distaste.

25 August.   It is the season of Congresses and Conferences in Moscow, when different delegations of specialists in every possible field descend from Britain and everywhere else. The British delegations expect, as of right, to be entertained in the British Embassy, and usually are. Tonight it is the turn of the Surgeons, and their hangers-on, the exhibitors of medical apparatus at an exhibition arranged to coincide with the Surgeons' Congress. The surgeons are all, apparently, Scottish, and the important ones are fat knights. They complain about the way the Congress is being organized by the Russians. There is no list of delegates, so they have no idea, when they read papers, whether they are talking to the world experts in their field or to people of no special knowledge; nor can they contact foreign colleagues because they have no idea whether they are here or, if so, where they are staying. Most of the speeches are made by surgeons from Eastern Europe who devote the first two-thirds of their allotted time to praising the achievements of the great Soviet Union. The medical apparatus exhibitors are a very different bunch (beer instead of whisky and soda) but they too have their problems. One who shows cheap plastic disposable syringes and surgical pipes has great difficulty convincing sceptical Soviet surgeons and doctors at the exhibition that these goods really are meant to be disposable – thrown away after one use. They wink and say knowingly, "Yes, but seriously, how does one re-sterilise it?" They also have a marked tendency to steal the exhibits from the display stand while the exhibitor's back is turned.

29 August.   Sunday. We go with the Ratfords and the Fields (he the Cultural Attaché, with a charming American wife who is a Dupont) to Zavidovo, a recreation area maintained for the Diplomatic Corps by the Soviet Government about 80 miles north of Moscow on the road to Kalinin and Leningrad. As it is more than 25 miles from the centre of Moscow, we have to apply for permission to go there three days in advance. Even then we are stopped once on the way out and once on the way back by militia-men who emerge from their glass kiosks at the sight of a diplomatic number-plate, flag us down and demand our documents (which they return only after bearing them off to the kiosk, telephoning to KGB headquarters and getting the all clear). Zavidovo is at a great curve of the Volga River, at its confluence with a minor tributary which divides to form a long island covered in pine forest and grassy clearings. There are pleasant beaches, boats to hire, water-skiing. We take barbecue equipment and plenty of the excellent beef which is sold by the diplomatic foodshop, marinaded in soy sauce and corn oil. It is warm and sunny. As I wade into the river to swim I am accosted by a large, cheerful Russian who, it transpires, has come down in a friend's motor-boat from Kalinin and chosen the island to camp, blissfully unaware that it is an official centre for foreign diplomats. We talk in my pidgin Russian until John Field, David Ratford, and then about seven children appear. The Russian – a science teacher from the polytechnic at Kalinin – observes this accretion of westerners with mounting dismay, and eventually asks pathetically: "Are <u>Russians</u> allowed here?"

3-7 September.   To London as escort to the Queen's Messenger with the diplomatic bags. Arrive home in Beckenham at 9 p.m. (11 p.m. Moscow time) to a splendidly warm welcome from the E.'s (who have been using the house as a base for their summer holidays in Europe before returning to New York) and M.C. Bed at 2 a.m. (4 a.m. Moscow time). Next day spent feverishly shopping in Victoria, the Strand, Piccadilly, Knightsbridge, Chelsea; then back to Beckenham for a party organised by the E.'s and M.C. at which almost everyone I want to see is present. Bed at 3 a.m. Next day down to Bristol to see H.B. and N. Both in very good form. Bed at 1 a.m. Next day back to London. More shopping. In the evening round to the D.-S.es. Bed at 2 a.m. Next day to the Office. Snatch bits of conversation with harassed colleagues in Eastern European and Soviet Department, all of whom seem to have eight visitors waiting to see them, telephones which ring continuously and mountains of files in their in trays. Decide that life in Moscow is relatively peaceful. In the evening meet GCS, drink beer in pleasant riverside pub, eat venison at pleasant King's Road restaurant, see Danish pornographic film of overwhelming starry-eyed innocence at the NFT, return with G to Coulsdon for slides, movies and bourbon, and so back to Beckenham. Bed at 3.30 a.m.

8 September. Leave London Airport soon after midnight on the Vanguard chartered by the FCO to take the new Ambassador, Sir John Killick, to Moscow to take up his duties. There are only about ten passengers (including the Killicks and self) but most of the cabin space is occupied by the Ambassador's heavy luggage, roped elaborately to the walls and floor, and baskets containing Lady Killick's loudly mewing cats. The flight is technically first class so we are plied in the traditional manner all night with champagne, whisky, caviar-laden snacks, supper, dinner, breakfast, etc. Just before take-off one of the engines stops working and we have a long wait while men in overalls tinker with it. At one point it looks as if we shall have to transfer to another aircraft: this, it seems, can be done in something like three hours…. At 3 a.m. we land in Stockholm for refueling (and also so as not to arrive too early in Moscow). Only a drunk BEA catering controller and I go off the plane into the big deserted airport transit lounge. At the far end a solitary barman, kept up especially for us, waits expectantly. We order, and get, two bottles of beer: sixteen shillings.

Back in the aircraft a deferential voice at my shoulder says: "Good evening, Sir. I hope everything is to your satisfaction?" It is Sir John Killick, a man bounding with energy and a sprightly sense of humour. More champagne, whisky, dinner, breakfast, etc. After six days of hot sunshine in Britain it is a shock at 9.15 a.m. to land in Moscow and find cold, driving rain and black clouds.

17 September. A dacha party given by the Fields and the Smiths. The dress for this party is "Fin de Siecle" or black tie. J. has tried all week to hire Fin de Siecle costumes for both of us from the Bolshoi Theatre, Mosfilm and the Stanislavsky Musical Theatre, but (to our intense relief) without success. However most of the guests have made even more effort or been more ingenious than we have, and there is a rich profusion of be-whiskered characters in flowing scarves, long coats,

BRIAN BARDER'S DIPLOMATIC DIARY

centrally parted hair, long skirts with bustles, plunging necklines and elaborately flowered hair-dos. Toulouse Lautrec all over the walls. Roulette in the garden room (I win three roubles and hastily quit). Dancing. Quantities of champagne, cold turkey, mousse, etc. The Head of Chancery is wearing a midi-kilt, some sort of military jacket, a pith helmet and a handle-bar moustache painted on with mascara. He dances energetically amid the traditional speculation respecting the kilt.

19 September. One of the new teachers [at] the Anglo-American School [...] comes to lunch. He has been to Africa and asks me whether I have too. I confirm that I have. He asks how many British colonies there are still in Africa. I say "Only Rhodesia, which is a rather special case." "Oh, really?" "Yes: you remember that it has declared itself independent, although we still regard it as legally a British colony." "No kidding!" "No kidding. The white minority has – well – assumed control. Illegally. You didn't hear about it at all?" "I sure didn't. Well, what d'ya know! Is that really so?" He seems profoundly shocked. Wonder what he will be specializing in when he teaches Current Affairs.

Sir John Killick (front row, 2nd from left) presenting his credentials to Soviet Head of State Nikolai Podgorny (to Killick's left), The Kremlin, Moscow 1972 (Barder is back row, 6th from left).

Top: Brian and Owen with our Zhiguli in the courtyard of "Sad Sam", Moscow 1972.

Right: Virginia, Brian and Dennis Blewitt of the Daily Express at Zavidovo, Aug 1971.

The family at Zavidovo, outside Moscow, Aug 1971.

Owen, Louise, Patricia ("our nanny), and Jane in Sadova Samotechnaya ("Sad Sam"), Moscow early 1970s.

CHAPTER 7

SEP-OCT 1971: MOSCOW

24 September.   Out to the airport, to see Ken and Gay Scott off on their departure for mid-tour leave, and also to spend a couple of hours with Malcolm Macdonald who is changing planes in Moscow on his way to Peking and wants to meet someone from the Embassy to talk about Soviet-Chinese relations. Ken Scott, the Head of Chancery, looks tired and ready for his leave. We talk about the possibility that while he is at home on leave there will be a crop of expulsions of Soviet KGB people from the UK which will be followed by a crop of counter-expulsions from our Embassy in Moscow: would the counter-expulsions include Ken himself, thus preventing him from returning to Moscow to pack up his belongings? Gay says she has taken the precaution of labelling some of their possessions in the flat in case the packing has to be done in their absence. Ken and I say that the likelihood is that there will be a round of expulsions and counter-expulsions while they are on leave. Gay says she wishes she had realized that this was so likely: she would have labelled everything. As I am to be Acting Head of Chancery while Ken is away, I express mixed feelings about the possibility of having to act for him for six months instead of six weeks: good financially, but back-breaking. We part amid expressions of doubt as to where we shall next meet.

Sit waiting for the Macdonald plane to arrive, in the transit lounge. Suddenly Michael Robinson (Third Secretary in Chancery) appears: I am wanted immediately in the Embassy, he will stay and look after Malcolm. A good start to my stint as Acting Head of Chancery! Drive back to the Embassy (about 40 minutes' drive) at a hair-raising pace. Walk through the main doors just on 6 p.m. to be greeted by information that Soviet Charge d'Affaires in London has just been summoned and given two weeks to get rid of 105 Soviet officials from Britain. The news is just coming through on the Reuter tape. Straight into emergency meeting with Ambassador, Minister and Administration Counsellor. Numerous aspects to be worked out: possible demonstrations outside the Embassy, question of counter-expulsions – how many likely? How to keep Embassy running? – and effects on staff morale if uncertainty on this prolonged; handling of press; who is to go with the Ambassador to receive inevitable Soviet protest and possibly also indication of Soviet counter-measures, and so on.

Spend whole evening answering feverish questions from the press. The Ambassador asks whether I can cope with being Head of Chancery and Press Attache and a desk officer in Chancery all at the same time: should someone else take over the press job? Reply that this is really not feasible: the press will ring up the person they believe to be press attache, whatever other arrangements we might make. Anyway I rather enjoy doing both.

26 September (Sunday).   The Ambassador receives a summons to the Foreign Ministry to see Kozyrev, one of the Deputy Foreign Ministers. As agreed at our meeting on Friday, I am to accompany him. A very chilly occasion, everyone very dignified and correct. Kozyrev hands over a statement strongly protesting at the British action against the 105 officials. If we do not withdraw these measures, the Soviet Government will have to take strong counter-measures. The Ambassador asks whether the Russians are going to publish their statement. Kozyrev gives no direct answer. We drive back to the Embassy to send "flash" telegrams, reporting, commenting and recommending. Barely time to get these off before the British press corps arrives: the Ambassador had already invited them round for a drink and a chat before the summons to the Foreign Ministry arrived. He gives them a pretty general account of what had occurred at the Foreign Ministry and declines to reveal the contents of the Soviet statement beyond describing it as a strong statement of protest. Numerous questions: "What car did you go in, Sir?" "Did you drive it yourself?" "Who went with you?" "Were you offered a drink by Mr Kozyrev, Sir?" Would you describe the atmosphere as tense?" Daniel Counihan of the BBC has time, just, to telephone his report for Radio Newsreel and the mid-day TV news, so we break up. On the way out of the Embassy David Bonavia of The Times notices that the teletype machine of TASS, the official Soviet news agency, is actually in the process of typing out the full text of the Soviet statement handed to the Ambassador an hour and a half before. So all the Ambassador's discretion and reticence are wasted.

5 October.   Eleven days since the expulsions. Still no news of what the Russians will do in retaliation. Clearly they will have to do something if only to deter other countries from following the British example, and to show that second-grade countries can't push them around with impunity. Enormous speculation everywhere: in the other Embassies, among the press, in our own Embassy. This fluctuates wildly. One day everyone is convinced that there will be no expulsions but that the Russians will break off all trade with Britain. The next day everyone is equally firmly convinced that precisely eighteen people will be expelled and that there will be various other severe measures. The other evening met Victor Louis at a cocktail party (VL is enigmatic and interesting Russian known to do jobs for the KGB, acts intermittently as accredited Moscow correspondent of the Evening News, married to English wife who was formerly an Embassy nanny, has performed various tasks for Soviet Government or KGB such as unofficial emissary to Israel and Taiwan, flogging a version of the Khrushchev memoires to Time-Life at a Copenhagen hotel, arranging publication in the West of one of Solzhenitsyn's banned novels – presumably so as to discredit him in the Soviet Union – and generally putting out planned leaks, advance trailers of information, flying kites and ballons d'essai, a little calculated disinformation, and a good deal of charm. He and Jennifer live in a luxurious dacha near Moscow, run four cars including a Mercedes and a Porsche, have thousands of roubles' worth of paintings, swimming pool, tennis courts …. When they came to dinner with us a week before the expulsions, he was talking earnestly and with evident sincerity of the mark left on him by his ten years in a Soviet labour camp under Stalin and how this affected his view of Khrushchev, under whom he was released. An interesting figure indeed in this otherwise rather grey society!) – and was assured that no British correspondents would be expelled, but that several members of the Embassy would. I asked whether I should start packing. VL: "No, why should you?" Wonder whether this means I can relax. Now VL has written a piece in the Evening News saying that between 12 and 19 will be expelled, including some in Britain on leave. Wonder (a) if this is true, (b) whether it will include the Scotts, condemning me to months of hard graft as H. of C. Decide that VL is just floating these figures to test the UK reaction: will the British respond by angry threats of counter-retaliation or will they say that 12 to 19 expulsions would be too moderate to be worth further action? Sooner or later we shall know: but how long does the uncertainty last? Is the uncertainty meant to be part of our punishment? It seems a rather low level of reaction for the Government of a super-power.

Telephone calls from numerous British newspapers in London flow in at all times of the day and (especially) night, both to my own private telephone at home and to me at the Embassy. One asks "Is it true that everyone in the British Embassy in Moscow is living on the knife-edge of fear?" Reply that much as we all like it here, expulsion from such a country as the Soviet Union is several degrees better than a fate worse than death. One telephone call is from WABC New York – a pop music station whose news bulletins never last more than thirty seconds, as I well remember. WABC nevertheless interview me (presumably on tape, and certainly at vast expense) for about ten minutes. The interviewer seems poorly informed even about the expulsions from Britain announced ten days ago. She keeps asking about these. Suggest to her that she turns up the New York Times for 25 September as a cheaper way of finding out about these events. Another caller telephoned on a Saturday afternoon – this time a British Sunday newspaper of low reputation – and asked for the telephone number of the News Department of the Foreign Ministry: they want to get the Soviet Government's comments. Explain that there is no such thing: Soviet Ministries don't have that sort of relationship with the press. Clearly the caller is not convinced. I give him various Moscow telephone numbers and warn that he is unlikely to get much sense out of any of them. He rings up much later again to say that he managed to get the KGB's telephone number from somewhere and rang that. He eventually got hold of someone who spoke English, only to be told that "the KGB is closed until Monday morning"! What a civilised secret police.

Actually we know that the KGB doesn't close down at weekends because they are intensively following me. Four of them, always in the same car, working in shifts (four at a time, three shifts, twelve in all – all to follow me. Flattering, I suppose.) They follow bumper-to-bumper – which is dangerous, apart from being mildly distracting. All wear raincoats and huge hats – presumably having seen from old Hollywood B features that this is the approved uniform. All are enormous thugs with faces that look as if they have shaved for 40 years in cold tea. When this surveillance began they were distinctly menacing and would follow me very closely indeed right to the front door, ignoring my amicable "Zdrastvuyte!" or else replying in a sneering, threating tone. Now however they seem to be more relaxed. On Saturday when I parked the car outside the bread shop on my way back from the Embassy and went in to buy bread, they parked right behind and trooped after me into the shop as usual, so I took the opportunity to say hullo, and "we are all going off to the country house and museum at Archangelskoye this afternoon – right?" Two of them, anyway, grinned broadly and said with satisfaction "Khorosho!" ("Good!"). They duly tailed along behind all the way to Archangelskoye and followed us amiably round the museum and grounds, pretending rather superficially to be looking at the pictures and statues too.

David Ratford, our friend from commercial section and the father of two girls who are Virginia's and Owen's closest current friends, goes off today for a week in England, leaving the older daughter (Karin) in the charge of Jane and another of the Embassy wives, since their other daughter is with David's wife, Ulla, in Sweden. The moment David has left it occurs to us all that he might be expelled while he is away and not be able to come back and collect Karin. Moreover Karin has no passport and no visa of her own: she is on David's. Fingers crossed.

8 October (Friday). As today is the day when the fortnight's notice to the 105 expellees expires, there is great speculation that the Russians will notify us today of their counter-measures. But the morning and afternoon pass with no sign of any summons. Return from the Embassy at about 7 p.m. to change, shave, bath, read Izvestia and go out to dinner with the Singapore Minister. At 7.30 get a telephone call from the Ambassador: he has been summoned to the Foreign Ministry for 8 o'clock. Can I come straight down to the Embassy? He has told them he is in the middle of dinner and won't be there till 8.30. Finish changing, telephone various people to arrange for the press to be told that the Ambassador has been summoned, call in three typists and telegraph staff, organize warning telegram to London, fix duty driver and car for Ambassador and self, get Embassy guard to ring round all heads of section in the Embassy and ask them to come to a meeting at 9.30, ring Singapore Minister and say we won't be able to come to dinner after all, and rush down to Embassy just in time to leave with Ambassador.

When we return the press is in the Embassy waiting-room in force. Ambassador goes off to scribble quick summary telegram to London while I go and "face the press" – notebooks, scribbling, frantic questions, people holding microphones under my chin: "Brian, are the Soviet measures very severe or just severe? Brian, when can you give us the names? Brian, how was the atmosphere this time? Brian, which car did you go in? Brian, did they offer you a drink …?"

One of those who is to be expelled arrives for the meeting – the one who is hardest hit by this expulsion, in fact. I ask him gently to pop into the Ambassador's study – so gently that he guesses at once. He is a university lecturer, a specialist in Soviet economics, and regular visits to the Soviet Union are the life-blood of his whole career. Now, through coming to work for the Foreign Office and the Embassy for a year, he has lost all: expelled and presumably not allowed to come back. It is a total catastrophe for him. The Ambassador tells him. The other victims also have to be found and told. Telegrams to London to ask them to find and tell those who are on the blacklist and who are in Britain – luckily not including the Scotts. More telegrams. More meetings. Press. Telephones. The Ambassador holds a further improvised press conference. "Sir, did they offer you a drink? Sir, may I take a photograph of you getting out of the car which you actually used…?" Return home finally at about 1 a.m. to find messages asking me to ring about half the Moscow press corps, whatever the time. "Brian, thanks for ringing: look, surely you can give us the names now, can't you? If you don't I'm going to miss my last edition…"

To bed with a great feeling of relief. To be expelled would not have been any great tragedy – it's a pretty tiresome place to spend two years, and in eight months we have seen enough to form quite definite conclusions about it. But expulsion now, with car unsold, advances and loans not repaid, allowances cut off, and so on, would have been pretty disastrous financially, disruptive for the children, and generally unsettling. Also one doesn't want to be treated like a thing – expelled and one's life disrupted not because of anything one has done one's-self but because one's name has been picked out of a (fur) hat to make up the desired number for public consumption.

19 October.   Buy a second car and become a two-car family. A sort of landmark, I suppose. It's a Zhiguli, jointly made at Togliattigrad by the Russians and Italians and indeed almost indistinguishable from the little Fiat. Costs £480 to diplomats, about £3,000 to the Russians. Moreover the Soviet authorities guarantee to buy them back from diplomats at only about £ 10 less than the purchase price. Price includes all extras: radio, numerous ingenious warning lights, excellent tool kit, two interior lights, engine and boot inspection lights, intermittent sweep setting for windscreen wipers, a first-class heater, front disc brakes and dual line braking, overhead camshaft, and a very neat, handy little 1100cc engine. A good, nippy little car, streets ahead of any other Soviet car (none of the others had Fiat participation). Now Jane can use the Cortina for shopping, transporting children around, visiting the university and all that, while I use the Zhiguli for commuting between the Embassy and the flat, visiting the Foreign Ministry (when on my own!) and other Embassies, and so on.

22 October.   Dinner with the Embassy doctor who lives at the Embassy. Leave his flat at about midnight and set off for home: find the bridge over the Moskva river is closed. Turn round, drive along embankment to next bridge: also closed. Back again (picking up a recently arrived colleague in his car who falls in behind), right along in other direction to bridge which as far as I know is never closed because it carries the main ring road. This too closed. Get complicated directions from militia-man on how to get across river – straight on 4 km, do U-turn at big house, right at bus stop etc. All in pitch dark. Set off pessimistically. Find that instructions cannot be followed because at every intersection there are militiamen forcing all traffic to go straight ahead. All bridges closed. At last find reason for situation: rehearsal for 7 November parade. Streets on other side of river filled with endless queues of nuclear rockets on transporters, tanks, personnel carriers, lorries full of men sitting stiffly to attention swaying like puppets in unison, rifles across chests, jeeps, large objects shrouded in canvas sheets, etc. At one crossing get a front seat view of all this as traffic is stopped to let it go by: for 25 minutes we watch this vast array of hardware rumble past. (Perhaps it is beginning to come round again, to fool the Western spies into thinking they have more than they really do?) Finally we are allowed to set off again and drive aimlessly around for another 40 minutes. Eventually stumble on the far end of the ring road, manage to get onto it and drive back round it – in the wrong direction. Home at 1.40 a.m.

23 October. Snow. How recent February seems! Out there with sprays, scrapers, brushes, penetrating oil. The din of cars trying vainly to start, batteries getting flatter and flatter. Chipping away at ice on windscreens. Slide hopelessly on way into Embassy: get snow-tyres fitted.

27 October. All snow gone. Mild and wet.

CHAPTER 8

NOV-DEC 1971:
MOSCOW, ARMENIA,
GEORGIA

4 November.   A newly arrived Sierra Leone First Secretary, BJ, to lunch. Very articulate and agreeable. He tells of his experience last week-end. Still living in a hotel until his flat is ready and his family arrive, he had a head-ache on Saturday evening and asked at the hotel reception desk where he could get some aspirins. They said only through the hotel doctor who was away until Monday. BJ went up to his room. Half an hour later two burly lady doctors arrived from the diplomatic polyclinic, knocked on his door, pushed their way in, laid him out on his bed and proceeded to give him a detailed and intimate examination. Eventually he managed to get it across to them (through an interpreter whom he telephoned) that he only had a mild headache. The doctors said they were not satisfied: would he please accompany them to the polyclinic? He finally consented on receiving a promise of transport back to his hotel. They took him by car to the polyclinic where he was subjected to an even more microscopic examination, with wiring up and machines and the full treatment. At the end they said: "You are suffering from rheumatic asthma. Take these pills." BJ: "But I have never had asthma in my life and I haven't even got a cough. All I have is a slight headache." Doctors: "Well, anyway, take these pills." BJ took the pills which proved to be powerful sleeping tablets. He passed out almost on the spot, slept the night at the polyclinic and was eventually delivered back to his hotel on the Sunday afternoon. As he says: "I suppose it gives them something to put on their file." Moral: "If you have a headache in Moscow, grin and bear it."

7 November.   The anniversary of Great October (the 1917 Bolshevik revolution – October under the old calendar, November under the reformed calendar). Big military and civil parade in Red Square. As is traditional, it is snowing and there is a razor-like wind. Watch it on television (only Counsellors and above get invited to watch in Red Square itself, where it is standing room only, there is usually a rotten view and you slowly freeze to death). The cameras keep returning obsessively to Brezhnev, up on the Lenin mausoleum with the rest of the Politburo and the main Red Army leaders. Big B. is as usual very animated and twitchy: he never keeps still for a moment. This time he spends a lot of time talking with much gesticulation and merriment to Kosygin, on his left, ignoring Podgorny on his right. The parade rolls by interminably underneath: enormous inter-continental ballistic missiles, tanks and armoured carriers, lorry-loads of soldiers sitting stiffly, swaying in unison as if they were all fastened to the sides of the vehicle; then selected units on foot, goose-stepping stiffly past at the salute, heads turned rigidly to the mausoleum. The cameras pan along a line of soldiers guarding the saluting base, snow gathering thickly on their fur hats: they look chilled to the marrow (and probably are, having been standing there since about seven in the morning). Just as the camera picks him up, one of the soldiers passes out – presumably from cold and tiredness – and pitches forward on his face. The camera immediately switches to Brezhnev. (The TV cameras in Britain or the States would of course have stayed riveted on the inert body of the soldier with close-ups of his face as the ambulance men come to take him away. But not here. The gallant soldiers of the Red Army do not faint.)

8 November.   The four Armenian students who have been in the Embassy for the last two and a half days finally depart today after an unheralded visit by the father of one of the boys and the mother of the other (the other two students are girls). This ends a tense and tragic episode for us. The facts as gleaned by the press are that the four pushed past the militia guards on the Embassy and ran inside to try to get to Britain. The Embassy explained the procedures for this and asked the four to leave: they refused. The press also spoke of them having razor blades and threatening to kill themselves. When the newspapermen asked us whether we were giving them food, we – meaning I, as press attaché – refused to comment: so at least one paper drew the conclusion that they were on hunger strike. They were four attractive and highly intelligent people, looking like students do anywhere in the world: long hair, granny glasses on one of the girls, midi skirt on another and smart well-cut slacks on the other; the boys with beards. We took it in turns to talk to them and try to help them to relax: when they first arrived they were in a state of exhaustion, hyper-tension and terror. To begin with they really believed that once they were safely inside the Embassy, we could get them to Britain without their having to go back through the hands of the Soviet authorities, but they eventually accepted that this was impossible. Someone lent them a cassette tape recorder and they played a Beatles tape for a few hours, delighted. In two and a half days some of us got to know them quite well. It was difficult to see how it would end, and impossible to see any but a tragic end to it. None of us guessed that it would be the tradition of tightly-controlled Armenian families that would break the log jam: but naturally enough the Russians thought of this. Half an hour with the two parents and they all trooped out, one in tears, the others stumbling. A group of us including the Ambassador and a couple of (British) newspaper correspondents escorted them across the Embassy fore-court. There were two cars waiting: a "taxi" – with taxi markings, anyway, but with a long radio aerial, and what purported to be a private car. They all climbed in and the two cars drove away. What their fate is, we shall never know. Denis Blewett, the Daily Express correspondent who has good contacts, was told by someone a few days later that the four had not even been charged but had been given a "ticking off" by their local KGB office in Yerevan and told not to do anything so silly again. But this was almost certainly a planted story to lull western press and diplomatic interest. Whether they are in prison, at a camp, or at a lunatic asylum, or whether for once the story that they had been let off with a talking-to was true, there's really no way of knowing. I hope they are all right in the end. They had a quality of innocence.

25 November. J and I fly to Yerevan, capital of the Armenian Soviet Socialist Republic, for a few days, mainly to visit the one British teacher at the University there, Dewi Williams. The Armenian in the seat next to us on the rather ropey

Aeroflot IL-18 turbo-prop plane asks if he may look at J's "Good Housekeeping". He goes through it fascinated, with me translating the advertisements, articles and captions into dog-Russian (with aid of dictionary). He strokes the glossy paper, delighted by its silkiness, and spends ten minutes staring at an advertisement depicting a pale blue bath with soapy water running out of it. A blue bath! He is entranced. When we invite him to keep the magazine to show to his wife and son, he is overwhelmed.

We arrive in Yerevan just as it is getting dark and get an Intourist car into the city from the airport. The Hotel Armenia is on the main square, inevitably "Lenin" square, with a huge chunky statue of Vladimir Ilyich on one side (mercifully not in the middle, for once) and fine pillared buildings all round, the Post Office, the History Museum, the Party Headquarters and so on. All have characteristic Armenian style balconies with intricately carved balustrades and pillars, mostly in Armenian "Tuf" stone, which has a lovely pink glow. The hotel is not bad by Soviet standards but the bathroom is the usual horror. Dewi arrives just as we do: Welsh, very boyish, full of enthusiasm and not at all deterred by his isolation from everything that is familiar. He lives at the University hostel which (as we later verify) is extremely primitive, and does most of his own catering and cooking with such materials as are available – chiefly spiced sausage and salted fish. He has been searching for three months for a spoon but there isn't a shop in the whole of Yerevan that stocks such a thing. (We give him the one we have, providentially, brought.) He speaks of the anti-Russian feeling in Armenia: he asked in a shop for batteries for his radio, using Russian of course (he speaks good Russian but so far only a few words of Armenian). The shop assistant just shook her head and muttered "NO". Dewi persisted: he was a teacher, he had bought the radio in this shop, he was British. The assistant said: "British? Oh, I'm sorry, I thought you were Russian. How many batteries do you want?"

26 November. Persistent telephone calls establish eventually that none of the local officials are prepared, or allowed, to see me: the Armenian Foreign Ministry keeps saying that the person concerned is out ("ring again tomorrow"), the Yerevan Gorispolkom (Town Council) says that the Chairman (Mayor) will receive me but when we all arrive at the incredibly run-down Council offices we are told by a very shamefaced official that the Chairman has been called away on urgent business, the Deputy Chairman is away sick, the Secretary isn't there at the moment – perhaps next week …? The Editor of the local newspaper promises to ring me back about an appointment, fails to do so, and when I call again, has his secretary explain that he is in a meeting and expects to be very busy for several days. It is obvious that the powers that be in Moscow have sent out the word that we are to be cold-shouldered, presumably as a mark of displeasure at the expulsion of the Soviet officials from Britain in September. I find it quite easy to take my punishment like a man since the absence of official interviews sets us free to do more sight-seeing and ordinary tourism than we could otherwise do.

27 November.   J, Dewi and I cram ourselves into a tatty local bus to go the 15 miles or so to Echmiazin, the ancient capital of Armenia, still the site of the Cathedral of the Armenian Church and its HQ. We inspect the Cathedral and watch a cockerel, held by an old Armenian peasant woman, being blessed by a priest before being taken out to be sacrificed. Then to the Palace for an interview, or rather audience, with the Catholicos (Archbishop, or Pope) of the entire Armenian Church, an immoderately dignified, patriarchal figure with a long white beard and piercing blue eyes. He turns out to be an Armenian from Rumania (there are almost as many Armenians living outside Armenia as there are in it) and he speaks no Russian or English: just Armenian, Rumanian and French. So we talk in French. He is very friendly, very ready to talk, but a bit guarded about the nature of his freedom of action vis-à-vis the Soviet authorities. However he claims that despite all the official discouragement of religion the numbers of Armenians attending church is steadily increasing. We drink Benedictine and Turkish coffee, exchange presents and depart. On the way out we are shown eight huge crates outside the Palace, containing 25 tons of Italian marble, the gift of the Armenian Church in Italy. Overseas Armenians, being smart cookies, tend to be well off, and support their mother church generously.

On the way out we go to have a quick peep at the big enclosed yard where the sacrifices are carried out: it is all very crumbling and broken down, like an abandoned builder's yard. Mercifully no sacrifices are actually in progress but a large and very cheerful Armenian family – about a dozen of them – are just embarking on a feast at a table down the middle of the yard, in the open air, at which the main dish is the sheep which they have just sacrificed and are cooking in a vast black cauldron tended by a witch-like old crone with a long hooked nose. When I ask if they mind me taking a photograph of this festive scene, they tell me they're delighted and then press us to join their feast: so we spend the whole of the rest of the day with them. As well as the boiled sheep (which is indescribably foul) there are huge quantities of cheese, flat Armenian bread, onions, cress, and apparently unlimited Armenian cognac and local vodka ("Try this – it's far better than that Russian stuff"). There are several bizarre touches. A radio on the table is playing the BBC World Service at top volume: it is Denis Norden telling some long and witty story. None of them speaks a word of English but a huge blowsy (dyed) red-headed woman of about forty assures me that they always listen to the BBC in English – "but we have to turn it off if anyone comes, of course." I point out a uniformed militia-man who is skulking rather shame-facedly in the background and ask whether it's really all right for them to be listening to the BBC so openly with him around? "Oh, don't worry," says the red-head: "that's my husband." (Later she says, pointing to him: "Look at him! He's a party member, but he believes in God!") A little wizened Armenian with one leg and a withered arm, who seems to live as a kind of parasite on the sacrificial feasts, joins the gathering and, fortified by cognac, begins to sing an Armenian folk-song in a high-pitched, whining voice with a grotesque leer in it. Everyone laughs loudly at the song, which is presumably highly improper: the two teenage girls (both piano students at the Yerevan Conservatoire – "My favourite composer is Bach") blush and giggle. The one-legged man cups his ear with his hand when he sings, presumably to guard against any imperfection of pitch. Later he confides to Dewi Williams: "I was a very literate man, you know. An intellectual. I used to be able to write Russian. But then I fell down a well in Russia…." The old crone who attends the black cauldron, also primed with cognac and vodka, begins to do a surprisingly nimble Armenian dance, cheered on by the assembled company. The one-legged man staggers out after her and hops about behind her, leering salaciously. One of the Armenians produces a camera and takes innumerable photographs of the whole party, arranged like a school in rows. Then it is my turn. Eventually we explain that we have other appointments back in Yerevan and excuse ourselves, amid effusive greetings and farewells, toasts to Peace and Friendship, Anglo-Armenian relations and the permanent good health of all present. From the taxi on the road back into Yerevan we get a good view of the twin peaks of Mount Ararat, which for once is not obscured by mist and which seems to loom over the city although in fact it is just across the Turkish border a few kilometers to the South. Although we are still nominally in the Soviet Union, Turkey and Iran seem much closer than Russia – as indeed of course they are. Moscow seems a million miles away.

29 November. By car over the mountains to Tbilisi. Yesterday it snowed in the mountains and the scenery today is wildly spectacular. The roads are very icy to start with and our Intourist driver seems to think the safest way with ice is to drive at it very hard – faintly alarming when you are negotiating a hairpin bend on a mountain pass with the road falling away thousands of feet at the edge. We stop and photograph the two ancient churches on the little island in Lake Sevan, all snow-covered in the frosty sun, and then stop again at a very unpretentious little restaurant overlooking the lake where we eat a huge lake trout each – a celebrated delicacy, found only in this particular lake, and very tasty indeed, washed down with Georgian wine (to our relief the driver declines alcoholic drinks). Later we cross the highest pass and the road drops steeply into a valley of breath-taking beauty, reminiscent of the Rockies or Switzerland and more unspoiled than either. The snow gives way to green hillsides and pleasant woods, with the occasional farm. We drive across the north-western corner of Azerbaijan and then into Georgia. An hour or so later we are entering Tbilisi.

The Hotel Iveria in Tbilisi is very chic indeed – sub-Hilton, very ambitiously conceived and not all that badly executed, although the details – curtain fittings, taps, door-latches – are as usual very poor and the long vaguely Scandinavian dressing table in our room has one end broken and slopes alarmingly. In the evening we meet Tamara Dragadze, an English girl of Georgian extraction who has come back to Georgia to find her roots and to do some research on the structure of the family in Georgian villages. She has learnt fluent Georgian and quite good Russian (but like everyone else in Tbilisi uses only Georgian). An interesting girl: now about 27, she wrote a novel while a student in England, is a qualified sociologist, and now occupies a remarkable position in the Tbilisi Establishment, by whom she is greatly lionized as one of the few ex-Georgians who has voluntarily come back to her homeland. Tamara appears frequently on Georgian TV, is friendly with all the local bigwigs (the Chairman of the Writers Union, the University heads of faculties and so on) on the cultural scene, and is now uncertain whether she is really a Georgian with a British passport or a British girl visiting Georgia. She is a very good and well-informed guide, interpreter and adviser, recognised at once wherever we go and welcomed with great enthusiasm. No problem about getting a free table in a Tbilisi restaurant when you are with Tamara!

Here too we are completely frozen out by officialdom, but none the worse for that, and free to roam around Tbilisi. It is a fine city, more like a real capital than Moscow, with more impressive shops and stores (even though they have nothing much to sell) and fine, wide, tree-lined streets. The old part of the city is very picturesque, with winding cobbled streets on steep hillsides, and houses with big wooden glassed-in verandahs and balconies on the first floors, rather reminiscent of Atlanta in the other Georgia. Tbilisi itself, the old city of Tiflis, has a superb setting, built in a bowl in the hills with the river flowing down the middle, so that from a little way up any of the hillsides you get a marvelous view.

1 December.   By Intourist car to Mtskheta, the ancient capital of Georgia and headquarters of the Georgian Orthodox Church (but much less autonomous and distinctive than the Armenian), and then on to Gori, Stalin's birthplace, about three and a half hours' drive from Tbilisi through fine rolling fertile countryside, hills and trees and miles of vineyards. A beautiful old church on the hill overlooking Mtskheta provides a striking skylined silhouette for miles. At Gori there is a huge statue of Stalin in the main square – probably the only one left in the Soviet Union since Khrushchev de-Stalinised in 1960-63. The Georgians have mixed feelings about Uncle Joe: he made bad mistakes, but – well, he was a Georgian, one of us, and he was a great man, wasn't he, known all over the world, and a great war leader.... The Stalin museum is huge, ornate, Moorish-looking with its minaret-like tower and intricate balconies; well-kept, reverently staffed, deserted. In front is the little two-room peasant cottage where Stalin was born: a classical style pavilion with pillars and pediments has been built over and round it. It is all rather stylish and tasteful by Soviet standards until you remember whom it is all meant to commemorate. The Georgian girl who shows us round the museum is only slightly embarrassed when we ask her the names of the characters depicted in a huge oil-painting showing the young Stalin's first meeting with Lenin, surrounded by old Bolsheviks, one of whom is plainly Trotsky: she names one or two at one end, but when she gets to Trotsky "the names of the rest have been forgotten, unfortunately."

2 December.   In the afternoon we board a twin-engined Aeroflot jet TU-104 and leave the warm bright sunshine of Georgia for the frozen slush and dirty fogs of Moscow. A superb view of the Caucasus mountains as we fly across them, seemingly far too close to the jagged rocky and snowy peaks, in the sunset. Then into deepening clouds and nothing more to see until we begin the descent before landing at Domodyedovo, one of Moscow's main airfields. A few minutes before we are due to land the stewardess clears everybody out of the front six rows of the aircraft and makes them all stand at the back; then turns all the interior lights off. Very alarming. However, we do a perfect landing and there is an Embassy car to meet us. The children are quite excited to see us again after eight days' absence broken by only one almost inaudible telephone call from Tbilisi, but we are rather dashed to find that they don't seem to have missed us particularly. There is a daunting pile of Pravdas and Izvestias waiting to be read. It's nice to see the children, and to have some ice for one's Scotch again, but otherwise it's difficult to raise much enthusiasm for being back in Moscow.

CHAPTER 9

Jan–May 1972:
Moscow, UK

27 January, 1972.   Impossible to catch up properly on five months' lost diary. So this will have to be pretty impressionistic, given the practical impossibility of turning myself into a full-time diarist.

A busy day today: lunch with the Greek Press and Cultural Relations Counsellor whose wife is said, not implausibly, to be the original model – or one of them – for Durrell's Justine; then cocktails and a film show with the Yugoslavs at their Embassy; then on to the Dom Jurnalistov, the HQ and clubhouse of the Soviet Journalists' Union, to which press attaches are occasionally invited. The "ki-no-coktel" at the Yugoslavs is not an unqualified success, at any rate technically. The embarrassed host announced that for procedural reasons the film he had invited us to see is "not available" and he will instead show some tourist films about holiday time in Yugoslavia. Then the projector insists on running at about half speed, gradually slowing to a halt. The deep bass voice of the (female) commentator turns inexorably into a growl, the movements become jerkier. Eventually and inevitably the film stops and at once catches fire, with quite spectacular effects.

The Dom Jurnalistov is hardly any better, when we eventually get there. Because of the technical difficulties at the Yugoslavs, we are pretty late arriving and by the time we get there all the Soviet journalists (meeting whom is the main attraction of the invitation) have gone. A few Eastern European diplomats and a Brazilian are eating herring and sour cream and drinking sweet white Georgian wine and vodka. Suddenly we see the (English) correspondent of the "Morning Star" and thankfully join him. He is a rather splendid old-style communist who occasionally reports surprisingly frankly about some aspects of Soviet life. We eat herrings and sour cream, etc. The only table free is in an icy draught. At last a Russian appears: a member of the Press Department of the Foreign Ministry, quite senior. At last, I think, we are going to have an interesting chat with a real Russian. But he pointedly ignores J. and myself, calls Colin W. away to a corner, and reads him a stern warning about his uncomradely action in writing a report on the exclusion of the press from the Bukovsky trial.

28 January.   A Christmas discotheque party, given jointly by ourselves and the occupants of the flat across the landing, the Assistant Naval Attaché and his wife. We drape curtain material across the lift shaft and the horrible grotty landing walls, and provide oceans of drink and continents of food for the medium-sized army of guests – a mixture of military attachés invited by the Dykeses and more or less louche newspapermen (plus assorted hand-kissing diplomats) invited by us. They all dance quite cheerfully and eat a good deal, but surprisingly little is drunk. Stagger to bed at about 3.30.

14 February.   We move from the biggest of all the diplomatic ghettoes, Kutuzovsky Prospekt, to one of the smaller ghettoes, at Sadovaya Samotechnaya. We have a larger flat, with an extra room, so that Virginia can at last have a room to herself; and altogether it's a definite improvement. But one side of the flat looks directly onto the Moscow ring road with a perpetual flow of traffic, day and night, including heavy lorries all the time. It's not so bad now when the windows (both layers) are tightly shut against the snow and cold but in summer how shall we hear ourselves think? The moving is of course hell as usual. The Embassy electrician, gas fitter, plumber and dvorniks or odd-job men, all Russians, turn up in the course of the day, grinning and nodding and doing the odd job until given the obligatory pair of cans of beer, whereupon they "run out of flex" or "need another pair of pliers from the Embassy" and disappear for the rest of the week. We fall exhausted into bed with the flat still looking as if a tornado had struck it.

15 February. I wake with a temperature and a memorably horrible cough. (Perhaps this is nature's way of telling me not to do anything further towards the restoration of the flat to a livable-in condition.) J. and Zina labour away, as does Patricia, while I lie sweating in bed with the BBC World Service.

In the late afternoon I am roused from a feverish doze by loud cries from the kitchen. I rush out in my pyjamas and find a vast jet of water shooting across the kitchen, bouncing off the wall and ceiling and rapidly flooding the flat. After a few minutes of ineffectual attempts to telephone the commandant in charge of the block of flats, supposedly on call for emergencies 24 hours a day (his telephone does not answer), to rouse the militia guards or the cleaning staff or someone who knows where to turn the water off at the mains, I plunge blindly into the icy jets – still in pyjamas – and grope frantically for the source (which turns out to be the washing-machine, supposedly "plumbed in" yesterday by the plumber). Eventually find a stop-cock which turns off the flow, peel off pyjamas, rub myself down with teeth chattering and crawl back into bed leaving the girls to try to mop up, using all available bath towels, buckets, saucepans, etc.

16 February. Worse. Notice that the Sadovaya cockroaches seem much bigger and blacker than the Kutuzovsky kind: they lumber, rather than scuttling. Attribute this to my fever, until J. remarks on same phenomenon.

17 February. Crawl out of bed to do my stuff (such as it is) as host at a party for Derek Day, Head of Personnel Department at the FCO, here on a short visit to see how our morale is coming along. Drink a lot of whisky and spend a long time talking to one of the Embassy Security Guards while the sweat pours down my face.

18 February. Worse.

26 February. Have Olga Sergeyevna Akhmanova, Professor of English at Moscow University, and a band of her teachers (those whom Jane conducts her weekly seminars for) to dinner. Also ask a man from Granada Television who is in Moscow to make some film or other and who rings me up during the day. He arrives for dinner got up as a sort of parody of an ad-man or TV-man (vast wide electric tie, stripey shirt, pink trousers, etc.) and spends the evening either lecturing Akhmanova – herself a woman normally forceful to the point of being domineering, but remarkably subdued tonight – or asking the younger and prettier teachers sotto voce about their sex lives. When the guests all rise to leave I offer a lift home to one of the teachers, a girl of about 25 or 30, who lives a few miles from Moscow in a small village to which, as it gradually transpires, she has never before been by car. She is adamant that it is just off the airport road. We set off in this direction. When we are only about ten minutes' drive from the airport, she whispers that she thinks we are on the wrong road. She meant that we should go past the air terminal, not on the road to the airport. It is a dual carriageway and there is no place to turn around. The time is about 1.30 a.m. Finally we come to a side turning which she claims to recognize and tells me to take. We thunder along this country road in the moonlight, the snow-covered fields on each side stretching away into the night, for what seems like about a hundred miles. Then off onto a cart-track in a village, along and round, right, right again, and left, and miraculously we are there. She gives me detailed directions for the return to Moscow, which I begin to follow very dubiously indeed. But they turn out to be quite correct and suddenly I recognize where I am. Amazingly am in bed by soon after 3 a.m.

8 March.   A sparkling, sunny, icy morning. Walk with Owen and the girls through the back streets around Sadovaya, finding charming little derelict churches and pocket-sized frozen parks. Back for lunch among the packing cases, and then off in the Embassy Zephyr to the airport for eight weeks' leave.

*   *   *   *   *

5 May.   At mid-morning we pile into the laden Cortina outside our familiar Lakeside front door, strap ourselves in, note down the mileage on the clock, and slowly drive away in the steady rain, waving to the forlorn figures of J's mother and V who stand in the front door dwindling behind us as we gather speed down the road. It seems a long way that we have to go before we drive into Moscow. The eight weeks have turned into nine, while we waited in vain for V to shake off her chicken pox and throat infection and finally got her a separate passport, transferred her Soviet visa to it (by courtesy of the remarkably efficient and agreeable

Soviet Consulate in the Bayswater Road) and decided to let her fly out on her own when she was fit to do so. She looks suddenly very small as we all drive away, leaving her alone for the first time.

As we sit in the appalling traffic jams on the road to Harwich we reflect mournfully on our good intentions for taking things easy on leave. The hours spent in the car: running it in three times, while a second and then a third set of pistons were fitted; miles of M1 as we thundered up to Scotland, and then thundered back again; miles of London suburbia and suburban traffic jams as we went to and fro between Bristol, Basingstoke, Frensham, Bedales, and Bournemouth on our various errands; a good deal of rather tense catching up on the cinema and theatre; as many evenings out, and as much eating and (especially) drinking in convivial company as in Moscow, except that the company was not only convivial but also congenial.

9 May.   We wave goodbye to the friendly, openly-commiserating Finnish border guards. The double white pole barriers swing up for us on the Finnish side, and then, a second later, ten yards away, on the Soviet side. In the Soviet immigration and customs building there are a few border guards and officials in uniform sitting around on bare wooden benches smoking; two are playing chess with an old broken chess set, half the pieces missing or snapped. No-one else is crossing in or out today, apparently. There is the usual Soviet smell of carbolic soap, sweat, cheap tobacco and drains. One unsmiling youth asks for my Soviet documents regarding the car. I explain that I am bringing the car into the USSR for the first time and have not yet obtained Soviet documents for it. He is intensely suspicious of this announcement and spends ten minutes laboriously writing with a blunt pencil in an immense ledger, fills in several forms in quadruplicate, takes them off to an invisible superior, makes three telephone calls, and looks for three minutes in total incomprehension at my UK car log book before allowing us grudgingly to proceed.

As we bounce along over the ruts and potholes we look back nostalgically at the past few days: the clean, comfortable car ferries from Harwich to Esbjerg and from Copenhagen to Helsinki; the superb food on the "Finlandia", her cinema, swimming pool, sauna, roomy cocktail lounges, duty free shops, spotless linen in the cabins; the fast, splendidly surfaced road across Denmark; the pleasant, rather old-fashioned hotel in Copenhagen and the familiar luxury of the Seurahuone Hotel at Hamina last night, just a few miles from the Soviet Union but still on the friendly, relaxed Finnish side. Now we have only the dreary grind of the dusty road through Leningrad to Novgorod, and tomorrow on to Moscow. Horrible petrol stations, consisting of rude old women in rusty corrugated iron shacks, often as much as 200 miles apart, dispensing smelly low-octane petrol; the staring unblinking gaze of the militia at the GAI-posts every few miles, straining to get down the number of the unfamiliar foreign car, hastening into their little hutches to telephone their reports, so that the combined might of the Soviet police was tracking our progress across their country; queues of ancient trundling lorries, many seemingly loaded with <u>earth</u> (why transport earth for miles across the countryside?); always the unsuspected pothole pounding the suspension to jelly, the patch of corrugation on the road, vibrating to the backbone and setting the teeth on edge.

Novgorod. The hotel is as crummy as ever, and the food in the restaurant is still cold.

10 May.   Tired and grubby, we drive into Moscow at about 4 p.m. Nothing seems to have changed. The cockroaches are drawn up in orderly ranks to receive us. Zina has worked hard, obviously, and the flat is clean and tidy and inviting. The traffic on the ring road is still thundering past. There is a message inviting us to a cocktail party given by the Ambassador that evening at 6 o'clock to say goodbye to David Bonavia, the Times correspondent, who has been expelled and is leaving the day after tomorrow. Can see no chance of getting even the first layer of grime off by 6 o'clock so ring up and make apologies.

11 May.   The Bonavias' farewell party at their home. It is a memorable occasion. Many leading dissidents are there, including the eminent and courageous Academician Sakharov, who hardly ever visits foreigners in their homes, and Pyotr Yakir, the son of the eminent general Yakir shot by Stalin when Pyotr was a boy (he was in a labour camp from the age of 14 until his release by Khrushchev). Shook hands with Sakharov, and wished there were not so many obstacles (not just linguistic ones) to telling him that it was a handshake I would remember. He said that he was working in a small institute somewhere, obviously the nearest thing to exile. His career as a scientist and Academician is finished because he has spoken up so bravely for justice and freedom. It is a tremendous tribute to David and Judy Bonavia that so many of these men and women valued his friendship so much, and trusted him so well, that they took the enormous risks of coming to his flat to see him off and to say goodbye to him, after he had been vilified in the Soviet press and expelled from their country.

16 May. V arrives from London, her first unaccompanied flight. She is a little pink in the face with the effort to carry it all off with calmness and confidence, but otherwise very cool and collected. That small figure standing in the rain in Beckenham, waving as we drove away to Russia, is at last exorcised.

29 May. President Nixon leaves Moscow today for Kiev on his way to Teheran after his Soviet trip. There was a great deal of activity before his arrival: whole streets were cleared of old houses and turf laid in their place by armies of old women; ready-grown flowers were thrust into empty flower-beds by further armies of indistinguishable old women; roads were repaired and houses white-washed, tatty old slogans taken down from factory walls and fresh new ones (new, alas, only in the most literal and physical sense) substituted; the Kremlin palace roofs were painted, and Vietnam propaganda in the press drastically curtailed. But once the great man and his travelling court were here, it made remarkably little impact, apart from the massive publicity on Soviet TV. The procession of cars carrying the Presidential party from Vnukovo Airport to the Kremlin (taking them right past the French Embassy, and only a few yards from the British) travelled at such a speed that no-one could be identified inside any of the vehicles and anyway his car (the bullet-proof Lincoln, flown in the day before) was surrounded by military motor-cyclist out-riders. Once he was inside the Kremlin he hardly came out again except to leave for good, although the Lovely Pat dutifully trailed around the metro ("very beautiful. So cute"). From our own Embassy we had an admirable view of the unusual spectacle of the Stars and Stripes flying over the Kremlin, just across the river: I tried to photograph it, but all the time I waited with camera to eye, it refused to blow out and identify itself.

Soviet TV today covered the farewell ceremonies at the airport as Nixon and co. prepared to take off in a big gleaming Aeroflot jet for Kiev, and rather surprisingly cut off the transmission as the great man and Lovely Pat disappeared inside the aircraft after the last ritual wave at the top of the steps, not showing takeoff as they usually do. Later it turned out that there had been technical trouble and he had had to transfer to another aircraft. A suitably ironical farewell to Moscow. Now we prepare to welcome Castro and Tito next month. (Not, alas, at the same time.)

CHAPTER 10

JUNE-JULY 1972: MOSCOW, LENINGRAD

7 June.   Surely it can't be a whole year since the last Queen's Birthday party ("QBP" to everyone in the Embassy)? This one was reprieved at the last moment from cancellation because of the court mourning for the Duke of Windsor, which – like that for the death of the King of Denmark a few months ago, only even more hypocritically – brought us a welcome crop of cancellations of attendances at parties and some pleasant evenings at home. But the period of mourning was shortened to allow us to celebrate the Queen's Birthday despite the ex-King's Deathday. As always on these occasions it was warm and sunny and the party was in the garden, the elaborate "Wet Weather Programme" proving once again wasted. The sprinkling of vaguely Ascot-like hats on some of the flowery-dressed girls (including one in dashing, if inappropriate, tightly-buckled black leather knee-length boots and a black midi-skirt), the lawn and flower-beds and the tinkle of small talk all create a distinct impression of an English garden party, but the image is a shade blighted by the unmistakeable knots of square, heavy figures in square, heavy suits, resolutely grasping tumblers of vodka and surreptitiously eying the British Embassy typists in the more audacious minis. I spend 15 minutes with one of these, Yuri Zhukov, Pravda's senior political commentator and a member of the Supreme Soviet. We exchange notes on what Sir Alec and Gromyko said when they met a few days ago in Berlin about the scope for improving Anglo-Soviet relations and I ask whether we shall see this aspiration reflected in "Pravda".

"Aha," Zhukov says roguishly, "time will tell" (one of the favourite catch-phrases worked to death by Soviet journalists). After this I have about half an hour with the Chinese Ambassador and his interpreter: all very courteous and friendly and without the smallest degree of communication in, I hope, either direction.

9 June.   Departure at the end of his Moscow tour of a Chancery colleague and friend, Graham Beel. We give him lunch and then drive him to the airport to see him off. As has happened much of the time that he has been here, he is being followed pretty ostentatiously by four large gentlemen in the usual whitish car, they fall in behind. I decide to try to take a short cut from our apartment block onto the Leningrad Highway, find I can't take an essential right turn and get hopelessly lost in a maze of back streets. Our friends stick doggedly on our tail. Quite unintentionally I find myself driving the wrong way up a one-way street: our escorts follow: I do a hazardous U-turn and shoot off down a side street: so do they: then, in a final burst of Keystone Copsery, I turn up another side street and find that this too is a one-way street going the wrong way. At this point our tails give up and park by the kerb, mopping their faces, until we sort ourselves out. I nip off to the right and find myself virtually on the Leningrad Highway, the original objective. We don't see the escorts again that day. My antics must have seemed extremely suspicious to them: no doubt they are unshakeably convinced that I was deliberately trying to shake them off.

18 June.   Spend the day at Yasnaya Polyana, the country estate where Tolstoy was born, lived, and is buried, about 120 miles south of Moscow near Tula. The big house where he was actually born was pulled down by Tolstoy as a young man and sold in pieces for re-erection elsewhere, to help pay off Count Leo's gambling debts. But the smaller, wooden house just next door on the estate where he subsequently lived is intact and preserved as a Tolstoy museum or shrine, very effectively. The whole atmosphere of the man, the place and the period comes across very pungently. Even Lenin is scarcely in evidence and Soviet Power seems a long way away – until I ask at the Tolstoy bookshop near the entrance to the estate for a copy of "War and Peace" and am told, with the shrugging dismissal appropriate to someone wishing to buy the Crown Jewels at the High Street jewelers, that they haven't got it. (It isn't available either in any of the main bookshops of Moscow or Leningrad, as I later discover.) But the main delight of Yasnaya Polyana is the huge grounds of the estate, its rolling woods and fields, lakes and streams, almost wholly unspoiled, and all full of Tolstovian associations (lovingly described by our English-speaking guide). Most moving of all is the simple grave – just a grassy mound, heaped with flowers, in a clearing in the Stariy Zakaz (Old Wood) on the edge of a gully, the place where according to Leon's admired older brother there is hidden the green stick on which is carved the secret of universal human happiness and where Tolstoy asked to be buried.

22 June.   With J and V by the night train to Leningrad, for the White Nights festival (so called because at this time of year it hardly gets dark at night-time) and as a treat for Virginia before we pack her off to boarding school in September. True to form, the Embassy car fails to turn up at 11 p.m. to take us to the station and we drag our neighbor, the Moscow correspondent of the Los Angeles Times, out of bed to transport us in his big Chevrolet, incongruous among the little Moskvitches and square Volgas of the Moscow streets. The fourth bunk of our 4-berth compartment is occupied by a rather pretty Bulgarian girl with unusually cosmopolitan connexions (siblings in the West, has visited Paris, mother half Swiss and so forth). She displays considerable skill in getting changed for bed, with me trying not to look as if I am looking, and rather to my disappointment shows no sign of trying to ensnare me into a compromising situation (not that this would be terribly easy in a space measuring about 7 feet by 8, most of which is taken up by four beds and my wife and daughter).

23 June.   Leningrad. The "Oktyabrskya" Hotel is just as awful as I had remembered it from my stay in May last year: shabby barrack-room style furniture, hard narrow beds and an indescribably squalid bathroom dispensing dark brown water from both taps. I check up at the Service Bureau about the Kirov Ballet: yes, she received a message from Moscow by telephone that we would want three tickets for Saturday morning. Spend the usual hour and half sorting out the reservations for our train journey back to Moscow on Sunday night, receive promise that tickets will be ready that afternoon, hand over our passports and depart with J and V to the Hermitage, where the Cezannes and the Picassos are as glorious as ever.

Walking afterwards in the gardens behind the Admiralty building, near the famous bronze horseman statue, V trips and falls, grazing her leg and getting a lot of earth and dirt over her. We then do a conducted tour of all the local cafes, refreshment stalls and shops to try to get a glass of water, a bottle of mineral water, or just a drink of some sort, to enable V to give herself a preliminary wipe down before we get back to the hotel: but without the slightest whiff of success, despite the fact that the temperature is about 85°, it is the middle of Leningrad's main festival, and the city is bursting at the seams with tourists. There must be a lot of thirsty people in this city, not to mention one blood- and mud-stained little girl.

In the evening, having cleaned up in the Oktyabrskya's brown water, we set off to find a pleasant restaurant for an evening meal. Each restaurant proves to have a sizeable queue of resigned-looking people, Russians and foreign tourists, waiting outside its closed doors. Attempting to apply the invariable practice in Moscow, I force my way in and show my diplomatic identity card, but this has no effect at all. Indeed, most of the restaurant door-keepers and managers jab a dismissive thumb at Virginia and say that even if we waited for three or four hours in the queue until our turn came, it wouldn't do any good because "we don't take children". We progressively lower our sights, trying every more disagreeable looking cafes, but get the same response at all of them. Eventually, getting by now pretty footsore, we trail back to the hotel, resigned to the prospect of a terrible dinner at the hotel restaurant of evil repute. But it is by now 8 p.m. and the hotel restaurant is shut – not only not accepting new customers, but empty, deserted, chairs stacked on tables and the lights out. It is also heavily padlocked. For 8 p.m. on a Friday evening in summer festival time at Leningrad's fourth biggest hotel, accommodating on that night alone several hundred foreign tourists, this seems somewhat uncalled for. We repair to our room and devour quantities of English tinned food which, providentially (meaning here "with foresight"), we had brought with us.

It is quite true, it doesn't get dark all night.

24 June.   Spend another hour at the service bureau failing to get our passports back or our return railway tickets: but they will "definitely be ready for you tomorrow" which is just as well since we are due to leave tomorrow. What about the tickets for the Kirov? Ah, no, that is impossible. But they were definitely promised to us: we ordered them weeks ago from Moscow! No, no, not promised. We promised to try, but unfortunately there are so many tourists in Leningrad, so many important guests, half the Central Committee is here, all wishing to visit the Kirov Ballet, you see, so it is definitely impossible. But here are three tickets for a very nice little ballet at a theatre just across the square from the Kirov – just as good, in fact thought by many to be better .... I stall, saying that I might consider buying the lesser ballet tickets if they can make me a definite restaurant booking for the evening meal. Much telephoning to restaurants: "Look, Misha, I have these English here, they will only buy the ballet tickets if I can get them a restaurant booking, otherwise I shall have to pay myself for the tickets, can you help me? .... No .... No .... I understand .... Dosvidanya, Misha." Eventually she twists the arms of the hotel restaurant manageress who reluctantly agrees to let us have a table at 5 p.m. provided we promise to vacate it by 6. I pay for the unwanted ballet tickets and the bargain is sealed.

We set off by hydrofoil down the Neva to the old Tsarist palace at Petrodvorets, a baroque extravagance of immense fountains arranged in enormous vistas stretching from the palace down to the sea, gilded Grecian-style statues, crumbling pavilions, ice cream stalls and joke cobbles which jet water upwards when trodden on. The whole place was completely wrecked by the Germans during the war (as photographs on prominent display show) and has been painstakingly and admirably restored. It is packed with sightseers, mostly Russian, all evidently enjoying the un-Soviet lavishness and style of it all. We are with a teacher from the Anglo-American school and his Bermuda-shorted wife, who happen also to be visiting Leningrad and who are fellow-victims of the Oktyabrskya. Neither speaks any Russian, and both have only the haziest notions about Russian history, concentrated in the main on Peter the Great and Catherine the Great. We stand in the palace Grand Hall admiring a huge oil painting prominently labelled "Archduke Nicholas". "Gee, there's a great picture of Peter the Great," he says. "Wow!", says his wife.

After a horrible 5 o'clock dinner in the hotel restaurant we make for our second-hand ballet across the square from the Kirov Theatre. As we are there ten minutes or so early we decide to stroll over and have a look at the foyer of the Kirov, this famous old pre-revolutionary theatre and the home of the world's ballet, if anywhere is. The foyer is already crowded and on impulse I go up to the cash desk and say that I suppose there is no chance of three tickets for tonight's performance. "Certainly," says the woman, "where in the theatre would you like to go?" So we do see the Kirov after all, in the beautiful, blue and gold, petite theatre where Nureyev and Makarova started. The ballet is "Gamlet" (there is no "H" in Russian), the dancing splendid, the choreography terrible. The last time J and I saw the Kirov company was at the Royal Festival Hall where we had been taken by a fat, jolly First Secretary at the Soviet Embassy who was later expelled as a spy.

25 June.   A Sunday's sight-seeing in this beautiful, non-Russian, Italianate, hot, dead city, with all its air of a great capital (so unlike Moscow's impenetrable provincialism), its superb show-piece buildings by such un-Russian figures as Rastrelli, Carlo Rossi, Rinaldi, Tresini and that Italianised-Russified-Scot "Kameron". Yet it is all like a vast disintegrating museum: the great facades are crumbling as fast as the palace next door is restored, nothing is used for the purposes originally intended, the life-style of the society which camps out in all this baroque splendour is all at odds with its spirit, and the only new buildings are a desecration. Peter tried to turn his people Westwards in his great westward-facing capital with all its echoes of Rome, Venice and Paris: but Lenin took the Russians back to the sprawling peasants' village of Moscow, whose centre is the ominous walls of the Kremlin and St Basil's onion domes.

A tour of the Peter and Paul fortress, including a visit to the cell where Lenin's older brother was imprisoned before he was hanged; a lot of walking; some photography in the magnificent Palace Square; a passable dinner, (booked by a triumphant Service Bureau which finally also produced, like rabbits from a hat, our tickets and passports) at the Chaika on the pretty Griboyedova Canal, with the head of the Embassy's registry and his wife; and off to the station at 11.30 for the midnight train (the Red Arrow) back to Moscow. This time the fourth bunk is occupied by an equally pretty but uncommunicative Russian girl who conducts her dressing and undressing activities in the insalubrious train toilet.

2 July.   We apply for permission to go to the diplomatic holiday area about 60 miles north of Moscow at Zavidova, for a day's picnic swimming and boating, as we did on several occasions last year, but are refused permission, at first on the ludicrous grounds that "there will be too many people there" (it is a huge area which includes a long stretch of the Volga and a sizeable island) and then, after we query this, on the less ludicrous grounds – which later however prove to be wholly fictitious – that there is to be "an important official function there on that day". In fact it turns out that Brezhnev was entertaining Castro at his dacha only a couple of kilometers up the main road from the diplomatic area, so presumably they didn't want any nosy British around. We go instead to the Bay of Joy, which is very crowded but within our 40 kilometer radius.

Earlier I had watched Castro's arrival as he drove in from the airport to the Kremlin. I watched at the back of the Embassy on the "Small Stone Bridge" (May Kammeniy Most) as the long procession of big sleek Chaika and Zill cars went past, Brezhnev and Castro standing together waving in the back of the leading car. Rentacrowd was out in force, holding but not waving little paper flags bearing the word "Druzhba" (friendship) – an economical gesture since the same flags, collected up after use by the group leader from each factory or kolkhoz, can be re-used on almost any future occasion. Brezhnev, for all his heavy Russian bulkiness, was completely dwarfed by Fidel, who looked like an enormous bear, in his usual battle fatigues and bristling with guns. They vanished at speed into the Kremlin through the Borovistkaya Gate and almost immediately the workmen appear on the bridge and start taking down the Cuban flags from the lamp-posts.

6 July.   We apply for permission to go at the weekend to Vladimir and Suzdal, two ancient towns not far from Moscow which are full of famous old churches and regular places for tourists to visit. Our application is turned down – apparently because the only hotel at Vladimir prefers to take the visitors who come under Intourist auspices since they pay in foreign currency. It really seems to be "Hate the British" week for those who decide whether and if so where we may travel. The heat wave which has been unbroken since our return from leave in May continues, with temperatures each day around 90° and a blazing sun. The Russians complain all the time that it is too hot. It is, but I prefer to save my complaints for the winter. We get through an awful lot of Pimms and Carlsberg. Luckily the Chancery is not too hot to work in so long as we open the windows, but since these are in three layers, each padlocked and protected by an inner steel grille, so that it takes about ten minutes to open or shut them, and since they have to be shut and locked every time the room is left unattended (for reasons of security), the air costs a good deal of effort.

29 July.   We are living all this week at the Embassy dacha (it costs about £27 for the week but it's worth it to get out of Moscow for a while and, for the children, to have a garden). This charming, dilapidated, faded wooden house with its four bedrooms and big airy living rooms is one of the Embassy's main assets and amenities and we all relax luxuriously, once having undergone the ordeal by packing-loading-unloading-unpacking that it entails: this is when the second car comes into its own. Our cat, Daisy, comes with us and rather surprisingly doesn't seize the opportunity to defect, as it were, to the Russians. The children swim in the river just behind the dacha, at a pleasant river beach, but Louise is up being sick all night afterwards and so, we later discover, are almost all the other Embassy children who came out for the day to swim at the same spot in Serebryanniy Bor: so the long heat of the summer and the pollution of the river and the low level of the water in the river (reducing the current flow) have all combined to poison half the Embassy. No more swimming here for the kids, alas.

Today, Saturday, we have about 25 people from the Embassy, including most of those who arrived during the last week or ten days, out to the dacha for a barbecue lunch. We get through a small lake of Pimms and an ocean of Carlsberg, then embark on the barbecue, using the dacha's big tin box from which the grill is now missing and for which we substitute a shoe-scraper grating. The thing uses up almost the entire 20 lbs. of charcoal which we had specially sent down from Helsinki and eventually develops such an intense heat that I, as chef, can hardly get to within ten yards of it, never mind turn over and remove the steaks, sausages and chickens. The sun beats down fiercely from above and the barbecue beats up fiercely from below, while I drip freely into it. Even my Nevada cowboy hat doesn't seem to provide any shade. However the lunch seems to be generally appreciated. Later most of us go down to the beach and swim, mouths firmly shut against the pollution. Although the dacha and the big island in the river on which it stands, Serebryanniy Bor, are only 30 minutes' drive from the centre of Moscow, they seem a lifetime apart, with the absence of traffic din, the virtual non-existence of militiamen (ubiquitous in Moscow, a harassing, nannying presence), the tall pines and the permanent atmosphere of weekend. Even though I have had to get up at 6.40 each morning to get Pravda read and then drive into the Embassy in time for the day's work, it has been well worth while.

Looking out through the wide open windows of the children's bedroom in the evening at the warm dry grass and the trees made pink by the summer sun, just beginning to go down, it is difficult to believe that the next time we are here there will be a blanket of frozen snow over everything, a roaring wood fire in the small living-room downstairs and skis and poles stacked in the porch by the front door. Meanwhile, there is August.

CHAPTER 11

AUG 1972 – JAN 1973: MOSCOW, MINSK, VILNIUS & MORE

I owe the poor diary an apology for so many months of neglect. A combination of much time-consuming, if mainly fruitless, activity, with a steady escalation in the manic social life, and indeed with my own natural idleness (now rapidly flowering into absolute <u>accidie</u>), has kept me from the labour of finding diary, carbon paper, typewriter and time. So I depart from the blow-by-blow, day-to-day format and just recall some particular impressions of these last months, in no special order.

Looking at Lenin. A recent announcement that the Lenin mausoleum was to be closed "for renovations" (what can be left now to renovate?) reminds me that I forgot to record our visit earlier in the summer. Louise wouldn't come, having no partiality for corpses, but Owen and V. did. The queue as usual wound in a crocodile from the brown marble entrance with the single word "LENIN" over the door (no trace now of "STALIN" which for a few years appeared below) across the corner of Red Square, down by the side of the History Museum and round to the edge of the Alexandrovsky Gardens which go alongside the outer walls of the Kremlin. Heaven knows who they all are, these endless queuers in sun and snow to see the new patron saint's holy relics: organised outings from schools and collective farms, private tourists, visiting delegations, anyone who is in Moscow and feels he or she must see the number one sight. Wedding couples too traditionally file past the cadaver after the ceremony, for good luck: there was a flushed bride in her white long dress just ahead of us. Brides and diplomats have immunity from queueing, and go almost to the front, where a militiaman shoe-horns a gap in the plodding mass and inserts his clients. So instead of waiting three, four, five hours, we waited about ten minutes, shuffling slowly forward. The Soldiers on guard at the door stand like West Point ramrods; the security guards just beyond them scrutinise everyone with X-ray eyes for bombs, cameras, umbrellas, paint-pots, evil designs on the shrine. (What a coup it would be, to blow Him up – or even just to crack His glass case a little!) Inside, all is marble and reverent silence. Along a hall, down marble steps, round a bend and into the presence. Beautifully lit, guarded by a soldier at each corner (facing outwards), lying there like the Crown Jewels, his face is small and waxy and has nothing remotely human about it. He is dressed in his smart, buttoned-up-to-the-neck little bourgeois suit with a neatly knotted tie, hands in the attitudes shown in the casts which one sees at his country house just outside Moscow at Leninskiye Gori. Not at all like a burning revolutionary; not at all like the all-watching father figure of the huge posters and the idealized representations; a little man with a neat beard. Much more like a wax-work than a human. Quite an impressive face, on its small scale, dogged looking and intelligent, not very likeable. We file past and out again into the sunlight, feeling simultaneously a sense of anti-climax and a sense of having viewed Jesus Christ, Genghis Khan, Hitler and Julius Caesar all rolled into one, in the flesh – what's left of it. After the forthcoming "renovation" there'll presumably be even less.

Eminent Visitors   The crop in this period has included Jim Callaghan and Vic Feather (separately, perhaps just as well). Callaghan came with the young and pleasant International Secretary of the Labour Party Tom McNally, who (so I thought) knows a thing or two. He – Callaghan – came to dinner at the Residence at the end of his talks with the Soviet hosts and got drawn gradually into a mara-thon, and fascinating, debate with a senior member of the Soviet Foreign Ministry who was also there. C. combined occasional apparent naivetes with very consid-erable shrewdness, even cunning, playing wide-eyed to draw his interlocutor onto favourable ground and then enjoying the leisurely kill. The MFA man is also no slouch at argument and made an infinitely more sophisticated case than some of his colleagues can ever do, but honours ended about even. Afterwards I drove C. and McNally back to their hotel and got an interesting private insight into how they had seen their visit. Pretty disillusioning, inevitably, but there were one or two necessary stars left in their eyes.

Vic Feather was also an obvious case of the downy bird who misses little and gives away less. He had several hours of talks with the Soviet trade union chief, Shelepin, one of the fifteen Politburo members who run this country plus numerous acolytes, and wound up (after a trip to Leningrad) early one snowy Sunday morning at the Residence for breakfast and to meet the Gentlemen of the British Press – whom I had invited a few days previously. But the Fifth Estate rises late on weekdays, and only for a few hours in the evening on Sunday, so the only takers for an interview with Vic Feather were the rather leathery, pipe-smoking correspondent of the Morning Star, an ageing and pretty disillusioned British communist: and dewy-eyed young Moyra Stramentova, the correspondent of the Financial Times, English and married to a Russian, so unable to take any risks. A Reuters correspondent was coming, but he couldn't start his car, and eventually came rushing in through one of the Embassy gates just as Feather drove out through the other. Anyway, he told Colin and Moyra what he thought of it all, in practiced and diplomatic language and in his splendid Yorkshire: "Ah toald the Roossians, ye see, yoor trade unions are different from ours. The Party tells you what to do: noa-wun tells uss what to do, that's the difference, I toald them." He's right, too.

Christmas and all that. The Embassy cabaret was rather more disastrously chaotic than usual, although much better organized and with less of a last-minute panic than in previous years. However flu and general dyspepsia laid low many stars, and censorship, applied late and without much discrimination, decimated the rest. My own appearance was in a maternity dress of Jane's (reaching to mid-thigh), an auburn wig belonging to the wife of the Assistant Military Attache, perilously high-heeled shoes (from the Assistant Visa Officer, a big girl) and a sumptuous bosom constructed from four socks. My fellow transvestites comprised the Administration Officer, the Third Secretary Chancery and the Assistant

Administration Officer who, in a mini-dress of his wife's, looked so gorgeous that it was worrying. Unfortunately the (male) star of the number succumbed on the previous day to bronchitis and had to be replaced at short notice by the Counsellor (Administration), who was also the compere and had too many lines to remember anyway. Jane appeared as a harassed Embassy housewife, a simulation requiring little if any artifice.

A few trips.   In December Jane and I had a few days in Minsk and Vilnius, mainly to visit the British teacher at the Language Institute in Minsk and the three girl students there (from Salford) and take them some films, books and records from the British Council to help out with the English teaching. Minsk, capital of Byelorussia, is the ultimate Soviet city, totally flattened in the war and totally rebuilt Stalin-style after the war, drab and uniform, with nothing at all to lift the spirit and nothing to gladden the eye. Nothing to do, either. Our appeals to the officials in the Byelorussian Foreign Ministry and the Minsk City Executive Council, on whom we called, to advise us what to see, yielded only the Museum of the History of the War, which, on inspection, proved to be a sort of sado-masochists' paradise – all whips, gallows, pictures of horribly tortured bodies, partisans at the end of Nazi ropes, Nazis at the ends of partisans' ropes, hand-cuffs, thumb-screws, mass graves, the lot. "Lest We Forget", fine, but this is ridiculous. A really very sick place indeed. One odd feature of Minsk was that no-one seemed to speak Byelorussian in the shops, cafes and buses – only Russian (whereas no Ukrainian in Kiev or Armenian in Yerevan would be caught dead speaking Russian unless virtually compelled to). The Byelorussians really don't seem all that different from the Russians – at least one of their component republics seems to enjoy it.

Vilnius, capital of Lithuania, is a very different kettle of fish. Where Minsk was wholly Soviet, Vilnius is wholly Lithuanian, and the recentness of Sovietisation is very apparent. The occasional Soviet-style building or tatty banner proclaiming "Glory to Labour" (in Russian) jarred horribly. The old part of the city, all winding cobbled streets, with a fine old university complex dating back to the 17th or 18th centuries, seemed totally western (or rather north-western: bits of it reminded us of Bergen in Norway) and there was even a rough imitation of a coffee bar, although western bourgeois spies like us evidently weren't served there and we finally walked out in a huff. Everyone spoke Lithuanian rather than Russian and some people, in the shops for example, seemed to have difficulty speaking Russian at all.

When we left the hotel in Minsk to get the train to Vilnius (it was 3 a.m. and the train left at 4 a.m. – the only time of day they would allow us to make the journey, presumably fearing that we would make rapid sketch-maps of the ICBM sites along the way if we were permitted to travel in daylight) we found that the hotel lift wasn't working. ("Why?" "Because it's night-time." Follow that.) Our case, as usual, weighed about four tons and we were on the fifth floor. Moments to remember.

In September we had driven for a long week-end to Yaroslavl, about five hours' drive from Moscow along pretty ropey roads. We couldn't leave until lunch-time on the Friday and so it was dark long before we reached Yaroslavl. It was also raining steadily and the roads were covered in thick black mud, much of which wound up on our wind screen owing to the presence just in front of us of about two hundred heavy farm trucks with loads of black mud and travelling at about eight miles an hour. Another memorable feature of the journey was that three hundred heavy farm trucks were coming the other way. Now there is no street or other lighting on these country roads and the edge of the road is just a strip of mud and a sheer drop into a ditch or stream and there are no cats-eyes or white lines down the middle. Moreover there are lots of people trudging along in the road in black hats and black coats and a lot more riding black bicycles without lights. And another funny thing is, the on-coming traffic just hates it if you have your headlights on, even dipped. So if you do, they turn theirs on, full beam. And their lights, on these big lorries, are about eye-level to a low-slung Cortina. So you're really blind, all the way. How I didn't mow down half the rural population of central Russia, I'll never know. Maybe I did.

Anyway it was all worth it in spite of the fact that the hotel at Yaroslavl charges the villainous "bron" (i.e. one night more than you are actually there for – quite apart from the fact that the tariff for foreigners is about four to five times higher for the same room as for Russians). Yaroslavl has a delightful central square with gracious streets radiating from it and quiet, dignified avenues with trees, lots of solid merchants' houses, and an admirable art gallery, plus a splendid promenade along a nobly broad stretch of the Volga. There are some excellent churches as well, some in good repair, others derelict. One, praised in the guide-book, proved to be virtually inaccessible except by wading through some hundreds of yards of deep mud (which we did) and then by breaking down several rusty padlocks and timber beams nailed across the doors (which we didn't). It has priceless Yaroslavl coloured enamel tiles on the walls and some magnificent onion domes. A few steps away they have thoughtfully built a vast factory complex which belches evil steam and smoke over the church. Even on Saturdays (we know, because it was and it did).

Back via Rostov (the Great, not on Don) with a fairy-tale Kremlin on the big misty lake, all superb towers and spires looming over solid fortress walls. And Pereslavl-Zalessky, with a great central Russian history but nothing at all to see now. And Zagorsk which is magnificent and needs, and got, a visit to itself. (We went there on another occasion with the Head of Accommodation Department from the FCO and two architects from the Department of the Environment, and after seeing the monastery and the churches we sat in the car in the yard outside drinking white Burgundy and eating salmon and egg-and-bacon pies while the Russian kids peered in as if at a manned space-craft. And you could smell the public lavatories behind the Church of the Trinity from the far side of the Cathedral of the Annunciation.)

Then, while we're on the subject, we went a couple of week-ends ago in December or January for a Saturday and Sunday to Vladimir and Suzdal, both hallowed old church and political centres of Old Russia and steeped in history. The Cathedral of the Assumption in Vladimir has magnificent frescoes by Rublev (pronounced Ru-bl<u>yov</u>) and a few kilometres beyond the town there's a superb little monolithic church in a field by a river, at Bogolyubovo: we tramped through the snow across a railway line and over a rickety wooden bridge and across about three fields of increasingly deep snow to see it, and did so, but had to content ourselves with a medium shot rather than a close-up: and it was by then too dark to photograph.

Suzdal is even more splendid: there can't be other places like it anywhere. It's a small church town along about a mile and a half of winding river, with meadows and steep banks on either side: and along the banks, churches (perhaps seventy or eighty of them) and five or six major monasteries, each with several churches and chapels, and a Kremlin with a marvelous cathedral, five blue domes with gold stars. From any monastery wall, by the river, one has a stunning view of all the others. An unforgettable scene from the remarkable Russian film "Andrei Rublev" was shot here, so there was an eerie sense of familiarity with it all. The whole place looks magnificent in the snow (and to judge by photographs, magnificent and totally different in the summer) but my slides, not yet developed, are unlikely to do it justice: too many white snow foregrounds, white wall subjects and white sky backgrounds.

Dissidents   One of our few contacts with the tiny, shrinking band of Soviet dissidents, at a party given very informally by the correspondent of an American magazine. They came to his flat in one of the buildings reserved for foreigners in groups of two or three, sitting in the back of correspondents' cars with their collars turned up and hats over eyes, the car spurting past the militia guard boxes: and hoped that the inevitable microphones in the flat wouldn't disclose their identities. We all used first names, although one was so celebrated that her identity must have been obvious. They were a good cross-section: Jewish historian and scientist prevented from emigrating to Israel and both dismissed from their jobs; a physicist trying to study psychology but unable to get the books or meet others in the field; the wife of a writer now in a labour camp in the far north; sundry others who are just brave and bright enough to see through the charade of Soviet life and not liking what they see.

Occasional contacts with westerners are obviously tremendously important to them, just for the assurance of talking to people who like them don't have blinkers (or at least have different blinkers). Above all it is important to them to keep in touch with the little band of western correspondents in Moscow because through them some account of their existence and their ideas gets back to the outside world, and is reflected back into the Soviet Union on western radio broadcasts – which means that their existence makes some dent on the great flat blind face of the system. But they are few, disorganized, uncoordinated, unsystematic and in many ways limited. Mostly are communists of some kind, pleading only for true and honest communism: and patriots too, ashamed of what the Stalin-Brezhnev kind of regime has done to them and their country (but with mixed feelings about Khrushchev and the miniscule progress made in this reign). One feels sorry for them and admires their great courage (the penalties for exercising even the modest freedoms they claim are horrific, usually involving the end of all family life and often years of hardship and suffering in hideous environments, even now): but it is difficult to imagine that their piteous trumpet note will bring the walls of Jericho tumbling down.

Random notes. Bread is still plentiful despite the disastrous harvest of last year, but the leadership has suppressed all mention of their vast grain purchases from the west in the Soviet press. Now this year too the snow is late and inadequate, so there will again probably be too little snow cover to save the winter wheat. Maybe another bad harvest this year. Already the Ministry of Agriculture has been sacked and a Deputy P.M. (Polyanksy, widely tipped as Brezhnev's successor) demoted to take his place – or has agriculture been promoted? Plenty of meat for the moment – because cattle have been slaughtered early through lack of animal feed. All the main 5-year plan figures for 1972 were well short of the target figures for the year. Brezhnev is thought to have had some kind of operation in November but is back on form now as Big Bouncing B. There's been a succession of air disasters at Moscow Airport but never any official figures. And one tired diarist will need a new back if he doesn't stop soon.

PART II

AUSTRALIA,
MID-1970s

CHAPTER 12

SEP 1973 – JAN 1974:

CANBERRA, MELBOURNE, SYDNEY, BRISBANE, DARWIN, ALICE SPRINGS, ADELAIDE

14 September, 1973.   Arrive in the BOAC VC10 at Sydney, bewildered by lack of sleep, an excess of free whisky, a total fouling up of my timing mechanism (I don't even know which <u>day</u> it is any more) and a throat dried by nostalgia after reliving four years of New York in four totally exhausting days. Totter off the aircraft with enormous cabin bag bulging with radios, cassette recorders and other electrical items too precious to entrust to the hold.

After repeatedly assuring solemn Australian officials that I have no rabies or diseased sheep with me, am hailed by Gordon Booth, Consul-General in Sydney, who drives me round to domestic airport for flight down to Canberra, mainly it transpires so that he can nobble me about various villainies being perpetrated by the High Commission in Canberra which he wants me to put a stop to. Promise to put stop to all. Quite unable to make out what he's talking about.

Met at Canberra on windy, sunlit village-style airport by large array of sheepish characters from High Commission, most of them seemingly about 6'9" tall and deeply tanned. Tallest reels off names. Shake hands and murmur inanities all round. Wonder who the hell they are. One giant passes me folder containing elegantly typed programme for my first few days: dinner tonight with so-and-so, lunch tomorrow with someone else, dinner with someone else again, lunch tomorrow with someone else, dinner with someone else again, lunch on Sunday with the Minister, dinner (black tie) with High Commissioner, picked up at motel Monday morning at 8.00 a.m. by so-and-so to be driven to High Commission, dinner with so-and-so …. List of Useful Telephone Numbers. Map of Canberra. Best Car Hire and taxi firms. Sheaf of invitation cards: At Home, for Dinner, for Buffet Supper, Luncheon, Informal, Black Tie, RSVP, RSVP, RSVP. Begin to murmur "Thank you very much" over and over again.

Suitcases (very obviously made of cardboard which has had a thorough wetting and dried unevenly) eventually appear from plane. Am led to waiting car and driven off by giant number 3 into Canberra and to motel getting vague impression of narrow winding roads, masses of greenery and space, long vistas and a few emphatic public buildings across an irregularly shaped lake, and strange rather ragged trees. Giant no. 3 seems to be telling me about some recent talks with senior officials in the Australian Ministry of Defence. Keep on murmuring "Thank you very much" whenever some response seems to be expected.

Arrive at motel. All American style (i.e. very nice indeed, with TV, coffee machine, fridge, bath and shower, room service menus, etc.). Sit gratefully on bed. Remaining giants begin to pour into room (their fleet of cars having just arrived) all carrying my cases, radios, cassette recorders, etc. Look for folder containing programme, invitations, etc., and realise have left it at airport. Room empties as by magic as giants set off in a roar of Triumph 2000's to rescue folder from airport. Take clothes off, throw them on floor, fall into bed and pass out.

25 September. Jane, Owen and Liz Deane leave London today: I leave Canberra for brief initial trips to Melbourne and Sydney, meeting J and O early on the 27th and flying back with them to Canberra. An agreeable day in Melbourne, a rich and dignified city with opulent balconied houses (their intricate wrought-iron railings made from the 19th and 18th century ships' ballast) and semi-tropical but orderly parks.

Do the rounds of the Consulate-General (assistant information officers, deputy visa officers, commercial assistants, telephonists, librarians, vice-consuls, receptionists). Very glad to meet you. Yes, just ten days ago. No, they're arriving on Thursday if the Sydney airport strikers let them land, ha ha. So what do you do here then? And how long have you been with the Consulate-General? <u>Twelve years</u>! Goodness. Well, very good to meet you and I'll see you again when I come back for a proper visit.

A very splendid lunch at the Melbourne Club (detailed replica of an expensive and exclusive London club) with E M and J R, the latter a former Marine Colonel who has settled in Australia and taken a job as a Senior Commercial Officer with the Consulate-General and finds himself as President of the Locally Engaged Staff Association of Australia (the trade union of the 200 or so Australians and British whom we employ in Canberra, Darwin and five of the six State capitals). We eat our magnificent Clyde River (near Sydney) oysters and steaks tournedos, washed down with three large decanters of heavy, fruity, narcotic South Australian red, staff side and official side, union and employer. It's an unfamiliar role, probably for both of us. We get on well and agree that we'll have a good relationship.

Decide that the Sydney airport strike makes the planned flight to Sydney tomorrow morning too uncertain so change to a booking on the overnight train instead (never used except at the admittedly frequent times of strike). Train leaves at 8 p.m. Dinner at Chinese restaurant with Information Officer, a gout victim – understandably, as it turns out. Drink a great deal of excellent vintage Wynns Ovens Valley Shiraz claret with the sweet and sour pork. Both realise simultaneously that it's 7.50. Run from restaurant to car, leap in and screech away, arriving at main railway station one minute before 8. Leap out, run onto platform and throw self into train just as it starts to move. Amazingly opulent, well-appointed sleeping compartment with own shower, WC, comfortable bed etc. Share with one other, an agreeable Australian banker. Accept his invitation to go and have a beer in train bar with colleague. Have several beers, ham sandwiches, etc., with banker, banker's friend, friend's latest acquaintance, etc. All agree that I don't "talk like a bloody Pom." Can't understand why.

26 September.   Sydney. A magnificent city, with the real feeling of a great cosmopolitan centre, raffish, busy, dirty, with glamorous shop windows, sky-scraper office blocks, parks full of palm and banana trees, an unforgettable harbour dominated by the massive bridge and the glittering white opera house all sail-shell flying panels in concrete and mosaic tiles. More New York than London (the traffic lights for pedestrians even say "Walk" and "Don't Walk") except for the advertisements and hoardings which are all for familiar British products.

Go round the Sydney Consulate-General Offices: assistant information officers, typists, vice-consuls …. Very glad to meet you ….

Administration Officer does some telephoning for me and discovers that Jane's flight, due Sydney tomorrow morning, has been diverted – to Melbourne.

28 September.   Jane, Owen and Liz begin to surface and consider their new environment and home. Two-storey white-painted house with green tile roof, two separate garages, sundry garden sheds, garden full of trees, bushes, plants, roses, wisteria, God knows what with tendrils and flowers and leaves: a couple of vines with bunches of tiny grapes and about three acres of mint. Fly-screens over all the windows and doors. A balcony outside the main bedroom and a sort of small verandah outside the (enormous) dining-room. Inside, furnishings much too rhetorical for family life but fine for entertaining: white damask, rose-wood, satin, polished mahogany. An agreeable study with green and gold leather topped desk. Plenty of book-shelves. Three bathrooms, four lavatories, two fridges. Deep freeze and dish-washing machine both bought from our predecessors, the latter flooding the kitchen floor during the last third of its operation. The whole in a leafy grass-lined road, opposite the Vietnamese Embassy.

We have a noisy motor mower (identical with everyone else's noisy motor mower in Canberra: on Saturday afternoons you can't hear yourself think), property of the High Commission. Am out mowing the "nature strip" (strip of grass between footpath and main road, for whose mowing we're responsible) when tanned gent in invariable Australian uniform of crisp mid-thigh shorts, long socks turned down just below knees, laced shoes, short-sleeve well-pressed shirt, crosses road and introduces himself as near neighbour from next to Vietnamese. He says he has a swimming pool. (Spirits rise.) Thought he ought to mention it in case our six-year-old wanders across the road and falls in. (Spirits fall.) Will we all go over for a beer? We do.

8 October.   Fly to Darwin to visit British Government Wireless Relay Station (relay point for virtually all our Asian and Far East Embassies and High Commissions and their communications with London). Flight goes Canberra-Melbourne-Brisbane-Mount Isa-Darwin. Between Brisbane and Mount Isa encounter most violent turbulence I've ever experienced anywhere: Boeing 727 bucks and rears, bottles crash in stewardesses' cupboards, beers spill, all sit strapped tightly in thinking about the Last Things. Pilot says over intercom in splendid Australian: Well, Lydies'n'gentlemen, we seem to've hit a few little bumps in the raoad, and it's a bit uncomfortable, sao we'll drop a coupla thaousand feet and see if we c'n find a better surface daown theer." We turn nose down and dive, straighten up, and miraculously it's all right again. More beers all round.

Darwin. A real frontier town, raffish, tough, hot as hell (it's well inside the tropics and indeed you can hardly breathe in the oppressive humid heat). All the men seem to have beer bellies, and hold an iced can in one hand to prove it, even while driving around town in their beat-up old Holden pick-ups. All wear shorts and T-shirts, no socks, and "thongs" (rubber flip-flops). Lots of aborigines, mostly pretty sorry sights, many drunk. Terrific palm-lined beaches but not useable for swimming for most of the year because of the dreaded and usually lethal sea-wasps, a kind of enormous jelly-fish with a poisonous sting. Have a quick swim in the motel pool but it's like swimming in warm brown window soup liberally laced with chlorine.

10 October.   Fly by Fokker Friendship to Alice Springs (on the "milk run", stopping at every little mining town in the middle of nowhere), then change to a jet for the rest of the trip to Adelaide, capital of South Australia. A fantastic trip: no other way, except driving, of getting an idea of the vastness and emptiness of this huge desert continent, with a few million people huddled along the southern and eastern edges of a landmass considerably larger than western Europe. You fly along the Darwin-Alice road which runs dead straight for hundreds of miles way down below across nothing, a white line across a white moon landscape. After Alice there's a lot more of the same until gradual greening signals the approach of the fertile plains of South Australia. Darwin to Adelaide is a little further than London to Moscow.

Adelaide: a civilised, stable, gracious, colonial-style city, pleasant rather than spectacular. Looks profoundly Tory but has a solid and seemingly immoveable Labor Government. Call on Deputy Premier, Leader of Opposition, State Secretary of Labor Party (and Whitlam's right-hand man at last December's successful election campaign, Mick Young), and a selection of Ministers. All friendly, unpretentious shirt-sleeves types, not terribly articulate, all patently honest and hard-working, sensible, not very radical, down to earth. Recall remark by rather plummy Pom in Melbourne: "Australia is just one bloody great working men's club." They are all either the salt of the earth or a lot of uncivilized hicks, whichever way you look at it. Certainly they have a nasty suspicion that it's the latter and are extremely sensitive to any sign that an over-cultivated class-conscious Pommy bastard is going to think so too.

Spend two nights with the Consul-General and swim in his pool, much impressing C-G and other locals who think it's still much too cold. Dinner at his house to meet political commentators from local press and TV and professors and lecturers in politics from University: all very young, lively and left-wing. Excellent value.

26 November.   To Brisbane, capital of Queensland. Something halfway between heat and brashness of Darwin, and small colonial town atmosphere of Adelaide. Much rebuilding everywhere, dust, heat, palm trees, tropical parks. Call on (Labor) Leader of Opposition in his squalid offices in State Parliament building, shared with two fat lady secretaries. Nice honest tired guy, obviously gave up years ago. On to State Secretary of Labor Party in crisp new Party offices, shared with highly profitable radio station run by Party in building looking like twenty-first century motel. Then to Trades Council (meet Fred, Joe, Jack, Wally, etc., all indistinguishable from UK counterparts) and to modern skyscraper office building housing main government offices to meet Deputy Premier and Leader of Liberal

Party who is a restless, neurotic tycoon type at a huge desk, who shoots questions at me for exactly 15 minutes, shoots glance at clock and shows us out. Just time for swim in C-G's pool before huge cocktail party in twilit garden for me to meet what seems to be entire Queensland Establishment (average age about 75).

28 November. Because of new airline strike have to leave at 6.15 a.m. Travel tourist class instead of First and have to wait for five hours at Sydney. Reflect that only consolation is that New South Wales electricity and post office strikes are over. Wonder what hysteria there would in UK if workers struck half as often and as long as here.

7 December. Take new Consul-General Melbourne (until last week British Ambassador in Nicaragua: posted to Melbourne on promotion), who is paying first visit to Canberra, to lunch meeting of National Press club where Prime Minister Gough Whitlam and Opposition Leader Billy Snedden are debating pros and cons of granting powers over prices and incomes to the Federal Government (as advocated by Whitlam's Labor Govt., resisted by Snedden's Liberal-Country Party Opposition and soon to be decided by referendum). General expectation is that Whitlam, confident debater with acid tongue and filthy temper, will eat Snedden alive. Snedden, vaguely pathetic figure with big bushy side-burns and big ears, surprisingly does rather well. Whitlam achieves unusual feat of ranting down at us. Very unconvincing and not very loveable. Have to pinch self to recall that price and income power obviously ought to be given to Federal Government despite Whitlam arguments for this.

8 December. Referendum. Huge majority in all states against giving powers on prices and incomes to Federal Government. (Whitlam-Snedden debate was televised nation-wide. Must prove something.)

15 December. Back to Sydney, this time with Jane. Dinner at Doyles fish restaurant on Rose Bay, in perfect setting. More succulent oysters and flinty Australian Chablis, then huge quantity of flounder and John Dory. Utterly delicious. Stay at High Commissioner's luxurious flat on Point Piper overlooking Double Bay and Rose Bay (flat is selectively available when High Commr. not using it himself). Lemon, avocado and banana trees in garden and huge vines.

16 December.   V. and L. arrive at Sydney from London. Both pale and exhausted after 35-hour flight through much turbulence: both were very sick much of the way. Fly back to Canberra with them by which time, after being invited to inspect the aircraft captain's cabin and flight-deck, they have cheered up enormously. They race round the house, every detail of which they already know from minute descriptions and floor-plans we have had to send them. Finally coax them into bed where they stay sleeping like the dead for thirty hours.

30 December.   Spend the day at their beach cottage at Guerrilla Bay, 200 miles south of Sydney and 98 miles over the mountains from Canberra, with the High Commissioner and Lady James (the latter French, well over 50 but v. fetching in pink gingham shorts). Although last few weeks have been roasting, today is grey with continuous rain. Nevertheless swim, go out in Sir M. J.'s little boat, walk along amazing black beach picking up black marble pebbles polished by sea, drink much (French) champagne, eat vast lunch (more oysters) and lose heavily to Virginia at Vingt-et-un.

3-6 January.   With the children in Sydney. Planned as lead-in to their departure on 6ᵗʰ from Sydney for home but flight is cancelled because of oil crisis. Drive back to Canberra in pouring rain (5 hours on appalling roads).

19 December (Sorry!).   Give party for entire High Commission staff, including Jameses and down to last driver and gardener. About 180 to 200 come. Gallons of wine, gin, Scotch: five hams, 3 tons chicken salad, 6 pates and 9 meat loaves, vanish instantly. Also several whole cheeses, 20 loaves, 3 cwt of crisps …. Paraffin flares flare and coloured lights twinkle in garden, and hi-fi blares carols and hard rock (no-one dances but atmosphere is all). Seven people say quite independently that this best party they've been to in Canberra. To bed triumphantly amid wreckage. Jane (who did entire preparation, all cooking, etc., single-handed: we had help in only to serve) prostrated.

10 January.   At last telegram confirms girls' safe arrival in UK: plane was 19 hours late, don't yet know why or where. Canberra temperature 27⁰C, sunny, plenty of petrol, no soldiers at the airport.

CHAPTER 13

FEB 1975:
ALICE SPRINGS, DARWIN,
PORT HEDLAND, PERTH

17 February, 1975. Alice Springs: drizzling rain, warm and muggy but not the blazing heat against which everyone warned me at this time of year in the hot tropical centre of Australia. (Not quite tropical, actually: "the Alice", as all the locals call it, is about 30 miles south of the Tropic of Capricorn. But it is tropical in its climate and style.)

Elderly American couple on bus from airport to terminal (he a pale version of Burl Ives, she a man-eating momma) seem to be only other out-of-season tourists in town. Almost all coach tours cancelled but we persuade someone to take us – Americans, self, and elderly English queer doing Australasian tour to celebrate retirement from BEA cargo office – by car tomorrow to local spot. Occupy afternoon investigating local shopping street: down one side, back the other. Dress: shorts, mandatory long socks, sandals, sports shirt and plastic raincoat. Lots of souvenirs, a few bits of Aboriginal wood carving, mostly of no merit, boomerangs and innumerable postcards. Swim in rain at motel pool.

18 February. With Mr and Mrs Burl Ives and BEA queer to Simpson's Gap and Standley Chasm in Holden station wagon driven by old Alice Springs hand who devotes energies mostly to denunciations of Aboriginal people as work-shy, drunken, lecherous, and molly-coddled by bloody idiot socialists in Canberra. All this lapped up by B. Ives and BEA man (former actually taking notes). Refrain from comment. Pass, in fact, several very drunken Aborigines – mid-morning – and several shanty settlements of indescribable squalor. Simpson's Gap an unusual gap in surrounding hills of MacDonnell Ranges, in river bed plus water hole, both silted up. Inspect extremely amiable, small rock wallabies scuttling about on remarkable rock formations around Gap (mostly immense granite slabs at 45^0 angles) but observe that they look like rats doing smart imitation of kangaroos, which sharply reduces charm. On to Standley's Chasm. Rain by now torrential. Lunch, advertised as available from kiosk at Chasm, not forthcoming "because we haven't got our health certificate back yet". Having foreseen something of sort, have brought sandwiches and can of Foster's. Drink latter and eat former surreptitiously while others are relieving themselves. Then squelch through sodden bush for 1 ½ miles to Chasm in rain. Very spectacular and worth a wetting: about 2 feet wide and over 250 feet high, sheer rock walls, in characteristic reddish stone. Sufficient water in chasm to prevent walking through.

Visits to Aboriginal reserve (rusting car bodies, more squalid shacks and new-ish brick or concrete one-storey houses in mid-destruction; old traditional rock paintings in Dulux paint; dogs), Alice Springs Museum, grave of founder of Flying Doctor Service, and the original Overland Telegraph Station just outside town where the Springs would be if there were any (actually it's a water-hole, or was, also silted up): the latter worth all the rest together. Nicely preserved, solid buildings, still with original 1870s furniture including a solid Victorian piano – everything brought up from Adelaide by camel, because the railway link was completed only in 1929 (original train engine preserved outside present railway station). Mrs Burl Ives keeps seeing Harvering Harks flapping in sky above us. Hope they are vultures.

Returning to town after tour we see Lord Snowdon strolling up main street with a couple of his film crew friends (he is here to plan a BBC TV film about the explorers Burke and Wills, which if it comes off should be fascinating): all in very tight jeans, denim jackets, desert boots and long hair. Very trendy. Americans both paralytic with excitement. Say they must remember to tell folks back home they saw Prince Snowdon on Royal Visit.

19 February. Walking across tarmac from aircraft to airport building on arrival at Darwin see huge steel letters welded to airport roof "DARWIN" all bent and twisted as if in fierce fire – first sign of effect of Cyclone Tracey which struck Darwin on Christmas Day, less than 2 months ago, with force of 200 mph winds and devastated town. Devastation is only possible word. Everywhere heavy steel lamp standards have been bent over double, and often bent at base to lie parallel with road a foot above it, twisted like straws by wind's force. Virtually every building is either demolished or badly damaged. Heavy roofs have been stripped off and flung against adjoining buildings, holing their skin and tearing out more debris which repeats the process. Corrugated iron and timber still lie about everywhere. Caravans which have been picked up and hurled hundreds of yards by the gales lie squashed and crumpled like matchboxes. All foliage has been stripped from trees, most trunks and branches snapped and torn off, a few more flexible ones still left like stripped nudes. Wrecked cars everywhere: most cars still being driven have smashed windows, stove-in wings, doors missing.

In the northern suburbs where the homes of our Darwin radio station staff were, and where damage was almost total, we drove through street after street of indistinguishable destruction, the wreckage sodden by the torrential rain since the cyclone. Most houses were built on stilts for coolness, and the superstructure has been stripped from the platforms which along with the stilts are all that survive. In some cases one, sometimes two, walls still stand, the roof and remaining walls blown out and away. Possessions still stand on what is left of floors, or lie in gardens amid heaps of debris and wreckage: a fridge, door torn off, still full of milk bottles and plastic containers; a drenched rocking horse; a shelf of books weirdly undisturbed; doorless wardrobes still full of women's dresses; odd shoes everywhere; smashed air conditioners and motor mowers. It looks as if there has been a war fought across the city, including a prolonged artillery bombardment. Of our 26 British Government houses, not one has anything left worth repairing: all will have to be bulldozed away, we'll have to start again. The wives and children we flew out by RAF Nimrod and Hercules from Singapore: most of the men have

BRIAN BARDER'S DIPLOMATIC DIARY

gone by now and a new team are here, without families, knowing what was in store for them. Four cyclone survivors are still here, all still obsessed by the experience, unwilling to think or talk much about anything else, still shell-shocked. Understandable not to be able to get out of one's mind a night only six weeks ago spent crouched in a surviving lavatory or tool shed clutching wife and children as the house fell down about one's head, the great fragments of roof and wall torn loose and sent spinning like missiles out into the howling night ….

20 February.   Calls on the Administrator of the Northern Territory, Director of Reconstruction, Deputy Mayor of Darwin (the Mayor is in Canberra!) and other local dignitaries. All cheerful and busy but worried about the thousands who were evacuated in the days after the cyclone and who are flocking back into Darwin where there is nowhere safe or adequate for them to live. The population of 47,000 was reduced by evacuation in about 5 days of massive airlift to just over 10,000: now already it's back to 22,000, and the authorities reckon there is living space surviving or patched up adequate, with overcrowding, for about 15,000. Where the surplus 7,000 have found to sleep out of the rain, no-one knows exactly, but there are signs of life everywhere: under wrecked platforms of what were once houses, under tarpaulins thrown across a few remaining rafters, in cars and half-wrecked caravans, the Darwinites can be seen beginning to resume their lives – many squatting in other people's abandoned but less completely destroyed houses. Everywhere men in shorts, boots and nothing else are nailing salvaged sheets of corrugated iron onto timber beams scrounged in the wreckage to make a new makeshift roof or to patch up half a missing wall. Any ideas of scrapping the old Darwin and re-building from scratch with new, better standards of design and safety will run into contemptuous defiance from those who are already using their bare hands to patch up what's left of their homes and who aren't going to stand and watch while Department of Words bull-dozers come and knock it all down again.

21 February.   Run into the Secretary of the Department of Aboriginal Affairs, the much abused Barry Dexter, at the canteen-style restaurant of the Travelodge, where virtually all visitors to Darwin are staying (since it's still the only hotel to have reopened). Ask him whether he has come from Canberra to see how the

Northern Territory and Darwin Aborigines are coping in the cyclone's aftermath. He says, Not at all: he's there to see how the white officials of his Department have managed and are managing! (Very well, it seems.)

22 February. Arriving in the evening at Port Hedland in Western Australia it seems strange to see undamaged buildings and upright lamp standards again. Met by a very chic middle-aged lady who is local representative of the State of Western Australia Department of the North-West: she drives me the 500 yards from the airport to hotel, a welcome courtesy in view of weight of my case. Swim and wash out innumerable soiled shirts of Darwin. Weather hot and sunny, but occasional torrential downpours.

23 February. Spend day writing up report on visit to Darwin. Manage to cook up no less than 25 specific recommendations on action needed to start getting radio station back into shape. Hope FCO in London won't take until next cyclone to decide whether to act on them.

In the evening British Consul-General from Perth, Ted Dymond, and Sam Fletcher from Department of the North-West, arrive from Perth to join me. Extensive sampling of admirable Western Australian beer, Swan lager. Also general admiration for minimally clad girl in hotel reception office whose proportions are quite remarkable. She turns out to be from Essex.

24 February. Visit the Port Hedland Harbour and docks – all created in past 10 years or so to handle iron ore brought by train from mines in Pilbara inland, loading into massive ore ships for Japan. Taken by Harbour Master up to top of harbor control tower with spectacular view of ore mountains awaiting shipment. Also mountains of solar salt, some discoloured by iron ore blown onto it (subject of major current legal suit by salt company seeking damages and injunction to restrain iron companies from letting their iron blow onto salt – but how?). Later visit two iron ore storage, processing, and loading installations – numerous massive scoops and conveyor belts and cranes and red dust – and then go round the solar salt works where salt water is dried out in the sun in a succession of huge lakes until it forms into thick white crystals big enough to break up with both hands. Driving across a field of solid salt in a land-rover with more salt, for all the world like old snow, as far as the eye can see, is a bizarre experience. The salt goes mainly to Japan, too, for chemical purposes.

25 February.   In a little twin-engined Otter aircraft with about 8 others to the mine and company township of Tom Price, about 250 miles inland from Port Hedland, in the Hamersley Ranges where Hamersley Iron is digging up the mountain of Tom Price and sending it to Japan to be turned systematically into steel. Lunch in the town's one motel where 2 bright young executives of the company lament the fact that about 180 days were lost last year through industrial disputes. Quick tour of mine and then on with Ted Dymond and Sam Fletcher in the Otter to Paraburdoo (pron. Parab'doo), the other and newer Hamersley mine about 75 miles south. We are driven in air conditioned car to company guest house where we are to stay night, leave cases and are taken on very thorough and, surprisingly, fascinating tour of whole mine process from blasting of hill-side, through crushers and screening, chemical sampling and storage, to stockpiles and computerized loading onto massive railway wagons for hauling to the port (not in this case Port Hedland, but Dampier). Quick look round town: Olympic swimming pool, TV station, supermarkets, cinema, squash courts, sports complex, very attractive air conditioned houses (same for all grades), schools and hospital, all provided by The Company, which loves all and asks in return nothing but the precious red rocks, and just a little love. They have terrible labour relations too.

In the evening half a dozen of the top management people come round to the house (after we have had an hour or so of drinks with the mine manager) for dinner. Wonder how dinner is to be provided in the guest house, a private dwelling fully equipped but not staffed. Problem solved when van arrives at 5.30 containing a chef in full rig, a lady cook, and enough food to feed small army. The nine of us dine sumptuously off lobster salads, whole roast chickens, filet mignon, and about a dozen varieties of cheese, washed down with black label Scotch, French wine (virtually unknown in Australia) and French brandy. All this in a science fiction township lifted bodily by the company into the middle of nowhere, amid miles of deserted tropical bush, where even the water has to be piped in from several hundred miles away over the mountains. Lost mah soul in the Company Store.

26 February.   Everyone at Paraburdoo talks endlessly about their local artist – a lad who drives one of the massive mechanical shovels at the mine and who, in his spare time, paints in oils and produces landscapes now selling at about $A200 each. Geoff Luckman, this prodigy, comes round to the house to show us some of his paintings. Alas, they are not very good. It turns out that he turns out seven or eight in an evening. Although from Melbourne, he is a typical stocky cockney, bare-footed in shorts and an electric blue open shirt, grinning sheepishly at his own success. (Just hope I'm not wrong about those paintings: it will be galling if they sell for thousands of dollars in a few years' time, but I hope they do all the same.)

To Perth in a Fokker Fellowship, which seems like a Jumbo after the Otter.

27 February.   Perth. A beautiful, sun-based city, built around water, a handful of sand's throw from Fremantle and long, luxurious beaches; gleaming white tower blocks and green parks despite the 76-day (so far) drought; palm trees, opulent Spanish-style houses, dignified public buildings.

Spend the day calling on various Ministers and other politicians (including tour of Parliament buildings and chambers, all lovingly modelled on Westminster), on Managing Director and Chief Editor of local Rupert Murdoch newspaper ("Rupert has given Britain up in disgust, I'm afraid, mate"), on Vice-Chancellor of brand-new University (also "Murdoch", no relation) where first ever students arrived 2 days ago, Vice-Principal of massive and magnificently equipped West Australian Institute of Technology, and on Principal of the older, Oxford-style University of Western Australia, with a superb collection of Sydney Nolan paintings bought a few years ago for £50 each.

Ted Dymond gives large cocktail party in evening for me at his enviable house, overlooking a view which must be among finest available to any member of the Diplomatic Service. Cocktail party begins at 7 p.m. and is expected to end at about

8.30, but in fact goes on until midnight. Driven back to hotel with Bev Bevan, a former colleague in Canberra who is back already on a visit from London, and we have a couple of late evening beers and some sandwiches with a recently arrived visitor from British Nuclear Fuels who appears in the hotel. To bed at 2.30 a.m.

28 February.   Back to Canberra, where it's cool for the first time in 2 weeks. How odd everyone looks in long trousers and ties.

A trip from Canberra via Darwin, Port Hedland and Perth back to Canberra is the equivalent in Europe of travelling from south-eastern Turkey to the northern part of Norway, thence far out into mid-Atlantic, back to southern Portugal, and across again to Turkey. Australia is a big country.

CHAPTER 14

MAY-SEP 1975: PERTH, SINGAPORE, HONG KONG, BECKENHAM, NYC, DC

31 May. Board the train at Sydney Central Railway Station for the 3,961 km. journey to Perth, right across the Australian continent from Sydney on the South Pacific in the East to Western Australia and the Indian Ocean in the West. Jane and Owen have a rather luxurious "twinette" with its own shower and toilet, converting into a comfortable enough sitting-room during the day; I am in a tiny single, with room for the bed or me but not both. Luckily the twinette holds me as well as the other two during the day.

We set off at a deliberate speed out of Sydney: Parramatta, Katoomba, through the Blue Mountains of New South Wales, Bathurst, Orange. We are hardly making any dent on NSW before it is dark. A remarkably good 4-course dinner with a bottle of wine, and to bed.

1-3 June. A marvellously relaxing experience, this: constructive boredom. No telephone, no callers, no social life beyond the bar and the restaurant car. Not even any scenery, in fact: trees (sometimes), bush (mostly), the endless scrub of the Nullarbor Plain. Here and there a few startled kangaroos bound away from the approaching train. There is the odd bird. The sun rises, swings around, pours blindingly into the airconditioned train, sets, gives way to what are obviously crisp cold nights. We pound along, still more steady than fast: the old mining town of Broken Hill (time to walk out of the station to look at the broad dusty streets, like a Hollywood set for a stereotyped Western); into South Australia, Port Pirie (time to wander round the town at leisure, this time, and admire the old harbour buildings), up between the lakes and onto the Nullarbor, endless miles of nothing except the occasional halt with a few prefabs for railway workers who work on the track, operate the water supply systems for passing trains, man the rare depots where the train stops for the driver to check in, collect instructions, move on. Part way across the plain the train, by now half a mile long, stops to enable the three of us to walk along its whole length to the engine for a visit granted beforehand by the Commissioner of Commonwealth Railways. We sit or stand in the big iron cab as it plunges on over the slight undulations of the Nullarbor, slowing occasionally to pass gangs of workmen on the track. Owen has a turn at driving, sitting in the seat for five minutes with his hand on the speed control lever. Eventually we stop at a depot and we climb down to walk the half mile back along the great silver tube to our compartment. On through the salt-bush and spinifex: Kalgoorlie, legendary town, and so through Western Australia to Perth.

3 – 5 June. Perth. A beautiful flavoury city, combining a sense of age and continuity with impressive modernity, quaint or beautiful old buildings alongside fine glass and steel skyscrapers, all set off by a splendid park and everywhere water – the Swan river and its mouth, the great basin, and the Indian Ocean coast itself, giving onto the busy port of Fremantle and Fremantle's miles of sandy beaches. We do some systematic sight-seeing, O. and I have a symbolic dip in the Indian Ocean (much chillier than I remember it in Dar es Salaam), we do bits of shopping in Perth's large department stores, eat magnificently in a Swedish restaurant dispensing, for some eerie reason, smorgasbord – a long way from the home of smorgasbord.

5 – 7 June. Our Jumbo arrives a couple of hours late, almost midnight, in Singapore, hot and steamy as always. Owen, who has slept rolled up in blankets on the floor of the aircraft by the emergency exit, is so exhausted that he can hardly stand or walk as we queue to go through health, immigration, customs … Happily there is a British High Commission car there, with smartly white-uniformed Malay driver, to meet us and drive us into town and to the hotel, where we roll into bed as if poleaxed.

The hotel proves to be one of the most luxurious and efficient we have ever encountered anywhere, though far from the dearest. O. and I swim before breakfast in the massive pool in water which, though luke-warm, is cooler than the outside air. A man comes cheerfully to the room to mend the zip of my small cabin bag. Breakfast appears on a large wheeled contraption which opens out into a full-sized dining-room table, all ready laid, fitting easily into our big room.

After breakfast Lim Chin Teong, a Singapore Chinese friend from Moscow days, arrives with his wife and an airconditioned Mercedes to take us out shopping. We describe what we need to buy and he works out an itinerary that will enable us to compare prices and find the most attractive bargains. Until late in the afternoon he won't let us buy anything in case we find something cheaper and better later. He bargains authoritatively for us in Chinese, lopping impressive percentages off the price-tags. We wind up with three large cartons of goodies at unbelievable prices, plus a lot of very smart luggage (mostly with wheels) which puts to shame our tatty old Marks and Spencers expanding suitcases, much bashed and held together with Sello-tape. Arrange with the RAF Movements Officer at the Tengah air force station Singapore that he will get our cartons flown by the Australian Air Force for us to Canberra in the course of the next few months while we are away. Lim agrees to keep them in his boot and deliver them to Tengah the following weekend. Hope we shall see them again one day.

Lunch with the Lims and an Indonesian couple just arrived from Moscow on their way back to Jakarta, in the Peking restaurant (where we are the only three Europeans present), a huge cavernous place that produces after a long conference between Lim and a tiny Chinese waitress a gigantic multi-course meal which is so meltingly delicious that it is heartbreaking to see half of it taken away uneaten when we are eventually conquered by its sheer volume.

7 – 13 June.   As we begin the descent into Hong Kong's Kai Tak airport, the green ribbed hills of the islands around Hong Kong spread out below, Owen observes: "Look, there's one of ours!" There indeed, just outside our window, fly-ing a fraction ahead of us and above, is an identical Boeing 707 in the same green colours of Cathay Pacific. Our aircraft captain explains that the sister aircraft has an emergency, the undercarriage not properly lowered, and that we have flown close to inspect it. The other plane lands first while we circle slowly out over the South China Sea. Happily all is well and at last we too can land, an hour late, swooping down onto the narrow runway alongside the harbor. Half an hour later we are in the 12th floor flat of the Beringers, Australian friends from Beckenham and Canberra, at Repulse Bay, overlooking the sea on the island side of HK.

HK has changed remarkably little, except superficially (more glossy skyscraper hotels and banks and ugly housing developments), since I was a pretend (National Service) Royal Tank Regiment subaltern here more than 20 years ago, sobering thought. I drag J. and O. into a prolonged bus trip up into the New Territories on a voyage of rediscovery to find again the green and gold bowl in the hills at Sek Kong where I used to work on the tanks in a sweltering stone cobbled tank park, in green army shorts and sandals, and the old Nissen hut officers' mess where we drank iced tea (with muslin nets weighted with beads over the glasses to keep out the flies and flying beetles) and cold San Miguel beers from frosted silver tankards. The army camp is still there, but of the old buildings only the tank park and the old parade ground remain: everything else is new airconditioned permanent looking structures, suitable for the New Army and a great deal more comfortable, no doubt: lacking, maybe, the Somerset Maugham flavor of the old huts and verandahs with their lazily turning fans hung from the ceilings and the filmy mosquito nets over the beds. We have a San Mig and a hamburger in the new NAAFI (even the NAAFI isn't called that any more) for old time's sake. Back by mini-bus to a station on the railway line which is as close as we are allowed to go to the border at Lo Wu (where I used to do border patrols in a scout car, revolver loaded with real bullets). By train back into Kowloon and the humid crowded bustle of Hong Kong.

The sea around the floating fish restaurants at Aberdeen is now too polluted to permit safe sea food dining, so the Beringers take us instead to another fish place, as yet virtually undetected by Europeans: cross by rickety sampan to a huddle of huts and shacks on a waterfront accessible only by water where we choose crabs and fish from tanks and barrels and take them to a Chinese café to be cooked and served. No-one speaks a work of English but our needs are universal and the meal is magnificent.

It pours with monsoon rain most of the time but between downpours I make my way to Sam's Tailor and Asha's in Kowloon to choose materials and get myself measured (a humiliating and depressing experience) for suits and shirts at still delectable prices, even though they have risen like comets in the 20 years. One fitting, much lubricated with San Mig, is enough, and the suits are an excellent fit. Sam's is only a door away from where Savalani, my tailor of 2 decades ago, used to be.

14 June. Back to an English heat wave. Driving in the hired car from the airport to Beckenham through the familiar streets we wonder where we can see evidence of the crisis and general collapse of which we read so much in the British newspapers and so much more in the Australian ones. Everyone wants to know why we have come back to the country when it is in such a state. Answer: because it is so agreeable, people are so nice, everything is on a manageable and humanized scale. It's very good to be home.

16 – 21 September. New York doesn't change either. We hitch a lift into Manhattan from Kennedy airport in a UK Mission car, a big American station wagon. Owen, complaining of not feeling well after the flight, suddenly vomits extensively over Jane and the back seat; the first time in his 8 years that he has ever vomited at all. He must have been saving it for the city of his birth.

There is more garbage around the streets than there used to be, but the difference is purely relative. Chaos and breakdown of control seem nearer the surface, but it's difficult to know whether one would detect this if one had not read so much about the collapse of the city's administration and solvency. The teachers end their strike while we are there, most of the policemen go back to work too, some garbage is being collected, the sun shines in the dirty charismatic streets, the fire escapes still adorn the remaining brownstones and the New York Times is still the best newspaper in the world.

J., who hasn't been back since we left NY in 1968, is entranced to find herself so completely at home in this familiar pungent place. We walk up Lexington from the Earnests' railroad apartment on East 87th St. just East of York, near Gracie Mansion, where we are staying, to look again at 1148 Fifth Avenue where we lived for nearly 4 ½ years all those centuries ago in the Sixties. 96th Street is the same, the same drug store on the corner, the liquor store and the deli just down Lexington, the supermarket and the underground garage where we kept the old green Cortina Estate car ("the liddle English station wagon"). One of the doormen at 1148 remembers us and we have a nostalgic chat with him; almost everyone we knew in the big apartment block has moved away by now. Over to Central Park and a bus down Fifth Avenue, past the zoo and the Metropolitan Museum and the Guggenheim, like a journey into one's own past.

We go with the Earnests to sample the group of art galleries newly sprung up in the East Village, just East of Greenwich Village: lots of garbage hung on the walls of cavernous rooms converted from old abandoned factories, mostly superbly and simply decorated and lit, but occasional delights as well. Then on to the San Gennaro festival in the Italian quarter at Mulberry Street, just south of Chinatown: delicious steaming hot meat and cheese pies and pastries from the little stalls, cheerful crowds trying their hands at the fairground competitions, barkers barking, bottles of Italian wine set out in rows as prizes, everywhere Italian girls with deep brown eyes and Lollobrigida faces and fat middle-aged Italian men with humorous lived-in faces like characters out of the Godfather. Don Earnest points out a big Italian restaurant behind the street stalls where a few weeks ago there was a big Mafia shoot-out. Filled up with pies, we take the subway to South Ferry at the Battery and pay our 25c. each (used to be 5c.) for the Staten Island Ferry and a marvelous view in the gathering dusk of the cluster of skyscrapers at the Wall Street end of Manhattan and of the Statue of Liberty, bathed in floodlight, green Queen of the harbor, majestic and serene. Hope Owen is suitably proud of his magnificent birthplace.

The express train on the subway back to 86th Street hurtles through the tunnels at such a reckless speed and with such a terrifying, metallic scream, that it seems like some experience of hell. Even Don and Barbara, hardened New Yorkers, are filled with horror. But the Sunday New York Times is as huge and full of good things as ever.

21 – 23 September.   Arrive in Washington, DC, rather queasy from a bumpy flight through the edge of thunderstorms: one of the stewardesses was airsick the whole way from New York, an unusual spectacle. The Brownings are there to meet us at the airport with their enormous American station wagon, and drive us back to their roomy suburban house by a pretty rural route along the Potomac river. After lunch we all drive out to Great Falls, a huge system of rapids and waterfalls, sparkling in the sun.

In the evening we go round for a drink with Ken and Gay Scott (he used to be Head of Chancery in Moscow and has just arrived as Head of Chancery Washington after a spell in London) at their big beautiful house and the following evening various old friends from Moscow come to dinner at the Brownings: Dean and Susie Wills of the Baltimore Sun, Stape and Sandy Roy from the State Department, the Scotts again. In New York we had had lunch with Rick and Ann Smith, he now National Editor of the New York Times, and author of a new book on (and entitled, simply) "The Russians", which has been selected as the Book of the Month Club main selection for next February – ensuring it success. Extraordinary how the special intimacy that develops in the odd circumstances of Moscow seems to survive and even flower in other places, Australia, London, New York, Washington. The intimacy seems to be vintage by the fact of more relaxed surroundings and the champagne-like fresh air of freedom to say what we like. When the dinner party breaks up we all agree that, nomads all, we shall see each other again somewhere in the world, some time. (Only a few weeks ago we spent a glorious sun-drenched day in Cambridge with Murray Seeger of the Los Angeles Times and Palma and Steven, he also ex-Moscow and now the LA Times Bonn correspondent. I took Murray and Steven punting and, just about opposite Clare, fell in, for the first time in my life.)

J. and I go for a walk in the afternoon between showers, past the White House, looking round drug stores and bookshops, just soaking in the feeling of being in the United States again. Even in Washington, which we barely know at all, we feel at home in a quite irrational but unmistakeable way.

At Dulles Airport we check in our baggage all the way to Auckland and go into the waiting room (comfortable chairs, big picture windows) to wait for the signal to board the DC 10 for Los Angeles. When the time comes, the whole waiting-room smoothly winds down a few feet and sets off, an enormous bus, across the tarmac to the plane. Amazing.

25 September. We arrive in Auckland, New Zealand, by Air New Zealand DC10, a plane to which we have become devoted since Washington: more spacious and airy, somehow, than the 747 Jumbos, and beautifully smooth. We have got from British Airways the name of a tiny local airline, Air North, which apparently flies from Auckland to Rotorua, our first destination in New Zealand. We find an Air North desk at Auckland airport but no-one is behind it. Eventually a small aircraft lands and a casual man of about 30 wanders in and opens up the Air North desk: he is the pilot. He accepts our British Airways tickets without a murmur and we are duly booked on the noon flight to Rotorua. After an hour's drive to the top of a gusty hill to see Auckland and its vast surrounding harbours, we return to the airport and the news that Rotorua airport is closed because of high winds. We get coffees in the little airport cafeteria and are immediately paged over the loudspeakers to come at once to the Air North gate as Rotorua has opened and the plane is leaving early to get there before it closes once more. We rush out to the tarmac and climb into a tiny 9-seater twin-engined Aero Commander. J., O. and I occupy the 3-seater bench at the back of the minuscule cabin. The Air North man, once again transmogrified to pilot, climbs into the front left-hand seat, turns round and asks everyone to put their seat belts on, starts up, lets in a sort of gear lever, trundles down the runway and coaxes the little machine into the air, swaying and lurching in the gusts of wind.

At Rotorua our motel room looks directly out onto the big geyser, spouting hot steam high into the air, and the little geysers and boiling sputtering mud of this amazing place. It feels as if the whole place is perched perilously on a thin crust of earth below which is a violent inferno of boiling steam trying with intermittent success to force its way up into a volcanic eruption. (This is indeed literally the case.) We have lunch in the motel, and decide to have a short nap after the long hours of flying and the massive time change. Fall into bed and do not stir until 7 hours later when the phone goes: David and Jan McDowell are on their way by car from Wellington and will pick us up from the motel next morning. O. can't be woken, but J. and I go and have dinner and a beer each, and I spend 25 minutes soaking in the hot mineral pool operated by the hotel, a blissful relaxing feeling. Back to bed for another 9 hours' sleep. By next morning (after waking at 4 a.m. for coffee and sandwiches) we seem to have shed the worst of the jet-lag.

The McDowells take us on a long tour of Rotorua's weird wonders, geysers (pronounced 'guy-zers'), boiling mud, Maori village, wood carvings, trout farm and Maori church; we all swim in more hot mineral pools, sulphurous-smelling (so much so that O. has to go and sit in the car), and steaming.

With Jan's sister and her 4 children, the McD.'s and their 4, and the 3 of us, we are a sizeable party. We pile into the 2 cars and drive over to Tokoroa, about an hour away, for dinner with J.'s sister and, for us, grateful bed in an unsuspectedly excellent motel, where we have what is effectively a small flat to ourselves, equipped with kitchen, living room, etc. Next day the McD. family splits, some going by train and the rest escorting us via Lake Taupo to Palmerston North through superb scenery, noble mountains and thundering falls, streams and valleys, sheep everywhere, brilliant sun and cloudless blue skies. We stop off for late afternoon tea with another sister and her farmer husband at an idyllic, vast, isolated farm, in glorious country. Owen feeds a new-born lamb with a baby's bottle. Stay at Palmerston North with D.'s father, a relaxed and energetic host. Next morning in the brilliant blue sky there is a big scarlet hot-air balloon, floating gently overhead, tiny pin-men figures in the basket that swings on cotton threads below it.

Wellington is unexpectedly beautiful, with a magnificent natural harbor, dizzy hills, and gentle architecture (including a new Basil Spence Parliament building, still under construction, in the shape of a giant bee-hive). We take the cable-car with D. to the botanical gardens and the observatory, high on the hill and soak up the air and sun and view like alcohol. Old friends from New York come to dinner: more nostalgia.

30 September. The Air New Zealand DC 8 touches down in Sydney. J. says, "Well, we made it round the world." The Acting Consul General, Brian O'Brien, is there to meet us (and the First Sea Lord, admittedly) and over a coffee at the other terminal while we wait for the plane to Canberra he tells us about the ups and downs of the past 4 months in Australia. At Canberra airport there are a dozen or so familiar faces who have come out to welcome us back and drive us in to the familiar white house with the green roof. We are astonished to find that it is good to be back.

Left: Brian, Owen and Louise panning for gold at Sovereign Hill, Victoria, Australia 1970s.

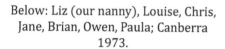

Below: Liz (our nanny), Louise, Chris, Jane, Brian, Owen, Paula; Canberra 1973.

Above: Brian ready to snorkel at "Big Bommie", Heron Island, Great Barrier Reef, Aug 1976.

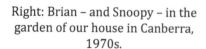

Right: Brian – and Snoopy – in the garden of our house in Canberra, 1970s.

CHAPTER 15

NOV 1975 – DEC 1976: CANBERRA, SYDNEY, HERON ISLAND, SNOWIES, DALMENY

11 November 1975. A sizzling day. Jane and I go to the Remembrance Day ceremony at the War memorial, sitting on plastic chairs in the broiling sun while soldiers are marched to and fro, military bands play, wreaths are laid, flags raised and lowered, hymns sung. The Governor-General looks as always like Mr Micawber, portly in morning coat and top hat, his thick snowy hair flowing out of it and setting off his florid petulant baby face, plum-coloured with tan or anger or both.

Soon after lunch, back at my desk in the High Commission, I am on the telephone to someone I don't know in an obscure Australian Government Department when he suddenly pauses in mid-sentence: "Wait a moment …. What? ….. sorry, I've just heard from my colleague here that the Governor-General has sacked Whitlam and made Fraser Prime Minister."

Chaos throughout the rest of the afternoon as we try to keep track of what is going on and to construct some sort of telegram to get off to London before we pack it in for the evening. Fraser's Senators have used their narrow majority in the Upper

House to pass supply, which they had refused to do for the past few months for the Whitlam Government's budget except on condition that Whitlam agreed to elections. The Labor Senators do not seem to have realised that their Government is out. The House of Representatives hears Fraser announce he is P.M., and promptly passes a vote of no confidence in him, calling on the Governor-General to reinstate Whitlam. The Speaker sets off for Government House to deliver this message but before he is granted audience, the G-G's Official Secretary, David Smith, arrives at the Parliament building and reads out an official Proclamation dissolving Parliament and declaring new elections – signed by Sir John Kerr and countersigned by Prime Minister Fraser. Smith ends his reading: "God Save The Queen." Whitlam, just behind and towering over him, shouts out: "Well may he say God Save The Queen, because nothing will save the Governor-General." He refers to Fraser as "Kerr's Cur".

In the evening Jane and Owen and I go down to the Parliament building (just down National Circuit and across King's Avenue) to see what is going on. There is a big crowd, perhaps a thousand or so, almost all in a state of dumbfounded rage at what has happened, still incredulous. They surge around the steps of Parliament House, calling and chanting for Gough and already waving placards inscribed "Shame, Fraser, Shame". After a while Whitlam leads out onto the top of the steps the whole Labor Caucus (ie all the MPs and Senators). A great roar goes up and Whitlam makes a short speech through a megaphone. Television cameramen rush about with microphones and cameras, getting cables tangled in the crowd. Billy MacMahon, the last Liberal PM until Fraser, bravely tries to address the crowd from the top of the steps in his weird quavery voice from between his enormous ears, but is shouted down. Although almost everyone there is in a state of high indignation and shock it is noteworthy that everyone is also very good-humoured and indeed clearly rather enjoying it.

Kerr had been a personal choice of Whitlam's for Governor-General, a clever and progressive lawyer who had been a personal friend. "Sic semper tyrannis!" "Et tu, Brute?"

13 December 1975. At the invitation of Frank Ley, the Chief Electoral Officer, whom we know quite well, we go round in the evening to the big central election tally-room in a Canberra suburban high school to see the first results coming in. The system is different from Britain's in that figures are issued as counting proceeds, enabling the pundits to start making projections almost from the time the polling stations close. Figures are going up on the huge boards and being changed all the time as new results and interim counting figures are telephoned in from all over Australia, from polling stations well over 3,000 miles away, some of them closer to Saigon than to Canberra. We are chatting to Michael Leapman, who writes the daily Diary in the Times and has come out to report the elections, when Frank Ley asks his deputy to take us round behind the scenes to see where the figures are received, collated and transferred to the vast board from behind. Although the press is excluded from this area, we manage to smuggle Leapman in (he interviews everyone feverishly, scribbling in a tiny notebook). There are closed circuit television screens everywhere, hundreds of people in T-shirts and shorts rushing about drenched in sweat, an atmosphere of barely controlled panic. The figures go on going up, filmed continuously by the batteries of TV cameras at the back of the hall.

In another part of the hall tiny television studios have been rigged up with as-sembled pundits sitting at tables with microphones in front of them watching the boards and interpreting the figures for their respective networks. We spot Bob Hawke, the President of the Labor Party and of the Trade Union Council, in a denim suit, with an outsize can of beer concealed from the cameras under his chair for surreptitious swigs when off-camera. Malcolm Mackerras, Australia's David Butler, is in another cameo-sized mini-studio talking away in his high-pitched voice. We try unsuccessfully to catch his eye. David Dimbleby appears from nowhere with a Panorama crew in tow, dressed in an immaculate white trop-ical suit, and greets Leapman who introduces us. We spend ten minutes trying to explain the intricacies of the Australian electoral system, complex in the House of Representatives, well beyond human comprehension in the Senate. Dimbleby (who seems an agreeable and unassuming young man) decides that it is all a bit complicated for his purposes. Am impressed by how much feel for the political and constitutional scene he and Leapman have obviously picked up in their short visits. Also struck once again by the remarkable similarity between the functions and techniques of diplomats and foreign correspondents, both trying to under-stand, interpret and report the funny goings-on of foreigners.

8 April 1976.   Woken by a telephone call from N. in Bristol: my father, 93 in a fortnight, has flu and is in a bad way, but no-one is prepared to say I need to come home. Telephone the night nurse at the old people's home where he is and get his doctor's number. Telephone doctor after many misadventures with directory enquiries in Bristol. Doctor mesmerised by getting telephone call from Australia at midnight but quite clear that I should return at once. Telephone Resident Clerk in the Foreign Office, and British Airways in Sydney. Wind up current affairs in the High Commission and get back home to pack and get off to the airport. (In a way the worst of it is that I am going to England when the girls are still here in Australia for what's left of their Easter holidays.) By mid-afternoon I am boarding the QANTAS flight to London in Sydney.

17 April 1976.   J., V., L., and O. are at the little Canberra airport to meet me as I get in on the 9.10 a.m. Ansett flight, having got in to Sydney at five past six on the BA 889, a good flight if any 26 hours spent on the same aircraft can be termed good, marred only by the strike in Perth (Western Australia) of catering staff which deprived me of the devilled kidneys and mushrooms for breakfast to which I had been looking forward ever since Hounslow. The girls leave for England and school a week tomorrow.

23 April 1976.   To Sydney for the week-end and then to see the girls off on Sunday afternoon. We install ourselves once again in the High Commissioner's flat at Point Piper, with a spectacular view from the sun lounge over the harbor and right out to the North Head: like the view from a penthouse apartment in a Hollywood domestic comedy.

A telephone message from Canberra: will I ring N. in Bristol? I know already: HB has died, barely a week after I left.

24 April 1976.   Fly back to Canberra to collect my passport and pack some clothes for the English spring. Henry and Lola De Mar, our splendid neighbours on the Sorrell Street side, take me back out to the airport in the VW and see me off.

25 April 1976.   Embark at Sydney for London with the girls – an unexpected bonus. Try to buy a tiny transistor radio at the duty-free shop in Sydney airport, am told that the model displayed is not available, have terrible row with shop manager. Girls desperately embarrassed. No radio but feel much better.

11 May 1976.   J. and O. meet me at Canberra airport once again. Have clocked up about 50,000 miles in past month and feel like it. Stick to rule 1 for minimising jet lag: stay on feet until time for bed locally, eschew day-time sleeping on first day after arrival. On the whole it works. The new High Commissioner, Sir Donald Tebbit, arrives the day after tomorrow.

16 August 1976.   To Heron Island, Queensland, on the Great Barrier Reef. Late winter in Australia but here we are just on the tropic of Capricorn and it is warm and sunny. We drove up a week ago through northern New South Wales, stopping at Coonabarrabran for the night to see the telescopes at Siding Spring next morning, high up in the Warrumbungles, where we were shown round by the British scientists who operate the Science Research Council telescope here. Admire the huge Anglo-Australian telescope with its massive lens ground in Birmingham or Manchester or somewhere. On through Goondiwindi on the Queensland border and then across Queensland, past thousands of dead kangaroos piled beside the road every few hundred yards (killed at night passing traffic), through Rockhampton on the tropic and into Yeppoon, a seaside resort in mild decline, the kind we seem drawn to as bees to honey. Five days of sun and (chilly) sea, in a well appointed caravan, barbecuing in the evenings and consuming immense quantities of good Australian wine from the casks (thick polythene bags in cardboard boxes with plastic taps, a gallon in each) which we have providentially brought with us. Then 120 odd miles south to Gladstone to catch the tiny boat, built as an oil rig tender, that takes us to Heron.

21 August.   Sadly we leave Heron after a memorable holiday, bronzed by the midwinter tropical sun and surfeited on unlimited reef fish, freshly caught and deliciously cooked, along with plentiful steaks and about everything else. But above all with the memory of the snorkeling: most spectacularly out at the "Big Bommie" (a fantastic coral cathedral about half a mile out at the edge of the reef) where the fish of all sizes and colours come to be cleaned by the cleaner-fish in huge numbers) but also just swimming out from the coral-powder beaches:

giant porpoises and turtles, a huge black and silver manta-ray, three medium-sized sharks gliding along close to the bottom minding their own business, coral trout, friendly and aggressive fish, small fish and big fish, golden, silver, bronze and scarlet fish, fish equipped with poisonous spines and venomous stings, transparent jelly-fish that raise a rash like nettles, huge goggling stupid fat slobs of fish that float past and roll their eyes at you as you lie idly on the surface with snorkel, goggles and flippers, looking down through the utterly clear water to the bottom shimmering in the sun. Since it's a literally indescribable experience I suppose it's a waste of time trying to describe it. The only trouble about a visit to Heron, as a scuba diver who had come specially from New York observed to me as we chugged out in the dive boat to the Big Bommie, is that it spoils you for anywhere else. (The New Yorker, Henry, nearly drowned next day. The dive boat had to go off after him as the current carried him away, leaving us snorkelers wondering if we would make it back to the beach.)

The coral is only a hint less amazing than the fish: fantastically shaped, like giant brains and antlers or rock gardens, in pinks and mauves and blues. It is inescapably reminiscent of bones, to the touch especially ("Of his bones are coral made," evocative if ungrammatical). Perhaps because it is literally made of the bones of the millions of polyps that create it, forcing up mounds of coral and coral debris which eventually form whole islands such as Heron. As we sail away from it in the early morning sun, it has a dream-like quality, and we listen for the heavenly choir to fade in from the Hollywood bowl (in vain, fortunately).

5 September 1976.   Less than 2 weeks after leaving Heron Island, our skins scorched and tingling with sun and coral sand and salt, we are ski-ing in the Snowy Mountains, 3 hours' drive from Canberra in NSW. There have been good falls in the past week and the snow lies deep and crisp and even, to coin a phrase. We get the skis and poles off the roof rack in crowded Smiggin Holes, where the smart down-hill ski set are doing their thing in their smart ski clothes, queuing in polychrome for the ski lifts, and ski round the edge of the hill to do our Russian style cross-country lope in utterly unspoilt and deserted country. The sun, in a brilliant blue sky, is so hot in the hill's shelter from the wind, that we un-zip anoraks and untie scarves, creating our own ski tramlines in the dry firm powder. Only the gum-trees, crippled shapes in the snow, remind us that we are in Australia. In this setting and this climate you get drunk breathing the air.

31 December 1976. We toast the New Year in iced, dry, Australian champagne in Dalmeny on the south coast of NSW, staying in the ground floor flat of the beach house of ATG, Fraser's main adviser on foreign affairs. We have been roasted and burned by the sun, pounded and pummeled by the crashing surf, lulled by the warm waters of the inlet, gorged on oysters at 30 cents (20p.) a dozen, dazzled – some of us – by the magnificent girls. Roll on 1977.

CHAPTER 16

JAN-MAY 1977:
WEE JASPER, SYDNEY

29 – 31 January 1977. A week-end with Owen and our neighbours from next door in Sorell Street, Henry and Lola De Mar (Australian despite the exotic names) and their children, at Wee Jasper, 3 hours' drive away in the Brindabella Mountains. Borrowing the tent which belongs to the British Defence Liaison Staff and using the Cortina station wagon, the De Mars' camper van and their beetle VW, we get ourselves set up in a gorgeous spot under willow trees beside a wide but fairly shallow creek, just deep enough to swim in (and wash, bath, etc.) – highly necessary as it is sizzling hot. We have masses of the obligatory Australian "Eskies" (expanded polystyrene insulated boxes) full of ice, beer, white wine, etc.

The drive across the mountains has been fairly hair-raising with a lot of dust, some alarming gradients and many hairpins, although nothing like as frightful as the notorious Araluen Valley road along which we once brought Jean and Arthur George protesting and appalled from the coast. Almost all dirt, the road occasionally degenerates into jagged rock and large stones. Much of it is impassable after rain. Wonder what we shall do if it rains heavily while we are at Wee Jasper. Monday is a holiday (Australia Day) but I really need to be back at work on Tuesday.

On Sunday morning we swim and walk alternately up stream to some very attractive waterfalls, gushing foamily into wide and deep rock pools with sheer sides where the swimming is superb. Find a place where one can enjoy a free pummeling from the thundering water funneled down onto one's shoulders by a 'V' in the rock – like massage without the sex. (However some titillation is supplied by several typically nubile and healthy looking Australian girls in characteristically minimal bikinis, besporting themselves in the cool water of the creek and the hot sunshine.)

Because of the long drought and hot dry weather there are sporadic notices dotted about the countryside forbidding fires in certain parishes. In the evening we decide to take a risk and light a barbecue fire, partly because we have no idea what parish we are in and partly because we have no other means of cooking the steaks, chops, sausages, chickens, etc. that we have brought. I get charcoal fires burning gaily in our two barbecue bowls on their tripods while Henry constructs a mighty wood fire surrounded by boulders from the creek across which we can balance a steel grid for the cooking when the wood has burned down. As it gets darker the flames leap joyously in the air. I start some steaks on the charcoal. Suddenly a land rover drives along the river bank and pulls up with a flourish at our camp site: it seems to have machine guns and mortars mounted all over it (on closer inspection they prove to be sirens, hose nozzles, searchlights, etc.). Two men climb out and swagger over to us. They are dressed as Texan sheriffs or possibly Royal Canadian Mounted Police without their mounts. They make several comments of a critical nature about our fires. I move the charcoal barbecues inside the tent (from which savoury-smelling smoke billows forth) and apologetically start emptying buckets of creek water over Henry's fire while Henry demanded to know the law (short title, number, section and sub-section) under which the rangers were claiming the right to deprive us of our sovereign right as Australians to barbecue what and where we liked, when we liked, and did they realise that he was a land-owner in this parish (he has indeed bought a tiny plot of bush on a steep hillside on the other side of the creek and plans to build a holiday house on it one day) and he will bloody well have a barbecue if he bloody well feels like one? The rangers, instead of punching Henry's face, produce a dog-eared copy of the Fires Ordinance from their fortified land rover and they and Henry spend what seems like an hour or so trying to read it by the light of a small torch, while the steaks on the barbecues in the tent slowly turn to coal.

2 April 1977.   To Sydney in the car to celebrate our wedding anniversary and to meet the girls who are due in to Sydney airport at 6.10 a.m. tomorrow morning. Just before we leave Canberra the telephone rings: British Airways, to say the flight is delayed by several hours, will we check again in the morning? Then a message from GG in England, to the same effect: there has been a bomb threat, the plane has had to return to London, they will be four or five hours late. Set off for Sydney, grinding along the winding narrow roads, taking our lives in our hands every time we pull out to overtake a massive semi-trailer groaning along at 15 km. an hour, wondering why they call these frightful roads the "Federal Highway" and the "Hume Highway" for all the world as if they were Australian versions of the Jersey Turnpike.

The High Commissioner's flat at Point Piper, overlooking the bay, is as good to arrive at as ever. The bay and harbor are full of sailing boats and the water glitters in the sun. We eat Chinese food from the take-away in Rose Bay down the road and wash it down with a lovely crisp South Australian Elizabeth Riesling. Nineteen years.

3 April 1977.   Sunday morning. The telephone rings in the Sydney flat. The girls' plane will not be in before 7 p.m. and it may be later. Because of the Sydney airport curfew the plane is being diverted to Melbourne first and only then brought to Sydney. Jane says "Why not get them off at Melbourne and fly them to Canberra from there?" Sublime brainwave. (Sancta simplicitas.) B.A. girl agrees and promises to organise matters. This leaves us barely enough time to get back to Canberra before the girls arrive there. Rush about packing up everything from the flat, hurl it into the car, and drive off at high speed. Pause momentarily for hot pasties at a roadside café at the top of the Macquarie Pass, with a coke for Owen and cans of Fosters for us. On through Moss Vale, Goulburn, Collector, Lake George …. We drive into the car park at Canberra airport three minutes before the plane lands. As usual the girls look about four years older than when we saw them off three months ago and we are not absolutely sure that we have identified them correctly.

24 – 26 April 1977.   Back to Sydney with the girls for a last couple of nights in the Point Piper flat before the girls leave Australia for the last time – well, the last time in this series. Spend an agreeable warm sunny autumn morning at the Taronga Park Zoo, communing with the wombats and wallabies. In the evening we go to the Opera House to see 'Caesar and Cleopatra'. As parking for the Opera House is virtually impossible unless one goes several hours early, and as Owen has a leg in plaster from breaking it at football (he crashed into a large American boy, showing the dangers of tangling with the super-powers), we arrive at about 6 p.m. for the 7.45 performance, find a lucky meter space in Macquarie Street on the hill above the Opera House, and all sit in the car with the interior light on listening to the radio and eating turkey sandwiches, while interested passers-by gather on the pavement and peer in.

'Caesar' was splendid, with lots of two-way inner-and-outer revolving sets and elaborate costumes and a satisfactorily kittenish Cleo. One of the players (Britannus) was Wallas Eaton, all the way from "Take It From Here", now pretty ancient, very polished and professional, very camp. To get seats on the aisle for Owen's leg to stick out into we had to take seats in the front row, right up against the edge of the apron stage, staring up the skirts of the Roman soldiers.

Spend much of Monday morning organising a week on a houseboat in Kashmire for our journey home in July. The Indian Government Tourist Office in Sydney is more charming than helpful. All the brochures and price lists are about nine years old and the man says that as the Indian Government is a non-profit-making organization he can't make any bookings for me. Luckily profit-making American Express is more practical.

Lunch at the Old Spaghetti Factory, the children's favourite eating-place in Sydney, and out to the airport for the last of many departures by the girls. The Jumbo gets off after dark, 90 minutes late ("due to technical factors" – i.e. it was broken), floating up like a huge floodlit ship and disappearing into the black sky until only the sawn-off Union Jack on the tail, still floodlit from the fuselage, is visible like some portent.

4 May 1977. Definite confirmation at last that I am going in September for eleven months to the Canadian National Defence College at Kingston, Ontario. The plan had been that I should return to London for a spell as head of a Department in the Office, but with many moves and changes suspended while everyone awaits the report of the CPRS Review, and little movement in the Counsellor grade for several months, there is nothing suitable coming up, so the Canadian course is offered as a useful and agreeable stop-gap, which I agree to with alacrity: much better than the other possibility which had been towed tentatively across my front, a sabbatical year at a UK university (no allowances and probably not even any help with the cost of accommodation, and no-one in the least interested in whatever subject I cooked up to study). The Canadian course is a general one in international affairs with a Canadian and defence orientation, about half of the college being from the Canadian and a few other armed services (Brigadier and Colonel level) and the rest civilians, officials and others. There is a lot of travelling, all over Canada and including Latin America, the US, Eastern and Southern Europe, Africa, South-East Asia, and probably Australia. The FCO man on the course this year has already found us a house in Kingston and to judge by the National Geographic Atlas Kingston is a comfortable day's drive from New York (not to mention Boston and Detroit). It will make a change from telegrams, files and briefs, anyway.

7 May 1977. All flights into, out of and within Australia grounded by a strike of air traffic controllers in support of their claim to a 36% pay rise (they were originally demanding 76%). No air mail, no bags, no mail at all. Embark on what must be a world record for 12,000-mile telephone calls. We are really too far away.

PART III:

CANADA, AND AROUND THE WORLD, LATE 1970S

CHAPTER 17

SEP-NOV 1977:
CANADA, EVERY PROVINCE
& TERRITORY

Sunday, 25 September 1977.   The Canadian National Defence College leaves
for its first trip of the year, round the Atlantic Provinces of Canada, Quebec and
Ontario: "the Eastern Canada Field Study". We are about 50 in all, comprising
the Commandant (a Rear-Admiral), the Directing Staff, 41 course members (we
avoid the term "student", being all rather staid middle-aged gentlemen and two
hardly less staid ladies), the Commandant's wife and 5 wives of course members
and Directing Staff, chosen by lot. My failure to draw a lucky number for J. for a
trip during the year is, I suppose, quite unconnected with the accident of having
13 as my officers' mess number.

We queue obediently to get into the bus at the College, and are driven off to the
Canadian Air Force base at Ottawa for the flight by RCAF Hercules to St. John's
Newfoundland, where we arrive at about 6 p.m., having fed on Canadian Air
Force sandwiches and beer en route.

26 September.   We are bussed around St. John's on a glorious crisp cold bright
day, the air like dry white wine. Up on Signal Hill where Marconi received the
first ever radio message (from Cornwall), it blows hard and exhilaratingly. After

we have had a session with some Newfoundland Ministers (once their resources begin to be developed, they will become the richest area of Canada), we are received en masse by the Mayor of St John's, a remarkable young woman called Dorothy Wyatt, with frizzy Afro hair, enormous granny glasses, a skimpy sweater and pedal pusher breeches. She is preceded into her chamber by a solemn character in Toytown uniform bearing the Mace of office. In the course of her address to the College the Mayor mentions, as an aside, that she was once asked whether she wore a padded bra, and replied that of course she did. She tells us with modest pride that her technique with striking municipal bus-drivers has been to dismiss the strikers and take on new ones at lower wages (Newfoundland has over 15% unemployment so there is no shortage of applicants for jobs).

In the late afternoon the Hercules takes us on to Halifax, Nova Scotia. On a stroll by the docks in the evening before finding a fish restaurant for dinner (there seems to be only one, and that mediocre), we pass a Soviet trawler tied up at the wharf, impassive sailors lining the rails – obviously denied the chance to leave the ship. I call up to them "Dobriy Vecher!" ("good evening!"). "Dobriy Vecher!" they all shout back, amazed.

27 September.   Charlottetown, Prince Edward Island.   In the evening at the officers' mess there are more enormous lobsters than I have ever seen before in one place. (We are paying, though we don't yet know how much.) As the bridge on the main road is under repair, our bus tour has to omit the original house around which "Anne of Green Gables" was written. But Charlottetown has lots of character and history, with an atmosphere strongly reminiscent of the sleepy New England towns in the USA which, of course, come to think of it, are not very far away.

29 September.   All much inspired by a rousing address from the Premier of New Brunswick, Richard Hatfield. Am reminded at breakfast next morning by a Colonel who was until this year commanding officer of the Parachute Regiment that Hatfield presides over the most corrupt government in Canada. He's certainly very smooth.

30 September.   The Herc. flies us in to La Grande Riviere in northern Quebec to see the huge new hydro-electric project at James Bay. We see all the work in progress at "LG2" – the vast new dam site, the dam itself, the six massive tunnels down which the millions of tons of water will be forced by the weight of water in the reservoir, and (most impressive of all) the huge dank underground chamber, blasted out of the rock hundreds of feet below ground, where they are installing the massive turbines that will be turned by the thundering water and generate massive quantities of electricity for Quebec Province and also for the northern United States. The cavern itself is nightmarish, redolent of evil, echoing with the clang and clatter of the bull-dozers under the massive arc-lights in the damp chilly air. Can't help wondering how we would feel if there was a collapse of the millions of tons of granite at the tunnel entrance, leaving us trapped in this horrific place.

1 October.   Quebec City.   It's good to be back in this most civilised and flavoury of cities, as French as Bordeaux and more so than St Malo. Little has changed since February-March 1965 when we had a delicious family holiday here from New York: a few new skyscraper hotels (including the luxurious Loew's Le Concorde where we are now staying), an even more ubiquitous and insistent use of French, higher prices in the restaurants. It is an eerie feeling to walk in these winding streets, which I had thought to have forgotten almost completely, and yet to find that at each corner I know a split second before I turn the corner what I shall find around it. Literally Déja Vu!

Claude Morin, Minister of Governmental Affairs in M. Levesque's separatist Provincial Government, and the leading intellectual of the Parti Québecois, addresses us in the conference room of his Ministry, which is clearly organised as a Foreign Ministry. He is subtle, casual, articulate (in English), inflexible. English-speaking Canadians have failed for 200 years to understand the just claims of the French fact in Canada. Each reform, each change, has come too late to give to the people of Quebec the feeling that they have any place or role in Canada. Now only independence will satisfy their urgent need for national self-respect.

4 October.   Montreal.   A session with the Mayor, the celebrated Jean Drapeau, maestro of the Montreal Olympic Games which left the Montreal rate-payers with a massive deficit never likely to be paid off. He is a little dapper man, quick and bird-like, no mace-bearers or other formalities but a curious natural dignity of his own. He defends the Olympic Games decisions, all the follies and extravaganzas, to the last line of small print.

Later we hear an address from Claude Ryan, editor of "Le Devoir", which is intellectually and politically one of the most dense and compressed statements of a very intelligent man's view of society that I have ever heard.

5 October.   Toronto.   Sky-scrapers, neon lights, five-lane highways. Could be anywhere.

6 October.   Ottawa.   Wish I could pronounce the name of the Canadian capital city in the Canadian style without sounding as if I am sending them up: "Arda-WAH", in the middle of a sentence otherwise spoken in BBC English, sounds affected. So I say "Otter-wer" which sounds just as affected.

The British military members and (especially) their wives are much disappointed by the informality of the reception given by the Governor-General and Mme. Leger for the College. (The UK contingent is a Brigadier, a Captain R.N., a Group Captain RAF, and myself.) No hats, no gloves, no bowing, no curtseys. The RN wife thinks all this very unsuitable. "After all, he is supposed to represent Her Majesty. This wouldn't do at Buckingham Palace." The Legers do indeed seem admirably informal and genuine, despite the lunatic magnificence of the Government House Ballroom in which the reception takes place.

7 October.   Sessions with the Chief of Defence Staff and a Judge of the Supreme Court (separately – the latter in the courtroom itself, followed by sandwiches and whisky in the judges' chambers). Then back into the bus for the 2 ½-hour journey back to Kingston. We have all got to know one another all too well; no fisticuffs yet, but there are still 14 weeks of group travel ahead of us.

24 October.   Barely two weeks later and we are off again. Mid-afternoon our Hercules lands at Frobisher Bay in the Canadian Arctic. We emerge from the aircraft like Disney figures, wrapped in huge Arctic parkas (issued by the Canadian forces supply store in Kingston), fur hats, padded mittens and massive vinyl boots, and clump across the snow to our waiting bus like figures from a film about life in a Siberian labour camp. It's bloody cold, but surprisingly invigorating. There is a little rather thin sunshine. I spent the last hour and a half of the flight in the cockpit of the Hercules, looking down on this endless white vista. The sea is not yet frozen over, but it won't be long before it is.

The little hotel serves us all Arctic Char (a pleasant fish, distantly related to salmon) for dinner. It is pronounced "Arrrdikcharrr" as if by a yokel from Zummerzet. The fish has been liberally doused in garlic salt, rather uncharacteristically one feels. We are charge $17.50 a head for it, too (about £8.50): much muttering at this, but we recognize that the overheads must be high.

In the evening we pick our way gingerly over the frozen snow, muffled against the icy wind, to the Frobisher Public Library for a briefing by a local Eskimo. The Eskimo, whose English is not very good, manages to convey touchingly the message that white Canadian culture has taught him to need canned food and cigarettes without providing him with the means to buy them. In questions afterwards he is asked patronizing questions by the Canadian Colonels, who (having called all previous speakers "Sir") address him as "Joe" and congratulate him on his realism in recognising the benefits of white civilisation.

25 October. Resolute Bay. Because of strong cross-winds, the pilot of our Hercules is doubtful if we shall be able to land at this tiny airstrip in the far northern Arctic (north of 74^0, virtually at magnetic north), but he goes in anyway. The airstrip manager says that no civilian plane would have attempted to land in such conditions. It is an eerie place, in permanent twilight at this time of year, desperately cold but with a surprisingly thin snow cover. Humans seem to cling to it by the skin of their teeth, unconvinced that anything can be permanent in such a temperature. The commander of the little base tells us that if the electricity supply fails, they have a maximum of six hours in which to fly everybody out – everybody – before they die of cold. Luckily there are only about 200 of them.

On to Inuvik this evening – still well inside the Arctic Circle. Here we are addressed by a beautiful thin blonde girl, pale with passion for her cause – the leader of the local Eskimos (there is a hint of high cheek-bones if you look hard enough, but she would pass muster easily enough in Idaho). Her name is Miss Nellie Cournoyea and she is very articulate indeed. Much relieved that none of the Colonels addresses her as "Eskimo Nell".

26 October. Whitehorse, Yukon Territory. The Deputy Administrator, one-third of whose population in the Yukon are American Indians, admits in answer to a question about the legal status of the Indians that he doesn't know. It isn't quite as cold.

28 October. The Hercules takes us in howling winds and driving rain from Comex Air Base on Vancouver Island to Powell River on the mainland of British Columbia to visit the pulp and paper mill. The little runway at Powell River is 1,700 feet long. I ask one of the Canadian Air Force Colonels what is the minimum runway length for a Hercules to land. "1,700 feet," he says. Sure enough we have to land by virtually nosediving onto the runway to slow us down before we go off the end. There is an almighty jolt and we are there.

29-31 October. Vancouver. Everyone is right about Vancouver. It is a glorious city, snow-covered mountains behind and the Pacific Ocean in front and all round. Echoes of Sydney, Hong Kong, even New York. The great suspension bridges are even reminiscent of San Francisco, as is the physical configuration of the city. Alas, it is raining almost all the time we are there, and clouds obscure the mountain backdrop. On Sunday afternoon and after a bus tour with an over-poweringly folksy bus-driver and guide ("You folks don't want all that historical garbage that some guides dish out – we'll make this a family outing, OK?" – "No, you idle bastard, we're paying for the history and we're staying here till we get it"), the weather clears enough to permit a very pleasant walk in the sunshine around Gastown, the old part of the city, nicely done up and turned into a poor man's Greenwich Village or a clean man's Soho.

By bus and car ferry to Vancouver Island (again) and Victoria, capital of British Columbia. What a pleasant change to travel by something other than our rough and ready Hercules with its troop transport seating (improved in one way – they have installed powerful neon-type lights so that we can read, if we can stand the vibration).

3 November.   We have "done" Edmonton, capital of oil-rich and thriving Alberta, and the Canadian Forces Base at Cold Lake in northern Alberta (where it pours with rain relentlessly). Now to the Great Canadian Tar Sands at Fort McMurray, even further north, where they chew thousands of tons of sand and earth out of a bleak hillside and boil oil out of it. Forewarned about the likelihood of getting black sticky tar-oil on our shoes, we clump about with billowing plastic bags tied over our feet. Getting oil out of earth is not very interesting.

5 November.   Saturday outing to a ranch outside Calgary. This certainly appears to be the real thing. The bus edges cautiously through the big wooden entrance ("O.H. Ranch") and up to the ranch house and the cattle pens. Displays of "cutting" cattle (mounted cowboys in Stetsons, one of them 88 years old, sorting calves from heifers), then some serious drinking and a magnificent lunch of barbecued steaks and salad in a huge marquee thoughtfully erected by the Canadian army (which also supplies the barmen, waiters, etc.). As we drive away, sated, in our bus, I wonder if they are taking the whole ranch down already and rolling it up in readiness for the next lot of gullible visitors. Certainly the cows looked real. But I wasn't too sure about the cowboys and ranch hands.

6 November.   Sunday outing from Calgary into the Canadian Rockies – Banff and Lake Louise. Another day of improbably Hollywood set. The mountains, snow and lakes defy description. Note that the glacier at the far end of Lake Louise is distinctly blue. The grandeur of the mountains is overpowering, and they seem somehow more sharp and jagged than the Rockies in Colorado, as I recall them; yet the whole effect is of a rather shallow prettiness, I suppose because our capacity to respond to natural scenery has been corrupted by technicolour travelogue films and countless postcards, so that we can no longer distinguish between the arty representation (complete with superlative-laden sound-track) and the real thing.

Calgary, rapidly becoming Canada's financial centre as well as the expanding centre of the cattle and oil industries, is a brash, rich, bouncing city. I'm glad to have seen it, but "I wouldn't like to live here."

7 November.   The President of a potash company outside Regina, Saskatchewan, on the endless rolling prairie, spends an hour complaining about punitive taxation. The course member from the Imperial Oil company remarks as we leave that these lamentations would be more convincing if the man hadn't lit a succession of cigars with $100 bills.

8 November.   An excellent morning with the Royal Canadian Mounted Police, whose training depot is here in Regina, with their museum – yards from where Louise Riel was hanged for leading the rebellion of the Métis. The Mounties really do seem to have a social awareness and dedication not commonly found among cops in the UK or US.

9 November.   In the cultivated and civilised but perishing cold city of Winnipeg. Tomorrow we fly to Trenton air base and bus back to Kingston, having visited every province and territory in Canada.

CHAPTER 18

DEC 1977:
WATCHING IN NEW YORK
(BY JANE BARDER)

"My life is in danger," a voice whispered urgently in my ear. We were paying a nostalgic visit to Manhattan and were buying a takeaway lunch in an upper West Side Chinese restaurant. I had moved across to look up a friend's telephone number. I shot around and found a well-dressed New Yorker speaking into a dome-shielded telephone. He was put through no doubt to the section fielding zany callers. "Mr. Brown?" he said. "This is John Does. I am being irradiated by my Bell telephone installation. I can't get any law enforcement agencies to take any action because my story sounds so intrinsically unlikely …. No, I'm not calling from my own telephone. I've had it disconnected."

I moved away. I didn't want to be around but it was good to be back in articulate if crazy New York.

Later that Saturday were in a Broadway self-service liquor store choosing a bottle of champagne for our hosts. A young upper West Side housewife was pushing a supermarket trolley with a fair number of bottles of assorted wines in it already. "It's so difficult when you don't know what to buy," she said appealingly. "Well, as long as it's alcoholic —", I started to say. "No: I've got this wine rack, you see, and I need to fill it." The manager appeared. "I thought a bottle from every country," she said. "Well, we have wine from all over the world," he said. "South Africa…." "No," she said, "that's the wrong shape." "Chile," he said, producing a bottle. "That would fit my wine rack," she enthused. That's New York again, we thought.

I was on a crowded cross-town bus. I had got on at the start of the route but was preceded by large numbers of people with transfers. The bus before must have broken down. A frisson ran through the bus. We were hurtling down Central Park West and crossed at 79th instead of 86th. People started ringing the bell urgently and calling, "Driver, I want to get out here." I realized that because of heavy rain overnight the park must be flooded in places. The driver wasn't about to stop until he hit his own route again. The middle-European man on my right told me to watch my purse because there were pickpockets at work. The man on my left either heard him or noticed them himself and pointed them out to his wife. The four of us sat and watched them. A tall good-looking black man who had got on with me, and the two younger men, moved up and down the bus three times in all – banging into people and, presumably, picking their pockets. I didn't see the pockets picked but I saw their progress up and down and back again. What is the etiquette in this situation, I wondered? As a foreigner, I left it to my fellow-passengers. When we eventually stopped on 86th and Madison the tall man and his colleagues got off and, under instruction from my neighbour, I watched while they got on the bus which had pulled up behind us. The etiquette must be to watch and guard your own property.

The sign in the supermarket on 100th Street said: "These candies are not free. Help yourself and put 2c. in the honor jar." There was a large table with bowls of wrapped candies and a big glass jar with a few cents in the bottom. A tiny old lady buried some candies in the bottom of her hand-bag. She didn't put any cents in the glass jar and she glared with hatred at me, watching her.

I had been warned by my friends that New York had changed since 1968 and that I must be very careful. I was staying at 101st. Street and was invited out to dinner on W. 86th Street. Against all the advice of my well-meaning friends and the wishes of my husband, I walked. I passed lots of interesting-looking New Yorkers; nothing terrible happened. It's good to be back in New York again.

December, 1977

CHAPTER 19

JAN-FEB 1978: AROUND THE WORLD IN THIRTY DAYS

Thursday 12 January, 1978: Kingston, Ontario.

6 a.m.: yellow lamplight on the frozen snow, waiting for a lift from the house to Fort Frontenac where the bus will take us through the cold dawn to Trenton air force base. The Canadian Forces Boeing 707 is waiting on the dark strip of tarmac amid the endless wastes of snow. As we file on board it is snowing lightly. We have a good view of more snow on the American mid-west and then majestically rugged on the Rockies. After this, cloud obscures any glimpse of San Francisco and we take it on trust that we are headed out over the Pacific.

Hawaii. The ultimate tourist heaven. Warm sun, the golden sand of Waikiki Beach, just across the road from the Hyatt Regency Hotel. Matching golden girls. Youths who look as if they have been born and raised here scour the sand for valuables, using metal detectors wired to batteries slung over their shoulders. We swim, then linger over Budweisers on the balcony outside the hotel bedroom while the sun sets pink and gold behind the skyscraping hotels and the palm trees. It looks more like Hawaii Five-oh than Hawaii.

Sunday 15 January: Tokyo.

Our only totally free, unprogrammed day of the entire tour. We sally forth into the higgledy-piggledy maze of Tokyo's curiously unprepossessing streets, eat raw fish and drink sake in Shinjoku, mingle with the crowds on the clean, rapid subway trains, note the expensive and tasteful clothes on everyone from snappy teenagers to middle-aged mums. In the evening to the Nichegeki music-hall, a kind of Japanese Mayol – not quite as glamorously elaborate as the Folies Bergères, but more sexy in a conservative way. The girls, clad and un-, seem beefier and healthier than the men, who are mostly weedy specimens looking as if they need a square meal. A delicious meal afterwards of tempura (fish and vegetables deep-fried in batter in front of you as you eat it) at a Tenichi restaurant in the Sony building. Telephone Jane in London: the gales have killed a woman in the same road. In Tokyo the temperature is around freezing but there is pleasant sunshine and no wind.

All the Canadians rush to buy Seiko digital watches in the International Shopping Arcade. These have tiny alarms. For the next few days, until the Colonels have mastered the controls, all our briefings and lectures will be interrupted periodically by piercing whistles from embarrassed soldierly wrists.

Wednesday 18 January: Atami, Japan.

The bullet train is off the track for maintenance so we are taken on an endless bus journey from Tokyo through the dreary suburbs, the stench of diesel fumes (no wonder the Japanese so often wear surgical face masks) and the thick snow to Atami, where we arrive an hour and a half after the scheduled time. We are welcomed in our traditional Japanese rooms (four mattresses on the floor of each) by a poker-faced kimono-clad lady of indeterminate age, billed as "ready to help us dress in traditional Japanese gowns for the evening". Ours drapes the voluminous gowns unceremoniously over our shoulders and scuttles out of the room before we can remove our trousers. We shuffle out in our plastic slippers to sample the traditional Japanese communal baths – alas, sexually segregated. The men's baths are unromantically tiled, the water is just hot enough to be mildly uncomfortable, and the diminutive flannels provided, however often wrung out in traditional Japanese style, prove predictably inadequate as towels. We drape ourselves again in our gowns and troop damply into dinner – preceded by a dispassionate display of traditional Japanese samurai sword-play by two young men (mostly ceremonial salutes and re-positionings, interrupted by occasional symbolic lunges) and some spirited banging of enormous drums by a small troupe of teen-aged boys in loose blouses and skin-tight white shorts, on a garishly-lit stage at the end of the dining-room with an enormous Canadian maple-leaf flag draped across the back-cloth and lit by a spotlight. We squat or recline uncomfortably on the floor in front of our plates of raw fish, beer and sake, tutored in the appropriate rituals by kneeling geishas. As I am sitting next to the Canadian Defence Attaché, who has organised the whole expedition, we are served and instructed by the Head Geisha, a po-faced woman of about 55 who dumps some food on our plates and at once lights a cigarette whose smoke she puffs in our faces as we eat. Fortunately she soon retires to the stage with three of the other geishas and they set up a background of tuneless but vaguely mournful traditional Japanese music, accompanying themselves on small de-tuned banjoes, while we help ourselves. The raw fish is not to the taste of all the participants: I find it quite tasty, but soon monotonous.

After dinner, when it is evident that we are not going to buy any more beer and sake, the Counsellor of the Canadian Embassy stands at a microphone at the end of the dining room and tells jokes, some of them moderately funny, for several hours. Most of us creep away to our "bed"-rooms and consume generous quantities of duty-free whisky by way of anaesthetic in preparation for a hideously uncomfortable night on the traditional Japanese floor. The general consensus is that we have been comprehensively and decisively ripped off.

Thursday, 19 January: Atami to Nagoya.

A much better bus ride in bright sunshine through rolling countryside, past the delectable Mount Fuji, volcano-shaped and snow-capped, seeming to float above the surrounding countryside exactly as in the familiar pictures of it. Forty expensive Canadian cameras click busily, and four cheap British ones a little more selectively. The Americans and the Australian are bitingly funny about the awfulness of Atami.

Friday 20 January: Nagoya – Shanghai – Peking.

Our 707 lands in Shanghai to pick up the mandatory Chinese "navigator" who is to escort us through Chinese airspace to Peking: but for some reason we have to while away a couple of hours in the huge drab marble halls of the empty airport building before we are allowed to re-board and get on our way. We pass the time by collecting sheaves of (free) pamphlets in English and French with obscure polemics by Mao, and Little Red Books – the Little Red Covers of which, in sturdy plastic, are detachable, presumably so that revised editions of the contents can readily be substituted in the event of a change of line. (One earlier edition, now a collector's piece, had a Foreword by Lin Piao.) The airport is so reminiscent of Sheremet'evo Airport at Moscow that I suspect it of being a Soviet gift from the friendly Fifties.

Peking is icy cold, a dry penetrating cold that seems to attach the marrow of the bones. The city is hazy with thin yellow dust through which the wintry evening sun barely penetrates. The view of the roofs of the Forbidden City from my hotel bedroom in the Peking Hotel is correspondingly romantic, with their hint of pagoda curves in the pale haze. Dinner (together with the other Brits) with Sir E.Y., who used to be my Head of Chancery in New York 12 years ago, and Pam, in their comfortable and elegant Residence, full of Chinese and British treasures.

Saturday 21 January: Peking.

Visit a Chinese tank unit, about 30 miles outside Peking on a freezing plain. Even with People's Liberation Army great-coats draped over our own top-coats we are chilled through. The tanks seem primitive and antiquated, but they are put through their elementary paces with a certain gusto. After a delicious Chinese lunch with the tankists, we re-board the buses (seen off by a cymbal-clashing band and lines of PLA soldiers holding streaming scarlet banners and clapping enthusiastically) and drive on another 20 miles to the Great Wall. This is as majestic and stunning a sight as anyone could reasonably expect: what is less foreseeable is the extreme steepness of the section of the Wall which we are allowed to walk on, but the climb is rewarded by a superb view of the Wall winding its way over the crests of the mountains until it disappears in the distance: the barrier between the simple nomads on the outside and the sophisticated citizens of the Middle Kingdom on the inside.

On the way back we visit the Ming Tombs, driving down the line of humorous animal statuary that adorns the approach avenue. Only one of the 13 C.XV-XVI tombs has been discovered, excavated and restored: somewhere in those hills are another dozen, slumbering in the eternal dark, loaded with unimaginable treasures.

The PLA (our hosts for the whole visit) gives a banquet for us in the evening at the celebrated Peking Duck Restaurant. We consume virtually the whole of numerous ducks, subdivided into a dozen or so courses: even the webbed feet are sliced and braised deliciously. We wash down numerous toasts in Mao Tai, that burning liquor distilled from maize with which the Chinese are amused to make tiddly their respected guests.

Sunday 22 January: Peking.

An eerie visit to the Military Academy, near the Summer Palace. The PLA clearly thinks it mandatory to visit our sister institution, but we find it without students: the academy has been closed 18 months earlier following the disruptions of the Gang of Four, i.e. a student take-over and the purging of the Directing Staff as part of the second Cultural Revolution. Now the staff are back, new curricula are being prepared, and soon there will be a new generation of students. Wherever we go – factories, communal farms, shipyards, museums – we are given impassioned accounts of how years of work have been lost through the sabotage and interference of the Gang of Four and their adherents: testimony to the mad disruptive ideas of the ageing Mao and his frightful wife.

Peeping through a curtained window of the Military Museum, during an interminable blow-by-blow tour of the Chinese "Liberation" from 1928 to 1949, we see lying shattered in a stone courtyard an American U2 aircraft.

Mao on tactics: "When the enemy attacks, we retreat. When the enemy halts, we harass. When he retreats, we follow. When he is tired, we attack."

At our return banquet I ask the PLA host at my table, through our PLA Foreign Relations Bureau interpreter, why in all the Military Museum there is no evidence of any part being played in their revolution by Lin Piao or Liu Shao-Chi: whatever their subsequent careers, surly in their early days they must have done the Party some service? After earnest consultation, the answer comes back: "We have no objection to mentioning the early careers of Lin Piao and Liu Shao-Chi." Delphic. As is the reply by Mr Wu, another PLA interpreter, who has spent 2 years studying at Kingston Ontario, at Queens University, to my question about how the Chinese reconcile their expressions of friendship towards western countries such as Canada and Britain with their belief that war (i.e. between the west and the 3rd world led by China) is inevitable. Wu replied simply: "We hold that war is inevitable but we know that the Soviets and many in the West do not agree."

We queue up to view the cadaver of Chairman Mao in his glass case. The building and mise-en-scène are much more vulgar and tasteless than the Lenin mausoleum in Red Square, but otherwise it is a carbon copy. The religious aura is as strong. Lenin is in a neat bourgeois suit: Mao, appropriately, in a Mao jacket, buttoned at the collar, and draped in a huge red flag with a hammer and sickle embroidered on it. Lenin I remember as waxy white in the face: Mao looks like a dark yellow plasticine doll. Lenin's expression is composed and grave. Mao's face is contorted with what appears to be horror.

Monday 23 January: Peking - Hangchow.

A PLA Trident (bought from Britain some years ago) takes us from Peking to Hangchow, stopping en route at an isolated air base to enable us to see round the base, watch a (rather routine) air display by the MIGs, and inspect the small chemical plant where the wives of all the airmen from the Commanding Officer downwards work every day at loading medicines into bottles and ampoules. After seeing the air base we re-embark in the Trident, which is on the point of take-off when we suddenly change our minds and taxi back to the little terminal building. There is some cock and bull story about Hangchow airport being closed temporarily by bad weather, and we soon return to the runway and take off. But in that interval we refueled! Perhaps there was a sudden message that the Trident would need to carry enough fuel to get it back to Peking?

Hangchow (pronounced "Hung-Joe" – but why not spell it accordingly?) is a gorgeously pretty resort area, on the edge of the famous West Lake, dotted with pagodas, little temples, islands with ornamental bamboo gardens, pleasant walks and boat rides everywhere. We visit the main local silk factory. Primitive machines churn out miles of silk patterned with black and white pictures of the 4 patron saints, those European villains Marx, Engels, Lenin and Stalin, with Mao and Chairman Hua bringing up the rear. An elderly lady in the universal blue smock and baggy blue trousers sits placidly at the end where these silk portraits spew from the machine, patiently chopping them up with a huge pair of scissors. As her speed of operation is about a tenth of that of the machine, the pile of uncut portraits beside her gets higher and higher.

We are put through a film show in the evening, with the entire PLA garrison of Hangchow sitting spellbound behind us: a film on the growth of bamboo roots, one on circus animals, and a 2-hour allegorical folk story involving characters called Monkey, Pixie and Monk, all of whom do a lot of loud singing in a tragic high-pitched atonal chant. A daunting ordeal.

Wednesday 25 January: Hangchow – Shanghai.

On our way to the shipyard in the buses we get tantalizing glimpses of the Bund, the famous old water-front street where the western merchants' offices, banks and clubs were. The names of some of the old Dutch and German banks can still be read on the fronts of the solid stone buildings. The western style is evident everywhere. We try to get a taxi from the hotel at lunchtime to visit the Friendship (foreigners') Store, with the real intention in my case of slipping away and looking at the Bund, but our hosts decline gently and firmly to allow us to roam so far afield. The shops around the hotel seem better stocked than corresponding shops in Moscow: quite good quality shoes and clothes, plenty of food. Everyone seems adequately dressed, and here where the weather is milder than in Peking and people are not encumbered by heavy coats, everyone looks more brightly and cheerfully dressed, the women in varied blouses (though nearly all in trousers).

The shipyard is a chaotic mess of live cables and old iron, spinning lathes with no guard rails, men grinding and even welding without goggles. No-one wears safety helmets. There is little activity. At the commune (collective farm area) things are more orderly but chillingly regimented. There is an economy which is virtually independent of cash: wages are derisory, most basic services (but not health) are provided free, there is only a rare opportunity to leave the commune and get work elsewhere and then only with Party approval. The whole commune is run by the Party Committee, which itself determines and controls the membership of the Revolutionary Committee, which in turn has no powers of any significance anyway. Although this is clearly a special display commune (the guide admits to an average of five or six visits every month), its facilities are very limited; the "hospital" is in a poor state with new-born babies alongside people with what appear to be quite serious and presumably infectious diseases, and two gloomy individuals undergoing electric acupuncture and obviously not enjoying it at all. However, the pigs seem to be in good shape.

Friday 27 January: Shanghai – Canton – Calcutta.

After the aseptic regimented orderliness of China – or at any rate those glimpses of China we were programmed to enjoy – the bus journey from the airport into Calcutta proves traumatic for those of our party who have not seen Third World squalor before. The teeming streets and crippled beggars, hovels and dirt, rags and animals all jumbled in a colourful malodorous poverty-stricken steaming mess, bring one sensitive franco-phone Canadian civilian to the verge of tears, and several of the Colonels to explosive disgust. Weeks later some will still be saying that what India needs is a solid dose of Chinese communism (discipline, leadership, motivation, hard work, and the other military virtues). I strongly suspect but can't prove that there is similar squalor in China and that people suffer similar deprivation, but of course we were not allowed to see it. However this may be wrong: and if such hard-core degradation has really been eliminated, perhaps the 2 million people doing forced labour in Sinkiang are a fair price to pay – not to mention those still being executed for persistent political deviation? If so, the Colonels are right. But I can't swallow it.

We visit an "improved slum", i.e. one where some basic communal services – sewers, drinking water, washing facilities – have been provided. It is primitive and overcrowded but not degrading. A tall Indian is leaning against a wall in a teeming slum courtyard with a transistor radio held to his ear, listening rapt to a commentary in Hindi on the India-versus-Australia test match in Adelaide. Our Australian Group Captain pricks up his ears and the Indian gives him the score in English.

One of Mother Theresa's mission refuges for destitute and dying old people and orphans rescued from the streets proves a little less grueling than expected. The kids all seem well fed and cared for and we see few of the old. Some of us reluctantly tour the ward for mentally sick people, which is as piteous as such places anywhere. The neat bird-like Indian Sister in charge of this ward points to a darkly muttering young woman in a corner, and says that there has been a problem with her: one of the other patients bit off her big toe while having a seizure. "But this one didn't mind: she thought it was part of the treatment."

Sunday 29 January: Calcutta – Agra – Delhi

What can one say about the Taj Mahal, except that this is the way to see it – specially closed to the public for our (and, admittedly, the President of Ireland's) visit; flying in to the little Agra airport in our own 707, touring the Taj and the old fort, and flying out again to Delhi?

In the evening of our arrival from Agra in Delhi we go out to the big square in front of the government office buildings to watch the Indian forces Beat the Retreat at sundown. Soldiers on camels with lances silhouetted against the evening sky, a solitary bugler playing a melancholy lament from the turret of a high tower, the parade advancing in line abreast and halting in front of the President on his saluting base, massed military bands marching and countermarching, drummers with leopard-skins twirling their drum-sticks, the three Chiefs of staff in their uniforms flanking the Minister of Defence – the whole thing is almost comically British in inspiration and tradition, pungently redolent of the Raj. It seems a very far cry from the People's Liberation Army in their baggy trousers.

Wednesday 1 February: Delhi.

We visit three villages some forty miles outside Delhi. In the last of the three we are greeted by the whole population of the village assembled in a small square, elders in white turbans, a choir of doll-like small girls in brilliantly coloured miniature saris, the village head man and the local school teacher as interpreter. After speeches of welcome and description of the life of the village, some of the villagers ask questions about Canada: do all the huts in Canada have electricity? How many bowls of milk do Canadians drink every day? Does every Canadian own a cow? The effort to relate us, visitors from Mars, to their daily lives is incredibly moving. We are decorated with garlands of flowers and given drinks of Cola (not Coke: Coca-Cola has been expelled from India for failing to reveal its formula to the Government under the partnership deal). We visit a well-appointed orphans' home and the house of a retired Congress Party MP, who reclines on a settee in his yard, surrounded by his womenfolk and cows, slightly drunk and very amiably loquacious.

Dinner with an old friend now in the Australian High Commission in Delhi: I have enjoyed his company in Moscow and Canberra (and played many hours of squash with him in both capitals): now we have a marvellously relaxed and bibulous evening in a third continent. Amazingly, he has become engaged. I telephone Jane from his house, using the just-inaugurated STD service.

Friday 3 February: Lusaka, Zambia.

The warm, green, rolling countryside of Africa, uncrowded and unhurried, seems a balm to the spirit after these frenetic Asian glimpses.

Saturday 4 February: Lusaka / Livingston / Victoria Falls.

A bus journey of jarring discomfort and inordinate length through countryside of a numbing sameness. But a white plume of spray in the air 20 miles from Livingstone announces that we are approaching the Falls, three times the height of Niagara and twice as wide. We leave our overnight bags in our rooms at the Musi-O-Tunya Hotel, only a couple of hundred yards from the Falls, and walk over to view the spectacle. Luckily I decide to have a quick dip in the hotel pool en route for the falls – luckily, because the spectator on the famous Knife-edge bridge is soaked to the skin in spray thrown up by the thundering cascade of water, and swimming trunks are the ideal garb. The view is sensational, as is the total absence of guard rails or other protection at the various sheer drops hundreds of feet into the boiling ravine. They must lose a few tourists each year. Across the far end of the ravine, past the spectacular railway bridge (where Vorster and Kaunda met in a South African railway carriage above the Zambezi on the Zambian frontier), we get a good view of the Victoria Falls Hotel on the Rhodesia side.

For several minutes tonight there is a clearly audible rattle of small arms fire, followed by the crump of an explosion.

Monday 6 February: Lusaka.

Joshua Nkomo, Co-President of the Zimbabwe Patriotic Front, addresses us, only a few hours after his return from the Malta talks with David Owen and Andrew Young. He is calculatedly moderate, reassuring, statesmanlike. If only he could get the support he needs from the west, he could dispense with the aid he gets from the east. He has been brought up and remains a Christian, steeped in the western democratic tradition. Even those who have been talking of him beforehand as a murdering terrorist have to admit that they are deeply impressed.

In the evening we are received by President Kaunda at a Working Dinner at State House. The President addresses us for an hour or so about his (and Zambia's) philosophy of "humanism", none of whose tenets seems in the least controversial. Kaunda looks a great deal older and sounds a great deal vaguer than the brisk and purposeful figure whom I escorted around the Colonial Office in the late Fifties, and to whom I was presented (along with the rest of the UN committee of 24) in 1965. After the address and some weighty but unspecific answers to questions, we adjourn to the dining room for a buffet supper of Zambian food. The President hands out the plates as we line up for food; afterwards he pours out the coffee, for every one of us. A simple but irresistible gesture of humility and hospitality.

Wednesday 8 February: Tunis.

"You must admit, it's good to be back," says one of the Canadian civilians. Neither he nor I have been in Tunisia, or even North Africa, before. He means that the western ambience of the Tunis Hilton is comfortingly familiar: he can order, and enjoy, a grilled steak and salad, and knows he will not be poisoned by the ice cubes in his

Scotch. Some of us eat couscous in a last attempt to sample the food of the country. It is not, to be honest, particularly nice. (But the Mediterranean fish is excellent.)

We have a long session with the Prime Minister, M. Nouria, who speaks with understandable feeling and at great length about the "events" (there is a state of emergency, martial law, a curfew: at least 40, probably more than a hundred, people were shot by the security forces in riots, or demonstrations, only 10 days before we arrived). But he speaks very softly, each sentence fading into a dramatic whisper: in French, with no interpretation. Alas, few of us are able to benefit from his thoughts.

Lunch with the British Ambassador, JL, another friend from New York days when he was Head of United Nations Department. His house was given to HMG in perpetuity when its original owner, the Bey's Finance Minister, absconded with the Kingdom's cash. There used to be a small railway station at the bottom of the grounds, called "Consulate", for the sole use of the British Consul. Alas, it is closed now; but the house is still a splendid period piece in sumptuous Moorish style. However the Ambassador's chatty daughter (20 or so) can't wait to get back to Fulham where there is something to do. The curfew makes no difference because nothing happens in Tunis in the evenings anyway.

Saturday 11 February: Lajes, The Azores.

We stay overnight on this huge and once busy American air base, and this morning do our final shopping in the PX and visit the charming flavoury Portuguese town.

Trenton, Ontario.

The Canadian customs take 2 ½ hours to process the 50 of us; one old hand says he has never seen so much spending done by NDC members on a trip in all his years of collecting duty.

Kingston, Ontario.

The banks of frozen snow that line the streets are seven and eight feet high.

PART IV:

ETHIOPIA, MID-1980S

CHAPTER 20

SEP-DEC 1982:
ADDIS ABABA, LANGANO,
BAHR DAR, GONDAR

Tuesday 21 September.   Addis Ababa.   We emerge from the little Ethiopian Airlines jet, about four hours late, blinking in the golden morning sunshine, grateful for the dry warmth after the steam heat of Cairo in the past four days. The half-dozen or so Embassy staff lined up to greet us outside the terminal building tell us this is the first dry, sunny day and that we have brought the end of the rains. We shake hands with everyone, make polite conversation with the effusive gentleman from the Foreign Ministry Protocol Department who was at the foot of the steps to greet us, and soon climb into the Protocol Department car with him for the drive through the town to the Embassy compound, a Union Jack fluttering from the near-side wing and the Ambassador's Daimler following behind. We try not to sound as if we have been sitting up all night in Cairo Airport.

The Mercedes turns in to the compound and stops as the Embassy guards, drawn up in two ranks with ancient muskets at the slope, present arms. Someone opens the car door and gestures to me to get out. Clearly I am required to inspect this guard of honour. Their turnout obviously reflects hours of effort and practice. I tell the guard commander so. He listens uncomprehendingly. It is not clear how to terminate the ceremony. I do the embarrassed half-salute of the hatless civilian and say imperiously that the guard commander is to dismiss the men. Back into the car and up the gentle slope of the Embassy compound, past the trees and shrubs and flowers, past the trim colonial-style Chancery offices and some of the staff houses, to the Residence at the top, the Union Jack flying from the tall flagpole outside, and the ten Residence staff drawn up in two lines on each side of the steps to the front door. They are wearing amazing snow-white uniforms with brilliant sashes. More hand-shakes and welcomes, the Ethiopians grasping with both hands the offered hand, bowing low and murmuring in apparent ecstasy. They seem extremely numerous but remarkably friendly. Into the cool Residence, pausing to admire the columns of names of all my predecessors incised into the stone pillars; the Durbar Hall, with a signed photograph of Princess Anne (of all people) on the baby grand piano (brought up by camel from Djibouti in Nineteen Something); our own bedroom with its two adjoining bathrooms and my dressing room; the children's rooms and our private sitting-room (the "morning room"); around the first of the two internal courtyards to the three splendid bedrooms of the guest wing; through the large dining-room ("you can seat about fifty or a few more at a pinch") and back through the Durbar Hall to the Drawing-room ("nice to use this when you only have 15 or 20 to dinner"), on to the second courtyard, the study (I note the type-writer with appreciation), the corridor where the drinks are served from....

Just time for an hour in the huge double bed before we bath, change and are driven in the Daimler the 500 yards down the hill to the Head of Chancery's house to meet the UK-based staff and the senior members of the locally engaged (i.e. Ethiopian) staff for drinks and lunch. Hard to tell which of us looks with more apprehension at the other.

Sunday 26 September. Maskal ("the Cross") celebration in the main square, now Revolution Square, formerly Maskal Square. Tens of thousands of people, cheerful and orderly; we occupy seats in the diplomatic area which seems to be filled otherwise entirely by Russians and their blonde wives all obsessively taking photographs with their Praktikas. Troupes of well-drilled children chant and dance; teams of priests make and re-make formations, advancing, retreating. At the front in the centre the proceedings are watched by a Bench of Bishops: the Abuna of the Ethiopian Orthodox Church, the Catholic Archbishop, the Chaplain of the Anglican church in Addis, a visiting Canadian prelate of indeterminate sect wearing a good deal of purple. At the climax the Abuna lights a massive bonfire in the middle of the square and there is much dancing and chanting around it. High above the main stands a huge poster of Marx, Engels and Lenin benignly presides: opposite, a sign on top of an office block proclaims in English and Amharic the virtues of Proletarian Internationalism. Yet for all this huge crowd engaged in a purely religious ceremonial the evidence of state power is almost invisible. There are a few policemen and one or two soldiers, but they keep a low profile and there is none of that sense of tight armed control which is inseparable from large gatherings in the Soviet Union.

Monday 27 September. Maskal public holiday. We go off on a day outing with a picnic in the Daimler to Debra Libanos, Portuguese Bridge and the Blue Nile Gorge. The church at Debra Libanos, 100 kilometres from Addis, is reached by a narrow road on a ledge along the side of a steep gorge at the bottom of which is a tributary of the Blue Nile: the setting is spectacular, the scenery beautiful, everything green from the recent rains. My Ethiopian security escort, B.A., persuades a grubby priest loafing outside the church to let us in by a back entrance and to descend into the vaults where a funeral service has been going on since dawn. To reach the funeral chamber we pass through a catacomb which seems to be in total, utterly unrelieved darkness. B.A. leads the way, J. following and gripping his hand, me last gripping J's hand. We stand discreetly in the narrow entrance to the chamber, acrid with incense and the smoke of dozens of flares and candles. White-cloaked figures, all male, all with long staves, are swaying and crooning to the beat of a huge drum. The whole thing is hypnotic and disturbing. We are glad to be back in the brilliant sunshine again with the crippled beggars and the ragged children clamouring for coins for having allegedly guarded the Daimler in our absence.

We visit the 350-year-old Portuguese Bridge just up the road, climbing down to the weather-beaten old stone structure, crossing it, and clambering along a narrow ledge to an overhanging rock from which there is a stunning view back to the bridge and waterfall, with baboons sunning themselves on the rock face, and out beyond the escarpment onto a rolling plain dotted with thatched tukuls, the traditional round huts, and the occasional round church, its cross glinting in the sun. Back to the car pursued by friendly children anxious to show off their very passable English.

The Nile Gorge, another 100 kilometres away, is again a spectacular sight: a mile or so deep and about 2 miles across from rim to rim, it is reminiscent inevitably of the Grand Canyon but without the concrete viewing platforms and hot dog stands. We drive a mile or two down the rough rock-and-gravel road carved out of the edge of the cliff face and winding down to the river at the bottom of the gorge in a series of heart-in-mouth hairpin bends. Back to the top for our picnic of chilled white wine, cold chicken and salad out of the splendid wooden picnic box belonging once to Sir Douglas Busk (1952-56) and still reverently referred to by the Residence staff as "Sir Busk's Box".

29 October – 1 November. Lake Langano. A few days' welcome relief from the relentless round of official calls on other Ambassadors, lunches to be welcomed or to welcome others or to say goodbye to them, dinners ditto and innumerable National Day receptions. The Embassy owns – indeed, originally built – two simple but agreeable cottages on the shore of Lake Langano, one of the lakes in the Rift Valley and the only expanse of water in Ethiopia apart from the Hilton Hotel swimming pool which is free of bilharzia. Langano, being down in the valley, is about 2,000 feet lower than Addis (the Embassy compound is about 8,500 feet up) and occasional trips to a lower altitude are recommended for reducing the countless maladies and symptoms generally attributed to Addis's rarified air: insomnia (true – after 3 weeks in Addis J. and I regularly wake at 5.30 a.m. and can't go back to sleep, both of us hitherto effortless sleepers), headaches, wind, shortage of breath after even minor exertion (universal), propensity of self-winding watches to stop, capacity of sugar to sweeten with fewer grains… Every comment on some faintly disagreeable or puzzling sensation or passing vexation is met by a triumphant: "It's the altitude!" from one of the ubiquitous old hands. But at Langano the air is thicker, the sun more recognizably tropical, the dark brown water of the lake actually quite inviting. We share one of the cottages with my No. 2 and Head of Chancery, and are splendidly looked after by the two "zabanyas" (watchmen) paid by the Embassy to look after the cottages and their little compound, by A.B. (who works the radio link back to the Embassy), by the Residence cook who turns out excellent meals from the rudimentary kitchen hut, and by BWM, my official driver, who has driven every British Ambassador since the middle ages and indeed was the first, with the then Ambassador in the days when diplomats were travelers rather than tourists, to hack their way with machetes through what was then dense undergrowth to the lake shore and to clear the first lake shore camp site.

On the second day MFS (the No. 2 and H of C) sets off to visit another lake cottage in the small sailing dinghy which he and a couple of others own and keep at the lake. Instead of the predicted 15 minutes it takes him 3 hours. Trying to sail back in the late afternoon he is forced to make huge tacks and seems to us, watching through binoculars, to be getting steadily further away. With less than an hour to go before it gets (suddenly) dark, I take the landrover along the shore to the new hotel complex being built by the government tourist commission and persuade them to send out their one motorboat (liberated from a British company when it was nationalized at the time of the revolution) to go out and tow the sailing boat in. It is hard to be sure whether the poor chap is more mortified or relieved.

Next morning I go jogging on the dry scrub-land above the cliffs overlooking the lake, and in my efforts to shake off two tiresome dogs (Langano is no place to get rabies), I get mildly and very temporarily lost, overshooting the cottages by a couple of miles because they are invisible from the cliff-top. When I fail to return after an hour, there is general panic. B.A., personally responsible for my safety, hastily dons a natty Adidas track-suit and sets off after me. BWM leaps into the landrover and drives up and down the rocky track hooting. Both obviously have visions of losing their new Ambassador only a few weeks after his arrival and having to start toilet-training yet another new man all over again. (My occasional jogging expeditions in the early mornings with B.A., himself a former athletic instructor and pentathlon champion, have already given rise to astonishing rumours and legends in Addis. I am said to have been sighted running at high speed miles from my Embassy, pursued by an exhausted and terrified security man. Having heard this story for the ninth time, each one more imaginatively embellished, I begin to grow reluctant to deny it.)

BRIAN BARDER'S DIPLOMATIC DIARY

Saturday 6 November. Addis Ababa. At 8 a.m. the Foreign Ministry Protocol man arrives at the Residence with the Mercedes and the Union Jack on the wing to take me to the National Palace to present my credentials ("To Lt-Col Mengistu, Our Good Friend, Greetings! We have made choice of Our Trusty and Well-beloved Brian Leon Barder, Esquire, to reside with You in the character of Our Ambassador Extraordinary and Plenipotentiary...." – no exaggeration). Two earlier dates for the ceremony have been cancelled at the last moment because Comrade Chairman (his invariable designation) has gone off somewhere else instead. Now at last I'm actually On, but to present credentials to the Chairman's No. 2, Comrade Fikre-Selassie, the Secretary-General of the Derg. There are five Ambassadors to present today, and I'm on first because I arrived before the others: hence the dawn start. Inspect guard of honour outside Palace, stand to attention for fanfare and national anthem, escorted into Palace by dignified (female) Chief of Protocol, advance down long ornate Throne Room towards Comrade Secretary-General standing at far end: pause to be announced and then advance to Cde. S-G; hand over Credentials, shake hands, bow, introduce my three supporters (MFS, the 58-year-old lady Consul, the Commercial Secretary): am presented to S-G's retinue, including the Foreign Minister; sit in Louis XIV chairs and exchanges solemn little speeches, impromptu, about state of the world, our relations and what we plan/hope to do about them, fantastic honour and privilege, etc. Off to one side of the room for official photographs with Cde. S-G and respective retinues, out to the Mercedes and back to the Embassy with flag flying and motor-cycle outriders clearing the traffic for us: champagne and canapes for the Protocol man and my 3 henchmen, beer and a fiver each for the Mercedes driver and the motor cycle outriders. Finally I'm accredited and empowered to conduct business with the Ethiopian government. (According to local diplomatic lore and convention I haven't even been a proper, full Ambassador until now: pretty tedious for those, not a few, who are kept waiting for 3 or even 4 months before being able to present.)

Sunday 7 November. MFS and I jog the 21 kilometres from the Addis War Cemetery to the Cheshire Home for disabled and orphaned children, two out of the 2,000 or so Ethiopians and foreigners who do the Annual Cheshire Home Walk (some run, some jog, some walk). We are accompanied by J. and B.A. in the landrover loaded with dry clothes, spare running shoes, salt tablets, iced water and a cold-box (not Sir Busk's) full of Buck's Fizz. Having got 21 sponsors pledging – and eventually paying – a Birr a kilometer, for the Cheshire Home, I feel rather disagreeably virtuous as well as completely pole-axed by the mainly up-hill slog and – of course – the Altitude. (£1 = about 3.3 Birr.)

26 November – 2 December.   Bahr Dar and Gondar: Our first official trip outside Addis and Shoa Province (official permission having been secured with much hassle). After 12 hours in the landrover the 6 of us arrive in Bahr Dar pretty stiff and dusty: J., the lady consul, the Chancery secretary who is leaving soon, B.A. and BWM at the wheel. There are brand new and splendid hotels, identical inside, at Bahr Dar and Gondar: in both we are virtually the only guests. That in Bahr Dar stands right on Lake Tana: that in Gondar on the summit of a steep hill overlooking the town and the old castles, relics of when Gondar was the capital city. We visit the source of the Blue Nile (where it flows out of Lake Tana): Tississat Falls, comparable in grandeur with Niagara and Victoria Falls and quite deserted except by an ancient zabanya carrying a loaded Mauser rifle date-stamped 1896 (and with the safety catch off): and a Falasha Village where we buy extra-ordinary pottery figures from the Falashas, the Ethiopian Jews whose origins are such a potent mystery. Lots of official visits, too: two Producers' Co-operatives, Literacy Campaign centres, a rural water supply project, the Provincial Administration, a re-settlement camp for people returned from Eritrea and the Sudan, emergency food storage centre, and so on. Illuminating, often depressing, occasionally oddly uplifting: main impression, though, is the incredible poverty (Ethiopia is probably the poorest country in the world after Chad and Bhutan, and it is all too palpably true). Faced with deprivation of this order, where to begin? (No-one knows.)

We photograph village women filling their huge earthenware pitchers from the spring because the newly-installed taps in the village square are fenced off and padlocked. The pump, generator, pipes, storage tank and taps have been put in by a British company under a European Community Development Fund Project. (There are some coherent reasons for padlocking the taps, but the women at the spring probably don't know what they are.)

CHAPTER 21

JAN-MARCH 1983: ADDIS ABABA, KAFFA, WOLLEGA, ILLUBABOR, GAMBELA

Tuesday 11 January, 1983: Addis Ababa.   Another glorious, cool, bright sunny morning: breakfast outside on the terrace with our house-guest from East African Department, DHD – fresh orange juice, cereal with papaya, eggs and bacon, toast and (Oxford) marmalade, fresh fruit (bananas from the garden). Find I no longer notice as I used to in the early weeks the royal crest on all the china and silver. One can get used to anything in time. Crumble corner of a piece of toast for the little indignant squeaking bird with bright yellow crest and half its beak missing which comes every morning to be fed on the low wall of the terrace. Listen to 5 am (GMT!) BBC World Service news on Residence Sony while eating breakfast. Mustn't forget Paludrine.

Walk down the hill to the Chancery with DHD (3 minutes) through the eucalyptus trees, flowing shrubs, dwarf palm trees and flower beds, to read the telegrams before taking him off in the Daimler, reeking of petrol but flag flying, to call on the Deputy Head of the Relief and Rehabilitation Commission in his dingy office overlooking Revolution Square with a good view of the giant posters of Marx,

Engels and Lenin ("Holy Trinity", the Ethiopians call them – an echo, perhaps, of the familiar name "Power of the Trinity" or "Haile Selassie"?). Slide past usual crowd of nondescript people thronging concrete corridor outside the Deputy Commissioner's office and wait for a few moments in his ante-room chatting to the two (as usual strikingly beautiful) secretaries until beckoned in.

Later call with DHD on the American Charge d'Affaires and his very Ivy League (and very professional) deputy, as usual with his Brooks Brothers shirt and Phi Beta Kappa 3-piece suit. Admire again American capacity for sleek, comfortable and above all unmistakeably contemporary decoration and furnishing of their Embassy offices and residences.

Six or seven western (mainly EEC) and Commonwealth (mainly African) Ambassadors come to lunch to meet DHD. Very relaxed and informal, but somehow – perhaps it's the language barrier or lack of it – the Commonwealth people seem to feel more off duty than the Europeans, however friendly and fluent.

More calls in the afternoon (the dignified and impassive Head of European Department at the Ministry of Foreign Affairs; the Head of the Ethiopian News Agency at the Ministry of National Guidance and Information, who asks animatedly about the current place in the league table of Tottenham Hotspur; the Assistant Secretary-General of the OAU from whose 12th-floor office in the OAU compound one gets a good view down onto the Akaki prison where the most prominent remaining prisoners are held – it looks more like an animated village with a wire fence round it than a prison): and a big, polyglot buffet supper at six buffet tables in our long dining-room in the evening, noisy, polyglot, fairly generously lubricated with alcohol. Almost none of the Ethiopians invited are there: situation normal. The familiar oil painting of Charles I over the fireplace ("School of Van Dyke") stares down disapprovingly, as presumably he used to do in the days when His Imperial Majesty the diminutive Emperor was the guest of honour at glittering formal dinners in this same room, extended and rebuilt in 1965 to enable The Queen to give her return banquet for H.I.M. on the required scale. Did that dignified, upright little figure return the disapproving stare of the martyred – or anyway executed – English monarch?

Saturday 22 January.   2220 Ethiopian children throng the compound for the annual Embassy's children's Christmas party (Ethiopian Christmas is several weeks later than that of the western churches). All are supposedly offspring of our 70 or so Ethiopian staff: all supposedly between 4 and 14, although some can barely toddle and some have luxuriant macho moustaches. There are organized games, dancing, presents, Father Christmas (impersonated by the chaplain of the Anglican church, and a source of exotic terror to the smaller and more impressionable Ethiopian children), cartoons on video-tape at the Embassy Club. One of the most enthusiastically appreciated "events" is a ride for each child round the Embassy compound circuit in one of the landrovers, each taking about 20 at a time. All the Ethiopians and some of the more extrovert of the British hosts join with feverish energy in the dancing, which entails much squaring and vibration of the shoulders, Shoan dancing-style: on the more generously-endowed and nubile girl participants, the effect is electrifying. Each "child" gets a balloon, a pencil, a plastic top, some popcorn, a small scribble pad and a biscuit in a plastic bag. J and I enjoy seeing the delight occasioned by the pencils, having cleaned out the newsagents and stationers of Wandsworth to bring the hundreds we had been briefed to bring. As the light fades the children begin to depart, some crying as their balloons burst...

Thursday 27 January.   We visit Addis Ababa University. In all the administration offices there are ghosts: this was the Emperor's main working palace and residence until the bloodletting in the 1960 attempted coup while the Emperor was on a state visit to Brazil. Afterwards he could not stomach living in such a haunted place and he turned it over to the University. Now the Vice-Chancellor's outer office is where the Emperor's study was. After we had had a chat with the Vice-Chancellor (the British Council Representative who is also my Cultural Attache was there too) and some of his deans of departments, the old university museum, "temporarily" closed for refurbishment, was specially unlocked for us. First conventional museum displays of Ethiopiana: then, unheralded, the Emperor's private bedroom, with grandiose canopied 4-poster bed, a good deal of what appeared to be G-Plan bedroom furniture and some that might have been copied from the (first) "Queen Mary", and glass cases containing presents to H.I.M. from all over the world. Although he is officially reviled or, more often, written out of Ethiopian history, reminders of him persist everywhere: portraits and commemorative plaques all over the OAU and ECA conference centre, Africa Hall, which he conceived and opened: mosaics in the official church showing H.I.M. with a group of British staff officers re-entering Ethiopia after the defeat of the Italians in 1941. (Now it is the British who have also been written out of Ethiopian history: the speeches and articles celebrating Patriots' Day on 6 April will give not the smallest hint that the British and the other Allies played any part whatever in the liberation from fascism, and indeed the newly arrived and youthful Malawi Ambassador admits that his understanding from the celebrations was that it was the British imperialists whom the Ethiopian patriots and broad masses had defeated and driven out.)

Saturday 26 February. Farewell buffet supper for my Head of Chancery, who is off to be Sir Rex Hunt's deputy in the Falklands, and to welcome his successor. Once dessert is served and everyone has champagne, I make the obligatory short speech, almost wholly improvised, and meant to be mainly light-hearted. To my genuine surprise, this turns out to be a rollicking success, with much riotous laughter (not all, surely, sycophantic?). I experience for the first and almost certainly the last time the sensation of playing an audience like an instrument. It is rather humbling: so must Mark Antony, Mussolini and Max Miller have felt. Afterwards the Italian Ambassador, rather a formal colleague, comes up and offers his congratulations on "a very brilliant speech". The next attempt will infallibly be a flop. Luckily J. is a reliably brutal and frank critic.

Tuesday 1 March – Sunday 6 March: Kaffa, Wollega and Illubabor. J. and I, with my Second Secretary Chancery, B.A. (my security officer) and BWM (my driver) do a joint trip with JW, the EEC Delegate in Ethiopia (German), his delectable wife Ingrid, one of his technical assistance advisers (BZ) and their driver. The object is to visit 3 major EEC development projects (coffee improvement, a road built to open up a potentially rich agricultural area and a rural water supply project): and to see the romantic, rarely-visited town of Gambela down in the south-west and once part of British-administered Sudan, as the former British District Commissioner's office and residence, now those of the Sudanese Consul-General, eloquently testify: uneven wooden floors, high ceilings with clanking fans, green-painted verandahs around three sides, pure Greene-land.

Jima, our first day's destination, still bears signs of the Italian occupiers' short-lived notion of making it the new capital of fascist Italy in Africa, Nova Roma: grandiloquent official buildings, a crumbling piazza, a once fine main square. But all is now sadly dilapidated; Jima seems to have passed its peak. We walk in the evening along what was the main shopping street only 4 or 5 years ago: now it is turned over to seedy bars, brightly lit inside, some adorned with pictures of Chairman Mengistu, others with ancestors of Haile Selassie. All double unashamedly as brothels.

Next night in a small mosquito-infested hotel in Nekemte, capital of Wollega Region, and then along the new EEC road to Dembidollo where we spend the night at a surprisingly comfortable road construction workers' camp and get a bizarrely excellent dinner. First we visit the catholic mission at Dembidollo where those characteristically saintly Fathers and Sisters, all in civilian clothes, all cheerful and matter-of-fact, run their schools and clinics in the back of beyond and in the face of sometimes brutal harassment from the local authorities. They all seem genuinely pleased to see us, press on us cups of tea and jam tarts, introduce us to the stream of casual callers – visitors from the catholic mission coordinating committee, Cubans from the local hospital, a friendly little chap from the town administration office. Graham Greene-land again.

The road from Dembidollo down over the edge of the escarpment to Gambela on the Sudanese plain four or five thousand feet below is the worst we have ever experienced: how BWM gets the landrover down it we shall never know. The mere 40 km. take nearly 4 hours. On the way into Gambela we pass, stop and photograph, the Belgian war cemetery, sadly neglected and ruined, where (as the crumbling memorial still just legibly records) hundreds of Belgian and Congolese officers and men lie buried, "Morts Pour La Patrie" (which Patrie?). Later we find the one British war grave where an officer of the Royal Scots and the Sudanese Political Service lies buried where he fell: his gravestone is well tended in a peaceful, sunlit spot. The day before our arrival an old man who now works for the Sudanese Consul tells the Consul that he was there that day in 1941, helped bury the Englishman: but that he was killed by the English, not the Italians. When we meet him he refuses to repeat this, mumbling that he can't remember. Decide not to include this tantalizing little insight into my report to the Commonwealth War Graves Commission (who tell me later that mine is the first report on the Gambela grave that they have had for many years).

Afternoon: drive in the land rovers along the River Baro towards Itang. Local people all very friendly: most tall, well-built Sudanese types, quite different in physique from highlands Ethiopians. Few wear more than faded cotton loin-cloths, ragged khaki shorts or baggy swimming trunks; topless women are the rule rather than the exception. We find elephant tracks but no elephants; leave the landrovers to photograph the river only sparingly after hearing of a young Dutchman who visited recently, got out on the river bank, aimed his camera and was immediately seized and eaten alive by a crocodile. (A British couple who visit us in Addis a few weeks later, and who served in the Embassy at the end of the Sixties, show us a gruesome dog-eared black and white snapshot of what was left of an American Peace Corps volunteer who suffered a similar fate just outside Gambela: his parents insisted on his "remains" (unusually apt term) being returned to the States for burial.)

Next morning a breezy group of Canadians, few looking more than 19 or 20, who are doing an oil exploration aerial geophysical survey around Gambela, organize a couple of trips in their tiny plastic-bubble helicopter (Jane declines). The view from the little glass ball is stunning. Deep in the bush we spot a herd of elephant and drop like a stone to below the tree-tops to photograph them: most thunder off to escape from our engine din and down-draught dust-storm, but one huge bull elephant turns and stands squarely defiant, massive ears flared, as if posing for my camera.

Thursday 17 March: Addis Ababa. My Commercial Secretary brings a group of visitors from Tate and Lyle (involved as consultants in the Ethiopian sugar project at Fincha, financed by the Libyans) to see me. The face of the Managing Director and leader of the team seems instantly familiar, his name when he introduces himself even more so. He was the Adjutant of my tank regiment in Hong Kong in 1953-4. Only Proust or Anthony Powell could do justice to such an encounter, 30 years on in Ethiopia, our roles and personae utterly changed.

Tuesday 22 March: Addis Ababa.   Farewell lunch for the (bachelor) Netherlands Ambassador, Wieger Hellema, who among many other accomplishments has been a properly kilted adornment of the Embassy's Scottish Dancing evenings. In my lunch speech I suggest that he must have been Shakespeare's "Mr W.H." and claim to have found the following Shakespearean fragment which supports the theory:

> A spry Scottish dancer named Wieger
>
> Has a talent for reels that's not meagre;
>
> You can see he's well-built
>
> When he twirls in his kilt
>
> And his Rotterdam tartan's de rigueur.

> (I couldn't devise two adequate rhymes for "Hellema".)

Monday 28 March – Saturday 2 April: Dire Dawa, Harar, Jijiga (Hararghe Region).   The train leaves the station at Addis at 7.30 a.m. sharp (its punctuality perhaps a Mussolini legacy?). It chugs patiently, diesel-driven, through towns and villages, stopping at most in the middle of the market or main street: locals crowd round selling oranges, <u>chat</u>, bananas, nuts, coffee, injera and wat. Outside Debre Zeit we hit a car on a level crossing, but the train stops only for a minute or two. We stop for 45 minutes in baking heat at Awash Station for lunch, decide there isn't time to get a meal at the shady little "Buffet d'Aouache" and eat our sandwiches and drink our cold beer from the cold box we have brought. (There is a little bar in our one and only First Class compartment but by now the drinks are warm.) In to the historic little station at Dire Dawa at 7.30 p.m.: there on the platform are BWM, our driver, who set off in the land rover at 5.30 a.m.; GS, Oxfam worker, UK-educated, Manchester PhD, part-Ethiopian, part-Somali, part Maltese, Amharic speaker, polyglot, polycultural, comparable interpreter and not just linguistically; Lieutenant Ts., young head of the Hararghe Region Relief & Rehabilitation Commission (RRC): and the Dire Dawa representative of Mobil Oil, there as "back-up". All we lack is a brass band. It is warm and humid. The little square opposite the railway station is unmistakeably French. (Dire Dawa is the quintessential railway town, springing up around the station when the French-built line from Djibouti reached Dire Dawa in 1903. Evelyn Waugh provides a flavoury account of his stopover there in 1930 on his way by train to Addis Ababa for Haile Selassie's coronation: he stayed at the Continental Hotel, now a rather seedy-looking Espresso bar and café with some fly-blown rooms.) No hot water in the Ras Hotel but it's so hot that we don't really miss it. The beer is cold.

Next day we visit a leprosy and general hospital and a German-financed resettlement project just beyond Harar at Bisidimo: the latter founded by the son of the conductor Karl Bohm, a charismatic actor who suggested on a TV chat show that each viewer might send in one Deutsch-mark for the poor in Africa and found himself next morning with DM 2 ½ million. In the afternoon we call on the Administrator of Hararghe in Harar, an understandably harassed General, and then look round the old Muslim walled town of Harar, crowded by people, donkeys and camels, the women in brilliantly coloured dressed and shawls (we discover that the cloth for these on sale in the picturesque market comes from Japan – autres temps, autres moeurs). Sir Richard Burton (no relation?) was the first European to visit Harar in 1855, disguised as a Muslim, and it can't have changed much since. Many of the grave-stones in the little British war cemetery on the southern slopes below the town just outside the town walls are broken or missing: Owen carefully lists them from the copy of the Commonwealth War Graves Commission handbook we have brought. Nearby is Rimbaud's house, with a faded poster of the hirsute French romantic tacked up on the wall behind the balcony: he looks as mad as he must have been to choose this place as his home.

There is a lengthy argument with the local security authorities before we are allowed to set off for Jijiga, 1 ½ hours' drive beyond Harar down on the Somali border plain. There have been many attacks on this road by pro-Somali dissidents and shiftas (bandits), using the excellent cover provided by the bush and the strange rock formations in the Valley of the Rocks through which it passes; but there have not been any troubles there lately, there are plenty of soldiers along the road and so we are given the all clear on condition we get back to Harar by 4 p.m., well before dark. (As far as we know the few visits by Ambassadors and other diplomats to Jijiga in recent years have been by air.) Our driver covers the distance with unaccustomed speed and even the usually tranquil BA is noticeably on edge. Jijiga is a featureless town on the edge of the sun-baked plain, with burned-out Soviet tanks and APCs all around, mementoes of the abortive Somali invasion of 1977-8. We visit the RRC shelter at Sheikh Sharif on the edge of the town, where 5,600 people wait in tiny straw and stick wigwams for a chance to return to their semi-nomadic pastoralist existences if and when someone can provide the minimum number of cows, goats, camels and food to make them viable for the first few vital months. Others hope for some seed, an ox and a plough to enable them to resume farming. But water is desperately short and many have given up hope of leaving. Oxfam and Save the Children Fund workers have done wonders in improving the water supply arrangements and especially in reducing child mortality by properly balanced supplementary feeding schemes. We talk to some of the (Somali-speaking) people in the shelter through an RRC interpreter, and to the nutritionist in the little clinic; then visit the grain warehouse down the road where the food aid donated by the EEC, FRG, Canada, UNICEF etc. is kept. It is not rodent-proofed and there are losses from insecure bagging: but most of the food is in good nick and suitable for its purpose, unlike the boxes of Indian tea given by the UNHCR. At least there are no slimming foods of the kind found by a Save the Children Fund doctor in the drought area of northern Wollo in a relief food store (he threw it away).

On the way back we stay at the Awash National Park in an air-conditioned caravan. Unfortunately the air-conditioning works only when the electricity comes on at 6 p.m. when it is cooler anyway. J., who has been suffering from Dire Dawa tummy (or mild sun-stroke from walking across miles of tomato fields at an RRC settlement just outside Dire Dawa to inspect a non-functioning well), is almost baked alive in the caravan when she lies down there in the early afternoon. When it gets cooler in the early evening we drive in the land rover to the Awash River and see masses of game: kudu, water buck, oryx, baboons, wart-hogs etc. (The British Council Representative who is also there sees 3 lions loping across the dirt road but we miss them.) Magnificent water-falls and a breath-taking view down into the river gorge from the little bar and restaurant of the caravan park. Even at 6 o'clock the air conditioning is welcome.

2 April. Our silver wedding anniversary, and the last day of the trip. We stop for beers and a swim at Nazareth and for lunch on the terrace of the hotel at Debre Zeit, before driving into Addis Ababa (taking extra care as we cross the railway line) in the mid-afternoon. Back at 8,500 feet it is cool and cloudy and later in the afternoon there is a torrential rain-storm. The small rains have begun. It seems light years from Jijiga on its hot and dusty plain.

Elizabeth the Second,

by the Grace of God of the United Kingdom of Great Britain and Northern Ireland and of Her other Realms and Territories Queen, Head of the Commonwealth, Defender of the Faith,

To Lieutenant-Colonel Mengistu Haile Mariam, Chairman of the Provisional Military Administrative Council and the Council of Ministers of Socialist Ethiopia.

Sendeth Greeting!

Our Good Friend!

Being desirous to maintain, without interruption, the relations of friendship and good understanding which happily subsist between Our Realm and Socialist Ethiopia, We have made choice of Our Trusty and Well-beloved Brian Leon Barder, Esquire, to reside with You in the character of Our Ambassador Extraordinary and Plenipotentiary.

The

The experience which We have had of Mr Barder's talents and zeal for Our service assures Us that the selection We have made will be perfectly agreeable to You; and that he will discharge his Mission in such a manner as to merit Your approbation and esteem; and to prove himself worthy of this new mark of Our confidence.

We therefore request that You will give entire credence to all that Mr Barder shall communicate to You in Our name, more especially when he shall renew to You the assurances of the lively interest which We take in everything that affects the welfare and prosperity of Socialist Ethiopia.

Given at Our Court of Saint James's, the Eighteenth day of August, One thousand Nine hundred and Eighty-two, in the Thirty-first Year of Our Reign.

Your Good Friend,

(Signed) ELIZABETH R.

Above: Barder's diplomatic credentials to Ethiopia, 1982.

Above right: The British Ambassador's residence in Addis Ababa.

Below right: The British embassy's cottage on the shore of Lake Langano, Rift Valley.

Top: Virginia, Olly, Louise at Addis Alem

Bottom: Barder outside the residence, with Belew (bodyguard), Berhanu (driver), and Beyene (steward).

Above: Olly (on landrover), Berhanu, Jane, Gina, Belew; Ethiopia.

Right: The family on the residence terrace, Addis Ababa.

Below: Barder inspecting a guard of honour in Ethiopia.

CHAPTER 22

APRIL–JULY 1983:
ADDIS, KOMBOLCHA, DESE,
HAYK, BATI, NAIROBI

Monday 18 April: Addis Ababa to Kombolcha.   After weeks of pleading and nagging, our permission to visit Korem in northern Welo, where there is a small British Save the Children Fund team working on a medical and feeding programme for drought victims, materializes on the Saturday afternoon before our scheduled departure early on Monday. Libby G., head of SCF in Ethiopia, delighted at the prospect of a visit to her best-publicised operation but a little apprehensive lest the hoopla surrounding an ambassadorial visit should create boring problems of protocol and fuss, has gone on ahead to the SCF house in Dese and will come back down to Kombolcha to meet up with us this evening: tomorrow the plan is that we all travel up to Korem, spend Tuesday night there, return late on Wednesday to Kombolcha and back to Addis on Thursday. I look forward keenly to seeing these now quite celebrated SCF workers in the field. Television film of them and of the thousands of people gathered there in the fields like an illustration from a school Old Testament, waiting for food and medical care for the children, together with wildly varying accounts given in Addis by relief organisers of various nationalities and degrees of objectivity of the scale of the tragedy there, whet the appetite for seeing for oneself.

The drive to Kombolcha in the (as usual) overloaded landrover is long but spectacular: first to Debra Berhan, ascending steadily all the way past glimpses of huge valleys rolling away towards the edge of the escarpment; past the International Livestock Centre for Africa experimental and research farm where we had an agreeable night in the comfortable little guest-house only a few months ago with G and J as a base for visiting Debra Sina and the ancient capital of Ankober; on and still up, past hundreds of white- and brown-clad peasants working on a communal hillside terracing project and looking like an illustration in China Quarterly; a pause to go to the edge of a steep gorge and look out across the escarpment and down on the rolling plain rolling away beyond until it disappears in the haze (here one is actually looking at the beginning of the Danakil Depression from the central mountain plateau). The road climbs to nearly 10,000 feet with cold swirling mists hugging the surrounding mountain peaks, then plunges into a black, damp, concrete-lined tunnel gouged out by the Italians, one of the most dramatic of their road-building feats during the occupation. Out the other side onto a road clinging precariously to the sheer mountainside with a stunning view down onto the little town of Debra Sina, thatches and corrugated iron roofs glittering in the sun in their narrow saddle in the hills, with the gold and green sunlit plain beyond. The road winds its way down the hillside in a series of giant hairpins, the temperature rising perceptibly all the way down until, passing through the town and on down onto the plain, the sun's glow has become hot, even glary.

Now the road is, like the rain in Spain, mainly on the plain, occasionally climbing to the top of a spur from the escarpment and descending steeply again on the other side. The view of the escarpment and the mountains to the left and the rolling plains to the right is continuously glorious: what description escapes travel supplement cliché? The fields are green and fertile, the cows and goats, even the donkeys, look well fed. It's hard to imagine the bleak arid highlands up ahead where tens of thousands are starving or close to starvation, with no hope of growing anything to eat for another 8, 9 or even 10 months.

Kombolcha is a wild west sort of town, busy and crowded because this is the site of one of Ethiopia's few major road junctions: at the big fascist monument erected by the Italians in the main square at the far end of the main street (the monument now incompletely stripped of the fasces and inscriptions glorying in Il Duce, converted to a National Heroes' Memorial), opposite the crumbling but once-splendid Agip Hotel, the road forks right to run across the plains and deserts to the one significant seaport of Assab in Eritrea: and left, back up the escarpment to the sprawling mountain capital of Wele Region, Dese, only about 40 minutes away, on its hilly journey north through areas infested by Tigrean and later by Eritrean guerrillas and shiftas (bandits) to Korem and Mekele and eventually to its final destination of Asmara, the old Italian capital of Eritrea. We have a beer on the terrace of the Agip overlooking the square, and wander along the bustling main streets, nearly all the shops brightly-lit bars doubling as mini-brothels whose staffs lean against the doorways in the street smiling encouragingly at passing (especially white) males. All down the street big oil tankers are parked, the drivers spending a night and a half-day's rest here on the long journey south to Addis with a full lead from the Assab refinery, or north-east to Assab to fill up. A few militia with aged rifles loiter: Kombolcha is a possible target for guerrilla attack because of those tankers and the road junction, but they are not usually active as far south as this, even if incidents have been rumoured not far away and not long ago.

Libby arrives in her landrover from Dese just as we sit down to dinner in our new and picturesque little hotel on the southern end of the town: she has with her the Deputy Administrator of Welo, who tells us that there is now some uncertainty over the road to Korem on which we hope to travel tomorrow: a bridge is down, the telephone lines have been out, it is difficult to get a reliable report …. Perhaps we could go and see the Administrator in his office in Dese at 8 a.m. tomorrow and maybe by then he will have a better idea of whether we can proceed.

Tuesday 19 April: Kombolcha – Dese – Hayk – Bati – Kombolcha. The road from Kombolcha up the sides of the mountains to Dese is perhaps the most dramatic of all: magnificent engineering, a triumph of ingenuity over impossible terrain. The Administrator, by profession a General of Police, receives us soberly in his small cluttered office. It is most unfortunate but the bridge is still down. It is impossible to guess how long it will take to repair it or to build a diversion. Also there have been shifts in places near the road recently; soon the army will get them under control but for the moment…. "We don't want to lose an Ambassador."

I agree cordially: "especially if it's me." The Administrator would ordinarily have been glad, he says, to have me visit Korem where my fellow-countrymen are doing such splendid work but the timing is unfortunate. Perhaps Miss Libby can bring us back later when things are more settled. Meanwhile he will be happy to give us an extended briefing on the problems and achievements of the Region of Welo including a detailed organization chart of the administration and some notably detailed statistics about the reforestation, drought relief, adult literacy and community health programmes. (I scribble diligently. So does C.H., my second secretary, who looks even more painfully disappointed than I feel about Korem. J. asks penetrating questions about Welo social services.) After the briefing we are very welcome to visit the famous and beautiful Lake Hayk: the Deputy Administrator will be so happy to accompany us and to act as our guide if that would meet His Excellency's wishes. (It would.)

Lake Hayk ("Hayk" being, imaginatively enough, the Amharic word for "lake") is indeed pretty as a picture: C. H. and I take several. A tiny peninsular hill joined to the lake shore by a narrow neck of land across which runs a high fence with a gate in it is topped by a small monastery nestling in trees. Hundreds of birds sit pensively along the top of the fence staring at us. Others float like toy ducks bobbing up and down on the lake. A majestic eagle sits in a tree, head turned in profile like an American coat of arms on a speaker's rostrum. Women are no allowed through the gate onto the peninsula because, according to the Deputy Administrator (he has come along presumably in case we might be tempted to make a sudden unauthorized dash for Korem), when there were nuns as well as monks in the monastery they kept getting pregnant and this distracted the monks from their devotions. The men walk round the monastery and photograph the women standing rather forlornly by the landrovers beyond the fence. I give a tentative tap with a pebble on a big granite slab suspended by a chain from a wooden frame: rather surprisingly this produces a very loud clang like the stroke of a giant bell which reverberates across the lake and sends flocks of birds wheeling and circling above us.

After a beery lunch with Libby in the SCF house back in Dese, we drive back into Kombolcha down the mountains, reorganize our hotel bookings and set off down the other fork of the road (direction Assab) to visit the town of Bati where there is a Relief & Rehabilitation Commission feeding programme and a children's day centre funded by SCF which Libby wants to visit and check. The feeding centre is a rather pathetic group of poorly dressed people squatting in a dusty square with their camels and donkeys parked a few yards away, waiting for the weekly distribution from the bulging sacks of grain (stenciled "A GIFT FROM THE PEOPLE OF THE EUROPEAN COMMUNITY", "A GIFT FROM THE GOVERNMENT AND PEOPLE OF CANADA" and so on). The camels chew stolidly, looking prim. The donkeys look sorry for themselves, no doubt with good reason. Later in the big hut used as the children's day care centre Libby interrogates the evidently worried staff about how they use the money they get from SCF: why couldn't they raise enough locally to keep the centre going? What would happen if SCF ceased to fund it – would anyone be willing to pay to keep it going? Why are there fewer children attending than previously: Libby takes notes in a pocket note-book, looking rather disapproving. A small plump Englishman in spectacles and a suit turns up and is warmly greeted by the locals: it turns out that he is an assistant bank manager or some such thing from somewhere like Beaconsfield who, in his spare time, runs an evangelical church relief and charitable good works organization and, during the drought and famine of 1973-4 which helped to prompt the revolution, lived in Bati and ran a famine relief operation in the area, earning – evidently – much affection and respect. Contrary to first impressions he proves to be very perceptive, energetic and capable. Not for the first time in one's dealings with relief workers, diplomacy is made to seem a superficial, shallow, almost shameful occupation. Definitely not one of the caring professions, anyway.

Back in Kombolcha we say goodbye to Libby who returns for the night to the SCF house in Dese determined to press on to Korem on her own in the morning, confident in the belief that the Administrator's warning applied only to an ambassadorial visit, either because the presence of an ambassador in the area might be thought liable to stimulate Tigrean rebel activity, or because the authorities would quite sensibly apply a more rigorous security criterion to an ambassador than to an inconspicuous relief worker. I urge her to leave it for a couple of weeks and to come back with us to Addis Ababa but she is quietly dismissive of all the fears and fuss.

Saturday 23 April: Addis Ababa.   I am changing into my dinner jacket in the evening for the Embassy Gold Club's annual Golf Ball at the Embassy club when the telephone rings. It is H.G., the Oxfam representative in Ethiopia. He has just heard the news from Dese that the Tigreans have attacked and captured Korem, probably on Tuesday night or Wednesday morning, possibly later, and have rounded up all the expatriate relief workers (including the whole British SCF team) and driven them away to an unknown destination. I ask if Libby was among them. A pause; then, yes, she was. But it sounds as if they were all unharmed when last seen heading off into the mountains with the TPLF. The town administrator and some other officials have been shot, and there seem to have been a good many casualties in the fighting on both sides. Yes, it is terribly worrying and alarming. They are in an area stricken both by famine and by drought; anything could happen to them. It seemed unlikely that the TPLF would deliberately harm them, but ….

An evening of telephoning, the Golf Ball forgotten. To London. To Dese (fortunately I had noted the telephone numbers, including home numbers, of the Administrator and his Deputy). To the Foreign Ministry Duty Officer (several times). To the few Ministry officials whom I manage to track down on a Saturday evening. A few of the Embassy staff look in to ask what has happened and whether they can help (yes, they can). Someone sends up plates of roast pork from the Ball and we transfer most of the beer from the fridge to the study. Type out a telegram for the duty communications officer to transmit to London and Khartoum. More telephoning: to the Ambassadors of other countries whose nationals are among the hostages taken; Oxfam again; a return call from the Resident Clerk in London. Anger and frustration as the realization crystallises that there is going to be very little indeed that I or anyone else in Addis can usefully do.

No-one articulates the unspoken but obvious question: were they after us?

Tuesday 28 April: Addis Ababa.   Annual General Meeting of the British Community at the Embassy Club. The Community Chairman, Richard Wilding (an archeologist at the University) delivers his report on the Community's year. They miss our predecessors, welcome us. Everything is approved nem. con. Then the Chairman raises the question, originally put by J and myself on our arrival: should the name of the community magazine ("Bulldog", with a front cover depicting a Churchillian defiant dog in front of a wall-to-wall Union Jack) be changed to avoid confusion with, even contamination from, the notorious British Front organ of the same name – fascist, racist, especially inappropriate for a British community in black Africa, many of its members married to Ethiopians? The very suggestion of changing the magazine's name arouses intense indignation. Until the new Ambassador arrived, no-one had ever heard of this other "Bulldog". If anyone should change, it should be this National Front thing, not our magazine. Hands up all those who were personally outraged or angered by the title! There! No-one. I explain, so low-key as to be virtually inaudible, that it is not a question of outrage or anger but of the unsuitability of a title which would (for instance) make it quite impossible to leave a copy of the magazine out on a table in London, where there are a number of readers. The indignation is further aggravated by this intervention. The British Community should be non-political: the National Front were entitled to their opinions the same as anyone else. Suggestion overwhelmingly rejected.

Tuesday 17 May: Addis Ababa.   A stag dinner (something I take a dim view of in the best of circumstances, which these clearly are not) at the Residence of a western colleague whom I had better not identify. It is to say farewell to a departing colleague from a Muslim country and as a mark of respect no alcohol is served (although the nominally Muslim colleague is well known to enjoy a wee dram if it is offered). We stand around for an hour sipping orange juice, then sit down to a memorably unpalatable meal washed down with either mineral water or water. Speeches are even more tedious to sit through, I discover, without prior alcoholic anaesthesia. Coffee is prolonged to record lengths: no cognac. How to win friends and influence people. Golly.

Tuesday 31 May: Addis Ababa.   A hot and sweaty game of squash at the little sports club at the Addis HQ of ILCA (the International Livestock Centre for Africa): then off to the Sandford English School for the Annual General Meeting of the Sandford School Association, of which the British Ambassador is traditionally elected President. All the old hands assure me that it will be plain sailing:

knowing the entryist tendencies of some of the young British teachers, largely post-hippy Trotskyists, I am less confident. Sure enough there is a rumpus before the meeting: a group of the young teachers have nominated each other for election to the Board of Governors but have been disqualified by the (British, rather stern) lady who is Secretary to the Association, on the grounds that their applications for membership of the Association were received too late. They appeal, spoiling for a fight: a deputation calls on me at the Residence, jeans, beards and T-shirts, sitting on the chintzy drawing-room chairs and sipping weak tea out of royal-crested cups. Last year, they say, many applications were technically late but my predecessor allowed them: why should they be penalized? To the Secretary's disgust I made what is meant as a judgement of Solomon: just this once I shall allow them but I shall (and do) announce at the AGM that from now on the rules will be strictly – even harshly – applied. The deputation finishes its tea and stumps off, aggrieved at being robbed of their grievance. At the meeting itself there are various attempts to raise awkward issues and a ruling is required on a quadruple dead heat in the elections to the Board of Governors (I decide on a run-off, whereas my predecessor had claimed a non-existent Chairman's casting vote and declared elected the candidate he favoured). Sundry attempts are made to secure the adoption of far-fetched interpretations of the very loosely drafted statutes. It's all good clean fun but not quite the plain sailing I'd been led to hope for. Next year will the young Turks allow the Ambassador to be elected President again unopposed in accordance with hallowed tradition but not the statutes? Who cares?: next year I hope to be on home leave and sunning myself in the Bay of Naples while the factions wrangle with each other at the AGM.

Wednesday 8 June: Addis Ababa.   I watch from the "diplomats' gallery" as the OAU summit opens after days of argument and negotiation over the seating or – as it turns out – non-seating of the Western Sahara delegation. The eventual compromise is so offensive to the mercurial Col. Qadhafi that he storms out with his huge retinue (including, alas, his team of female bodyguards in leather or stretch nylon jumpsuits with revolvers in holsters slung low on their hips, one blonde, one black, one sun-burned, like the Mendelian theory), leaving only the Western and Libyan seats empty when President Moi finally calls the meeting to order just one year late. It is interesting to see so many familiar faces belonging to familiar names: Kaunda,

Obote, Nyerere, Mengistu, Masire of Botswana, Dieuf of Senegal, Sekeu Teuré, Moi, Sam Nujoma, Robert Mugabe, Staff Sergeant Doe, Machel…. The Canadian Ambassador and I arrive frightfully late for an intimate and elegant dinner party given by the Green Chargé, who by the time we get there is distraught, being comforted by our respective wives. Fortunately the Italian Ambassador arrives even later. But why didn't the Green call it off when he knew the Summit was opening that evening and that all Ambassadors were invited to attend?

Friday 10 June: Addis Ababa.   Libby and the other 9 expatriate relief workers are released unharmed in the Sudan (the TPLF wanted this to coincide with the opening of the OAU summit but floods delayed the arrival and anyway the Sudanese very sensibly refused to allow any press access). I shall never know either whether J. and I were intended to be in the party that undertook that 7-week Long March nor whether my appeals and representations and the assurances we extracted had had any effect in heading off military activity at the time and in places when the hostages might have been unintended victims. Anyway it's a happy ending.

Saturday 23 July: Nairobi – Addis Ababa.   Back to Addis from 8 days in Nairobi. A useful conference of a selection of British Ambassadors and High Commissioners on various African topics and a chance to meet the newly appointed FCO Africa Minister (Malcolm Rifkind). I bend his ear for 10 minutes about my views on Ethiopia and policy thereon. After the conference I go on a wild shopping spree as if rationing has just ended. Staggering off the plan in Addis I can hardly lift my official briefcase, enormous suitcase and BOAC bag, bulging with jars of Branston pickle, cashew nuts, jars of marmalade and packets of All Bran. What a treat is in store!

CHAPTER 23

AUG-NOV 1983: LAKE LANGANO, ADDIS ABABA, ARSI, BALE

Thursday 25 August, 1983.   Lake Langano.   Two days' local leave at Lake Langano in the little Embassy bungalows. Drive the landrover along the stream which flows from Langano to Lake Abiata and photograph innumerable Maribou storks, some as much as 4 – 5 feet tall and as ugly a thing as one can imagine, and magnificent fish eagles, more symbols than birds.

At night with windows open but shutters closed I feel something small and light moving on my bed. Try to shake it off, still 80% asleep. Seconds later it runs over my bare arm. Leap up, gibbering and groping for the torch. Jane leaps up too and unaccountably finds the bedroom door which she flings open, gabbling and panic-stricken. We switch on torches and light candles. Very gingerly I inspect the bedroom, the little living-room. Sure enough, a small black rodent scurries across the floor towards the bedroom, spots me and swerves away, disappearing out of the torch-beam. It seems to have no tail, certainly not a long one. After a protracted semi-hysterical conference J. and I turn off torches and lie on our backs, bedclothes drawn up to chins as if over corpses, waiting for the dawn. Conferences during the morning lead to a consensus that our unwanted visitor was a baby rat. This somehow makes it seem even more repulsive than a mouse.

As we pack up to go, J picks up her cardigan from a chair in the living-room and a large grey mouse with a very long tail shoots out and vanishes under the settee. All our Ethiopian staff, OC, and the Zabagnas (watchmen/guards) mount a hunt and finally bludgeon the creature to death in unseemly triumph. What a pity: it was nice going to Langano occasionally.

Friday 26 August.   Visit the Revolutionary Children's Amba (= group of villages) at Zwai, by prearrangement with the Ministry of Labour and Social Services. 5,000 children will eventually grow up here (only 2,000 so far) in a sprawling but isolated area – we drive over 100 km within the huge compound alone. Everything is based on segregation by age-group and sex, and regimentation. But the children look lively and stimulated and the staff of psychologists, nurses, house mothers, teachers and social workers, many western-trained, are extremely impressive and enlightened. In each "village" we are greeted by a welcoming committee of children with home-made welcoming flags, streamers and lapel badges. In one place about 60 girls in trim green dresses perform a welcoming chant and dance for us: lots of mutual clapping. We had expected to have a quick tour of about half an hour but find ourselves staying for 5 hours, culminating in a mouth-watering lunch in a big open-walled tukul commanding a spectacular view of hills and waterfall.

During our inspection of the various farms on which the children, mainly orphans of army families or victims of drought and the famines in the north, spend half of most days working, we are shown with understandable pride spruce modern piggeries inhabited by fat, engaging porkers. These are bred both for sale, we are told, and to feed the children. But, we point out, surely most if not all of the children must come from either Muslim or Ethiopian Orthodox Christian families for both of which pork is unclean. Is there not a problem inducing the children to eat it? "Sometimes, when they first arrive, but they soon get used to it." Shades of insistent pressure to eat lumpy, slimy porridge at boarding school during the war. You soon get used to it.

Tuesday 13 September.   Ninth anniversary of the revolution. Attend parade and speeches along with other Ambassadors, Army and Navy leaders, visiting foreign dignitaries, etc., in Revolution Square (formerly the Square of the Cross). Take with me camera and telephoto lens, hat, raincoat, orange squash, binoculars, spectacles and a book, plus a cushion for protection against the concrete ledge on which the VIPs sit. Find myself sitting only a few feet from what is in effect the royal box where Chairman M. takes the salute in lonely and magnificent aloofness, seated in an ornate gilt chair which has insistent undertones of a throne. The first marchers are small boys, in brilliant green and turquoise uniforms, goose-stepping jauntily with exaggerated arm movements that involve a sharp arm-blow across the chest with each step. Then small girls in tightly packed squads, kicking skinny legs martially into the air. Then a squad of young women in smart khaki uniforms, skirts just too tight and an inch too long to provide the necessary freedom for the high point of the goose-step kick. Soldiers, airmen, sailors, militia, then crudely but forcefully decorated floats bearing precariously balanced tableaux depicting Workers working, doctors doctoring, Peasants toiling, etc. The Chairman makes a speech, only an hour or so long this year: English texts are efficiently distributed along with Ethiopian Tourist Organisation brochures, calendars and a new glossy guidebook. A couple of girl members of the military band opposite the saluting base faint and are carted off. There is a substantial and colourful crowd which watches and listens without apparent emotion.

Later in the day the heavens open and the rain comes down in torrents. In the thick of this the Chairman unveils a gigantic statue of Lenin immediately outside Africa Hall, HQ of the UN Economic Commission for Africa and the conference hall where OAU summit meetings are held. A large visiting delegation from the Soviet Union and a smattering of Eastern European Ambassadors, steaming under umbrellas, watch. Lenin is portrayed with hand across breast, apparently taking the first (presumably symbolic) step – into the Future, perhaps, or as the Ethiopians irreverently suggest to one another in the succeeding weeks, possibly on his return journey on foot to Addis Ababa International Airport with his hand over his wallet. There are few outside or even modest statues in Addis, even of Ethiopian national or revolutionary heroes, and the appearance of Lenin writ large evokes much unfavourable comment.

Thursday 20 October.   Attend performance of "The Mousetrap" by the New Theatre Group (predominantly British but on this occasion fielding a polyglot cast, with faintly amusing side-effects for characterization) in the school hall of the English School. The identity of the murderer is apparent by the interval despite the author's flagrant cheating and implausibilities. The dialogue defies articulation. What an awful play! Why does it run and run? All the budding actors and actresses, even those who appear to have learned their lines phonetically and thus to have been spared any awareness of the inanity of what they are saying, seem completely floored.

Monday 24 October. Why this sudden rush of Art to Addis? Last week The Mousetrap, this week a performance in the National Theatre (started by the Italians, finished in the Fifties by the Ethiopians with western help in a style faintly reminiscent of the Festival of Britain) by an assortment of Soviet ballet dancers. Somehow this is not quite the Bolshoy. The Director of the Russian Hospital has told a colleague that during the rehearsals earlier in the day he has had to rush oxygen equipment to the theatre to revive dancers whose lungs have given up in the unequal struggle with the altitude. There is what appears to be a wet or otherwise slippery patch at the back of the stage on which one dancer after another slips, each thereafter dancing as if on an oil slick – rather inhibiting in regard to what might otherwise have been high, Nureyev-like leaps, entrechats, etc. The costumes are beginning to look as if they are approaching the end of an arduous African tour and the silver lurex tights affected by most of the all too evidently male dancers seem rather improbably to have shrunk since leaving Moscow. The music, played through large home-made-looking speakers, is mainly Tchaikovsky. One loudspeaker is positioned at the back of the stage where one after another of the members of the corps de ballet crash into it, staring at it resentfully as they pick themselves up. The Ethiopians in the audience watch bemused. Perhaps the Mousetrap wasn't all that bad.

Tuesday 1 November – Monday 7 November. Off again in the familiar landrover to make official visits to Arsi and Bale (rhymes with Farley) Regions – mainly to see the 1-man medical project of the British Save the Children Fund at the far end of our trip, the small town of Ginir. First night in the little Regional capital of Arsi, Asela, after an amicable hour's chat with the Administrator, who volunteers without inhibition that the reason for the booming productiveness of his small parish is the Swedish Government's agricultural development project and the expertise and mechanization that come with it, even more than the reliable rainfall and fertile soil. Of course there are problems – inadequate roads, poor coordination of under-equipped transport systems, not enough doctors or nurses – but in general this seems the most up-beat and successful area we have seen so far.

Next day we cross from Arsi to Bale at the bridge over the famous (but not very impressive, at this point anyway) Wabe Shebelle river. Past miles of sturdy-looking wheat and barley in giant State Farms to the little town of Dodola where we visit an Awraja (= County) Pedagogical Centre, supported financially by the EEC among others. Surprisingly, no-one in the town – the young Swiss ICRC representative, the town administrator, the local office of the Ministry of Education, the militia – has ever heard of it. We are about to give up and drive on to the game park at Dinshe when, on the outskirts of Dodola, I spot a small notice-board marked only "APC", with an arrow. Sure enough the entire staff of the little centre are there waiting for us. Their task is to develop and devise simple, cheap teaching aids made from local materials – mainly bits of wood and skin, nails and rubber tubes – which the teachers throughout the awraja can copy and make for themselves. Miraculous ingenuity goes into these artifacts, used not only to help with handicrafts but also to demonstrate blood circulation, isosceles triangles, etc. The pride with which all these crafty contraptions are demonstrated to us is oddly moving. At the end of our tour we sign the visitors' book, adding suitably admiring comments, and are presented not only with bottles of fizzy orange but also a home-made wooden shield with a cut-out plywood map of Bale Region indicating the awraja pedagogical centres and sub-centres, and an inscription to commemorate the visit of (as they put it with appreciative formality) His Excellency the Ambassador of Her Britannic Majesty.

The road to Dinshe traverses stunning and rapidly varying scenery: over a mountain which is pure Switzerland, with dark green pine forests on the lower slopes and little blue alpine flowers sprinkled over grassy meadows; across high plateau densely packed with ripening wheat, reminiscent of Kansas or Saskatchewan; up again over barer, colder mountains onto yet higher plateau and valleys like Kashmir; through a winding pass and down again into a broad valley where, after BWM has manoeuvred the landrover through thick wet mud, we see 20 or 30 nyala, the bulky dark buck-like animals which are unique to Ethiopia and virtually unique to this particular game park. Then on again through the little bustling town of Robe to Goba, the Regional capital, where we check into the big, modern, completely empty hotel – J and I going into the "suite" occupied by Comrade Chairman when he formally declared the hotel open in 1982. As in the big, comfortable, modern hotels in Bahir Dar and Gonder where we stayed last year, there are normally no guests at all and the numerous and attentive staff go mad with boredom and frustration. We have an excellent dinner, alone in the enormous dining-room, and go to bed under several blankets in a frigid temperature. Next morning an extended and useful call on the Bale Administrator elicits, later in the day, an invitation to be his guests at dinner in the hotel that evening, where there are about 20 of us altogether round the table – including 3 Danish nurses (one a white Rhodesian naturalized Danish) who in the matter-of-fact way of relief workers everywhere do an astonishing job driving round the often unhospitable and sometimes dangerous countryside doing clinics in remote settlements and villages. Next day when we visit a UNICEF water project in a little settlement just off the road to Ginir, a dignified old man mistakes J. and MP, my secretary, also fair-haired, for the Danish nurses and pleads with them for ointment and pills, even though both are a good 15 years older than the nurses. Trouble with white people is you can't tell their age.

On the way to Ginir we visit the caves at Soph Omar where a broad stream runs through superb caverns at the sun-baked bottom of a steep gorge. The caverns have massive granite vaults and stone walls sculpted by the currents and eddies of a once mighty torrent into delicately scalloped patterns. Outside the caves crocodiles on the river bank deter from a cooling dip but we picnic before climbing back into the landrover for the perilous climb back to the top of the gorge. By now the security authorities – perhaps fearing that we might be bent on another try at getting ourselves kidnapped as so nearly happened at Korem in April – have attached an escort to us; 4, sometimes 5, heavily armed plain-clothes cops sit in a Toyota pick-up truck just in front of us at all times. As they sit in the back facing backwards, their pistols and machine guns point right at our windscreen; the jolts and bumps as the vehicles lurch over the boulder-strewn dirt road seem more than enough to set them off, along with their grenades, but as this never happens we conclude that the weapons are probably and mercifully jammed. Armed guards are posted on our room in the hotel at Goba and on the doctor's house where we stay for 2 nights in Ginir, making his Alsations bark throughout both nights right under our window. Mahendra and Sheila Sheth are splendid hosts, miraculously producing exquisite Indian dishes out of extremely unpromising local Oromo ingredients and maintaining fastidious Indian standards in a house without electricity (except for a couple of hours each evening) or hot water. Mahendra – one of the SCF team captured at Korem and marched for 7 weeks through Welo, Tigray and Eritrea into the Sudan before release, losing a good many unwanted kilos in the process – does a tremendous job in the Ginir clinic and at the resettlement camps (which we visit with him on the following day) at Harawa and Melka Oda where his consulting rooms are disintegrating, dirty, fly-infested mud huts and his staff unqualified health assistants. At the inevitable briefing at Harawa by the enthusiastic Project Manager we hear how nearly 17,000 people have been brought hundreds of miles from the drought and war areas of Welo in the north to the fertile lands of Bale and organized into 2 big orderly camps where they all receive a predetermined ration of food, so many grammes a head, in exchange for their work in the fields, on reforestation projects, handicrafts, etc. I suggest that this really is "From each according to his ability, to each according to his need?" "If that is how Your Excellency cares to put it," says the Project Manager rather coolly.

Sunday 13 November.   I read the lesson ("And there shall be no more death, neither sorrow, nor crying") at the Remembrance Day service at the beautiful war cemetery on the outskirts of Addis Ababa, and lay the first of about 20 wreaths on behalf of Commonwealth and Allied governments who fought with Ethiopia to liberate her from the Italian fascists in 1942. The Ethiopian army band plays "Nimrod" from "Enigma" as one after another we lay our wreaths. Finally, I lay a second wreath jointly with a smartly uniformed officer representing the Ethiopian armed forces, this time in memory and honour of the Ethiopian dead. It is a moving moment, here in Socialist Ethiopia, performing the simple ceremony with a representative of the army of the Derg. He and several of the other Ethiopian officers attending have – to our surprise – accepted our invitation to come back to the Residence afterwards for lunch in the garden with the other representatives of allied countries who had laid wreaths and our whole Embassy staff, but – less surprisingly – they do not in the event turn up. A pity, but worth a try. We shall try again next year.

CHAPTER 24

CHRISTMAS 1983: ADDIS ABABA

(From a round-robin letter)

This brings you our warmest Christmas greetings and good wishes for 1984 from, for once, all five of us: unusually nowadays for when we are overseas, Virginia (and indeed Olly), Louise and Owen will all be celebrating what should be a warm and sunny Christmas with us here in Addis Ababa. It will certainly remind us of other overseas Christmases in the sun when we were all together, in Canberra.

From the end of the rainy (and chilly) season here in late September until the "small rains" in about March or April, the weather in Addis is really idyllic: cool nights and warm, sometimes indeed hot, sunny days and brilliant blue skies. From the end of September until Ethiopian Christmas (celebrated in early January) there is a great deal of social activity of every kind in Addis, both among the Embassies and the international organisations such as the OAU and ECA which have their HQs here, and also among the British community which possesses extraordinary talents and energies. There are various fund-raising activities such as the Cheshire Home Walk (which Brian trotted, rather than walked, last year, but had to miss this year because of a prior engagement to brief members of the Birmingham Chamber of Commerce Trade Mission after their arrival on the same day as the Walk, happily or otherwise), the traditional and very professional

British Community pantomime, the British Community Ball, numerous carol services and concerts, and of course a great many parties ranging from the formal to the very informal indeed. This year – and indeed next – we are doing a New Year's Eve party, to last all night and thus through the curfew, with a tent and a marquee up in the Residence gardens and Ethiopian champagne at midnight .... A few hours after the party (we hope) finishes, our old friends Graham and Helen Beringer will be arriving to stay with us for a couple of days, together with their two daughters. We have shared holidays with the Beringers in all 5 continents (London, Canberra, Niagara-on-the-Lake, Hong Kong, Cairo where Graham is now Australian Trade Commissioner) and we are keen to add another venue which will be a little more genuinely African than Cairo.

Another old friend whom we look forward to having to stay for a couple of days in December is Rex Browning, now Deputy Under-Secretary in the Overseas Development Administration where he is deputy to the Permanent Under-Secretary, Bill Ryrie, yet another old Colonial Office hand from the faraway Fifties. Even our children are beginning to show their age.

We plan a short holiday here and in Kenya on the Indian Ocean coast in February with yet more old friends, George and Jane Sutton, before embarking in late April on our mid-tour leave: 2 or 3 weeks in Italy on the way home and then the bulk of the summer in England, picking up the threads and refreshing our roots. There will be a lot of people to catch up with then, and we are looking forward to it already.

CHAPTER 25

JAN-MARCH 1984:
ADDIS ABABA, SOMALIA, KENYA, SIDAMO, GAMO GOFA

Sunday 1 January, 1984.   To bed this morning at about 5.30 a.m., the last of the younger, fitter and more intrepid revelers out of the 300 or so who celebrated New Year with us still ploughing doggedly through their fried eggs and kedgeree and coffee in the Durbar Hall or dancing very slowly on the terrace, waiting for the dawn. A few of those who have spent all night watching "Brideshead Revisited" on the video in the study are still there, several asleep. The Residence looks like a beerhall after a fight between mods and rockers. In the East courtyard, with its cheerful blue-and-white striped canopy and flower-encrusted steel masts, Dafaru is still serving the odd glass of dryish Ethiopian champagne or Scotch and Ambo (local mineral water, nearest thing to soda).

Up again at 7.am. to go to the airport to meet H & G and their two strapping healthy daughters off the plane from Nairobi. They are as bright and eager and en-thusiastic about seeing everything and going everywhere as when we have shared holidays with them in the past in the UK, in Australia, Hong Kong, at Niagara-on-the-Lake. The last occasion was when we stayed with them in Cairo, checking off the last remaining shared continent. It's very good to see them. But it would have been even better with a couple more hours in bed first.

Tuesday 2 January. News spreads that late on New Year's Eve, on their way back from Lake Langano to Addis, Daniel Hadot (the French Counsellor and No. 2, and a good friend), his wife Françoise, and one of their children, were killed when the car they were driving swerved to avoid a lorry parked without lights and hit an oncoming lorry head on. Another child was fearfully injured (and it was next morning after daybreak before they got him out). Yet another son, a teenager, was at our New Year's Eve party at the moment when his family was wiped out. At the Requiem Mass said for the Hadots they sing a French hymn to the tune of Auld Lang Syne – which we were energetically singing to celebrate the New Year at about the relevant time, glasses in our hands. Daniel was devoted to music; had the biggest loudspeakers for his hi-fi system that I have ever seen. We had long planned to swap evenings and play records to each other, but somehow never got round to it.

Friday 20 January. At 8 a.m. we go to the racecourse at Janmeda on the edge of Addis to see the climax of the Timkat ceremonies of the Ethiopian Orthodox Church (not Coptic, by the way). There's a big crowd of Ethiopians, all in holiday mood, marshalled by numerous good-humoured policemen, some on not very well trained horses that paw and wheel anxiously. Plenty of ferenji (foreigners) too, mostly with telephoto lenses like mortars. The priests and their acolytes are gorgeously decked out in lush-coloured robes, many carrying ornate Ethiopian brass and gold crosses and gold-tasselled, scarlet-and-blue silk umbrellas. Splendid bearded patriarchs with wild eyes move with dignity through the crowds. At the climax the Patriarch himself blesses the special pool of water below the ornate altar, and priests immediately start scooping it out and throwing it out over the crowd, which surges forward to get a chance of a few drops (even a drenching) of the now holy and potent fluid. The most holy and precious tabernacles from all the local churches are brought out of the marquees where they have rested for the night, and paraded high above the crowd's heads in ornately decorated and curtained boxes, looking a little like impending Punch and Judy shows. Speeches, mostly in Amharic or Ge'ez, but including one by a bearded Jamaican Rastafarian who sails fairly close to the political wind on the subject of freedom to practice religion in Ethiopia since the "Change".

Sunday 22 January.   Bekele, our friendly, dedicated Residence cook, barbecues a small pig, a gift to J. from the Stadium Grocers for Christmas in recognition of the remarkably high proportion of my frais which we re-direct to that establishment. We eat it with a dozen or so friends at tables in the garden by the bird-bath, in the area where (before our arrival, mercifully) Midsummer Night's Dream was once famously performed, the actors nipping back through the bushes to the Residence kitchens between exits and entrances for a quick one or three.

Thursday 9 February.   With Sir L and Lady A, visiting us on their way back to Nairobi, to the tiny village of Adada Mariam where there is one of the few complete and functioning Ethiopian rock churches, literally carved out of the solid rock below ground level. In the 13th century or thereabouts they hacked out a rectangle of deep trenches in the rock and from the trenches proceeded to hollow out a church, complete with arched doors and windows, inner sanctums, the lot: usually cross-shaped when viewed from above. This one is not a terribly good example but it's accessible from Addis, and the classic rock churches at Lalibela up in Tigray are closed to visitors this year because of the activities nearby of the Tigrean People's Liberation Front. We picnic on the way back near the banks of the Awash River, a delectable pastoral spot.

Tuesday 14 February.   Hand over a mobile X-ray machine to St Paul's Hospital, a gift of the British Government (and people, as I rather sanctimoniously add in my 'speech' at the ceremony, reflecting that involuntary charity is perhaps as meritorious as the other kind if our elected representatives have sanctioned it). The Director of the Hospital, the head of the surgical department, the Matron (trained in Wales), the technicians who have assembled the machine despite the absence of an instruction manual, doctors and nurses, all turn out in the entrance hall of the hospital to welcome the quite modest new arrival. The promised TV and still cameras of the Ethiopian News Agency, summoned by the Public Relations Officer of the Ministry of Health, fail to arrive, but there is quite a handsome acknowledgement in the form of a little news item on television that night and in the next day's press. The Permanent Secretary of the Ministry of Health and the Director of the hospital make graceful speeches recalling Britain's long-standing links with the development of health services in Ethiopia. Wish there was a little more to show for it. They have first class doctors but virtually no equipment and disintegrating hospital and clinic buildings. When they send medical students for training overseas only 10 per cent come back.

Tuesday 21 February to Sunday 4 March. Kenya: Diani Beach, Mombasa, Tsavo West Game Park, Nairobi. With G & J – two other old friends with whom we have shared holidays in some agreeable and spaced-out places from Greece to North Carolina – to the very edge of the Indian Ocean at a beach resort a few miles south of Mombasa. If one doesn't object too much to the massed ranks of German on package tours (I certainly don't object to their daughters sun-worshipping on the beach and round the two swimming pools, grabbing their bikini bras whenever a Kenyan cop saunters by swinging his truncheon and loosening his revolver in its holster), or to the British Tommies on R & R from the leave camp along the beach and allowed to use the hotel facilities, showing off their tattoos and their raw, burned, red adolescent faces looking as if they shave daily with an old baked beans tin lid, to the delighted and fluttery German girls, then this is a very good spot indeed for the kind of holiday depicted by the travel agencies: a magnificent beach, good snorkeling (I did) and wind-surfing (I didn't), clear, warm water, brilliant sun and cooling breezes, and some memorable meals at nearby sea-food restaurants – one in Mombasa with tables on a terrace overlooking the sea, under the stars, one just up the coast from Diani in an under-ground cave cunningly hollowed out and with a gap in the rock overhead through which to view the huge and stagey moon.

Kilaguni Lodge in the Tsavo West game park: lunch and dinner on the terrace of the lodge, and the evening and most of the night on the verandahs of the rooms, riveted by the parade of game only a couple of hundred yards away at the water-hole, floodlit after dark: zebra by the dozens, every kind of antelope and gazelle, wart-hog with tails up like pennants, hyena, water buffalo, but above all elephant – huge bulls with flaring ears, babies straight out of Babar, solicitous mums, macho adolescents trumpeting and dueling; wallowing in the mud, spraying themselves sensually, scratching those massive leathery flanks with evident satisfaction on a rock worn smooth with the friction of sandpapery hides. At one point we counted between 50 and 60 of these splendid beasts with their wise twinkling faces and legs like trees. Less welcome appearances from big yellow baboons which came loping along the verandah walls, peering into the bedrooms, baring their teeth: and the countless rat-like hyraxes scurrying around on and in the roofs and passage ways, snatching food from the tables, and no doubt carrying the horribly disfiguring disease leichmaniasis which the hyrax transfers to humans via the sandfly, destroying whole faces, eroding noses, etc.

From the bustling Nairobi, a day trip to Lake Naivasha in the Rift Valley, with some stunning views out across the rift on the way down to the lake shore and a good lunch at the Naivasha hotel. Here some of the earliest pioneering settlers created their farms out of the bush among the birds and the game, writing afterwards about it as if Naivasha spelled paradise, although it must have been rough for much of the time. Later we go for a drink to the Muthaiga Club, just round the corner from the High Commissioner's Residence where we're staying: it's redolent of the bad old settler days when the aristocratic and rackety, the good-timers and the crooks, intrigued and drank and took drugs and steered their unsteady courses between gambling and adulterous affairs punctuated by sudden eruptions of drunken violence. Certainly it all looks pretty tame now. No colour bar any more, of course, but not much sign of Kenyans apart from the servants. L A claims that not only a minority of the old white settler crowd at the Muthaiga Club were of the spectacular and dissolute kind one associates with the place, which I suppose is right, if rather dampening.

Sunday 4 March to Friday 9 March.   Mogadishu, Somalia.   The Kenya Airways Boeing 720 flies low along the Somali coast, beaches and surf below, wrinkled desert to the left, the green sparkling Indian Ocean to the right. Suddenly we're landing, on a strip next to the ocean, the grass on each side littered with the skeletons of long dead aircraft.

It's not as overpoweringly hot as I'd expected and there's a breeze which, though warm, doesn't actually toast the face in sand. The town is a rather attractively seedy blend of Arab and Italian, with campaniles and minarets, grandiose Mussolini triumphal arches, dusty piazzas, disintegrating clay houses with flat roofs; more middle east than Africa. The wood carvings and hide goods on sale are mainly tawdry rubbish but I find an acceptable meerschaum pipe, the wooden stem of which however seems to lack durability. There are a picturesque harbor and some inviting beaches but the sharks are out there with scalpel teeth waiting to zoom in to the shallows for Jaws III, so a cool shower is the best one can do. However 45 minutes down the coast there's a palm-shaded beach with a sharp reef a few hundred yards out which is claimed to keep the sharks at, as it were, bay, so we swim there with relief at washing off the sandy dust.

The Director-General of the Somali Ministry of Foreign Affairs gives a lunch, al fresco, for the British Ambassador, his wife and myself. It takes place under a huge acacia tree at a trestle table beside the road 13 kilometres outside Mogadishu and comprises boiled goat and roast goat, with a rather good honey sauce. We are warned to keep off the camel's milk, liable to upset unacclimatised stomachs, and to stick to Coca-Cola. It's an excellent meal.

The Alitalia DC10, comfortably half-empty, takes us right up to Hargeisa and Djibouti (without landing) before banking steeply and heading north and west back to Addis. Is it unsafe to fly over the warring Ogaden, or diplomatically un-acceptable to proceed directly from Somali to Ethiopian airspace without a sym-bolic de-lousing over Djibouti?

Wednesday 14 March to Tuesday 20 March.   Ethiopia – Sidamo and Gamo Gofa.   Last bit of touring for J and self before our mid-tour leave. IA, Embassy registrar, comes too. An agreeable drink at the hotel by the lake at Awasa with the Administrator of Sidamo Region, who started out as a shop assistant at about 75p. a week, studied to become a vet, and after the revolution moved into re-gional administration, having now become a figure of some power and influence – which he gives his full loyalty and gratitude to the revolution. He now sits where the Emperor's son once sat – an unlikely succession under the old régime. But he still belongs to a Bible study group and once went on a Bible study con-ference to Uganda.

South down the road that leads ultimately to the Kenya border, stopping off for a couple of hours' visit to a Catholic Mission at a remote spot in Borana country,

Dadim, where the American Father and one American Sister who looks like a bobby-soxer and another Sister from Belfast welcome us with huge mugs of coffee and terrifying descriptions of the rapidly worsening effects of the local drought. On to the Rangelands Development Programme project HQ at Yabelo where we are greeted like visiting royalty (not many visitors in these parts apart from relief people). We have been warned in Addis to bring our own food and water, but in fact a lavish dinner is laid on for us and a breakfast of stomach-turning rancid omelette next morning. The bath in the little guest-house has been filled by a water tanker which called in the previous week: from this we take as little as possible for flushing the loo and washing dry, hot, dusty faces. The local Regional Deputy Administrator, Awraja Deputy Administrator, the Woreda Administrator, the town Administrator and the Director and much of his staff from the Rangelands project all join us for dinner and many of them accompany us on a tour of the town before dark.

Next morning we set off on a dirt track leading westwards across a number of (we trust) dry river-beds and mountains to Konso. We seek local advice on the motorability of this route. All right, they say, so long as it hasn't been raining further north and if you have 4-wheel drive (we have). Also there might be a little problem over the local Borana fighting the Konso people along our route, as they have been doing recently, with several deaths from the ancient rifles carried by most adults in these parts. We are assured that the locals won't want to do us any harm, only each other. But our hosts will send an escort in another land rover behind us just in case. Are we carrying plenty of drinking water and petrol? (Yes.) The escorting land rover swings out of the compound behind us, drops back for a bit and then disappears; never to be seen again. There are moments during the trip when we could have wished it to reappear, as the track keeps petering out, leaving numerous indistinguishable options between the trees and over the sand banks. Luckily BWM, although he has never driven across this way before (virtually the first time we have found a road on which he hasn't driven before), has an uncanny instinct and we have to turn back and try again only twice. No sign of warring Borana or Konsos, but there's a dilapidated bridge which we are about to drive onto when in the nick of time a detachment of boy police appear from nowhere waving frantically to us to stay off the bridge, drive down into the river bed and up the course of the river to a point where we can drive up the opposite bank (no water, happily for us if not for the locals).

In Konso we walk round a remarkable African village, one of several around the outskirts of the small town and virtually unique to these parts, where several hundred families live in intense proximity to each other yet in the most structured and orderly housing and living quarters imaginable, built on several levels, with dense wooden fences and narrow tracks in a maze between the huts. There are guest-house huts for visitors, bars and coffee houses, places for cooking and for the children. Everywhere there are people from tiny babies to old crones. Everyone markedly friendly with much pumping of hands and amicable croaking and grunting. But these are very warlike folk who will go off with rifles and spears to beat up another village to avenge a fancied wrong at the drop of a goat-skin hat. We are on our best behavior.

On again in the late afternoon to Arba Minch ("40 Springs", but only two lakes visible). Grotty hotel, reminiscent of some of the more primitive efforts of Intourist in Soviet Central Asia (we are amused to hear a party of Russians rowing noisily with each other and with the hotel staff, admittedly an exceptionally dozy bunch), but with a stunning view down over the two lakes, the mountains of Sidamo beyond. We are now in the Regional capital of Gamo Gofa and I have visited 13 of the 14 Regions of Ethiopia.

More visits to Roman Catholic Mission relief and development projects, most of them like Dadim supported by Oxfam with money of which some comes from the British Government (so there is a professional justification for the trip!): wells, piped water supplies, clinics for mothers and children, reforestation and anti-erosion terracing done under food-for-work projects, a small earth dam and lake. After a day up in the mountains around Chencha, Father Jan takes us on a brisk walk round and up the village of Orcholo, where over 90% of the population have their faces disfigured or eaten away by leichmaniasis, the dreaded hyrax and sandfly co-existing happily here and local standards of hygiene being low, in part from extreme poverty and in part because of the total absence until recently of water. With help from Oxfam Father Jan has organised the villagers into installing a complete water supply system, fed by buried pipes from a spring two valleys away and a crucial 5 metres higher than the highest point in Orcholo. Jan's arrival with us in tow is like the arrival of Margaret Thatcher at the Conservative Party Conference. To the village people he is, quite simply, the saint and miracle worker who unaccountably one day brought them water. A shy, reserved, rather scholarly man, he blossoms and expands at this beatific welcome, hugging naked children and ragged old women indiscriminately. He strides up the mountainside looking like the Pied Piper. He says there is much puzzlement about the family structure of these curious people who are all fathers and sisters but who seem pitiably to have no children.

On Sunday we hire a small, shallow, fibre-glass boat with a small outboard motor and go out onto Lake Chamo to see the crocodiles. It takes us a few minutes to realise that what appear to be huge logs ¾-submerged in the water are the backs of crocodiles, which slowly submerge at our approach and disappear with a lash of the tail that produces a sudden swirl and boil of the water. One cuts it so fine that the bottom of the boat actually scrapes its back and we are given a great jolt; when the outboard motor is hauled back into the boat after our return, one blade of the propeller is badly bent. Most horrible sight of all is the giant crocs on the lake shore. We move in close to photograph them. Some, about 15 feet long or more, amble down to the water on surprisingly long legs, like dinosaurs, and vanish into the lake. Others lie there in the sun, huge jaws wide open as if waiting for a tasty duck or goose to fly inadvertently straight in. They seem the very embodiment of evil. Wish we had a steel boat: impossible not to imagine a pair of those jaws crunching up the fibre-glass like a match-box. Surprisingly, supercilious herons stalk about among the basking crocs without apparently turning a feather.

Saturday 24 March.   Addis Ababa.   J leaves for London to preside over L's and O's Easter holidays, the last before finals and "A" levels respectively. Return from the airport to the big empty house that so recently seemed packed with the young and the friends of the young. Being looked after by the whole Residence staff is a bit like being the only person in the audience for a concert given by a large orchestra and massed choirs. One feels guiltily obliged to make maximum use of this large resource even when all one wants to do is go to bed.

Seven weeks' solitary confinement begin. Ah, well. Not as long as Sarah Tisdall got.

CHAPTER 26

OCT-NOV 1984:
ADDIS ABABA, ASSAB,
MEKELE, KOREM

Saturday 27 October 1984.   The famine story has been steadily brewing up in the UK for months now and we've been getting a pretty good flow of grants from the ODA, the British aid ministry, mainly to enable Save the Children Fund (SCF) and Oxfam to fund their projects and start new ones. We've just made a suggestion about how best to spend a £50,000 pocket of money that someone in London has found somewhere and thoughtfully offered to us. Almost ever since getting back from our long leave in the UK in early September I've had a filthy cold and an intermittent flu-like condition, universally ascribed here like everything else to the altitude, and we have planned to go down to Langano to the cottages on the lake to relax a little nearer sea level, swim, sit in the sun and eat Bekele's delectable barbecues until Monday evening.

All at once on Saturday morning all hell breaks loose. The Ethiopian famine has bit Britain like a nuclear explosion. The press is suddenly clamouring violently for action. Parliament is wildly excited. Ministers are having to battle to satisfy the storm of demands. MPs are told that I have been asked urgently to make detailed recommendations on how best Britain can help – a request which actually reaches me somewhat after I hear a report of it on the BBC. The press start ringing up from London. The telegram traffic doubles, then trebles, then soars away totally out of control. Langano instantly becomes one of those good ideas that didn't quite come off. I suspect that this is going to prove just the first of a long line of week-ends that will be indistinguishable from weekdays (I'm right).

Last night (Friday) when J and I got back to the Residence after putting in our obligatory appearance at the latest production of the New Theatre Club (Barefoot in the Park, as usual remarkably skilfully done), the telephone rang as I was about to collapse into bed, nose streaming, throat burning, sinuses bursting: a name that rings no bells announces that "we" want an urgent discussion there and then at the Addis Ababa Hilton. I ask if the caller knows what time it is? What do "we" want to discuss? Caller enquires whether I have noticed that there is a famine in Ethiopia. I point out that a discussion late at night is unlikely to do more to alleviate the famine than a discussion at a civilised hour in the morning. It turns out finally that the call is from the associate of Tiny Rowland of Lonrho, who wishes to see me at my earliest convenience. Not about to tangle with Tiny, I agree to go – on Saturday morning.

Rowland and his group of acolytes have, naturally enough, a luxurious suite at the Hilton. Various senior Ethiopian officials, obeying similar summonses, come and go, or sit in capacious arm chairs drinking coffee. The Lonrho air fleet chief is planning to bring Lonrho 707s into Ethiopia to ferry relief supplies, to the evident consternation of the Air Force Colonel in charge of the Ethiopian Relief and Rehabilitation Commission's air operations, also in attendance. The Lonrho man confers with the Ethiopian Colonel in a low voice ("….we'll get the first aircraft in this afternoon … need fuel, what grade you got? – never mind, sort that out later, apron space OK? – we'll find a place, got a pencil and paper? – I'll give you the call signs and you can give me the frequencies, OK? …"). The chief henchman is permanently on the telephone to contacts in New York, London, Nairobi, Lagos, seemingly for the most part talking to Presidents and Prime Ministers, although identification is difficult. He periodically interrupts the boss's conversations with news of transactions complete, pertinent questions requiring instant decisions at the highest level, or simply acid comments on what is being said in some distant part of the room.

At some point while I am on the senior settee with the boss hearing a fullish account of his bitter disillusionment with the British Foreign Office, the Department of Trade, the Monopolies Commission, various City of London regulatory bodies, sundry British Ambassadors and High Commissioners, Mr Edward Heath, the British Government, and other personages and institutions dedicated to the destruction of Lonrho in general and Mr Rowland in particular, the henchman on the long-distance telephone announces that he has Robert Maxwell on the other end and Mr Maxwell wishes to talk to me ("Me?" "Yes, Your Excellency, you"). I hasten to talk to Mr Maxwell, not wishing to tangle with the Daily Mirror or Pergamon Press either. Robert Maxwell describes at length his project for bringing a Daily Mirror Mercy Flight full of relief supplies for the starving people of Ethiopia and outlines the duties of the British Embassy (including especially myself personally) in this regard. I make copious notes and demur as little as possible. Rowland then starts barracking from the settee, asking me to tell Maxwell that his mercy flight is a publicity stunt and that he should keep his ego out of the serious business of famine relief which should be left to people who knew about such things, including preeminently Lonrho and Mr Rowland. I transmit this message. Mr Maxwell, not surprisingly, invites me to relay to Mr Rowland a longish reply which touches on such matters as whether The Observer will be reporting Lonrho's provision of its 707s, the role of Daily Mirror publicity in stirring the conscience of the world, and certain alleged aspects of Mr Rowland's private life of which Mr Maxwell has become aware. I comply with this request. The boss on the settee becomes agitated. "Tell him – ", he begins. I demur, and offer him the telephone. The two newspaper tycoons and magnates continue their dialogue for a considerable time, at £3 a minute plus the Hilton surcharge.

Thursday 1 November. Arrival at Bole International Airport, Addis Ababa, of Mr Maxwell and his Mirror Mercy flight – a Tristar provided free by British Airways ("I had a word with King," as Maxwell explains to me later, making me wonder frantically for a moment which monarch has been enlisted in the Mirror's Good Cause of the Week). There is a large group of jeering western journalists on the tarmac anxious to discredit the Mercy Mission. They crowd round the bottom of the aircraft steps. Mr Maxwell appears at the top of the steps and announces that unless the arrangements for unloading the cargo and dispatching it instantly to the drought areas are to his liking, he will cancel the whole thing and fly the Mercy Mission back to Britain. He then withdraws into the aircraft cabin, presumably to confer with his associates. I join him in the cabin. A harassed Ethiopian identifies me to Maxwell. I tell him that I am confident the arrangements meet his specifications, as defined in the twice-daily telephone calls I have been receiving since the Saturday morning contact via Lonrho. The great man relents and consents to leave the aircraft. Miraculously, the arrangements are indeed exactly as demanded. Trucks have backed up to the cargo hatches even before the aircraft has come to a complete halt, and are busily loading up cardboard cartons of Horlicks and high energy biscuits (presumably for the starving to have at bedtime). Immediately the trucks are loaded, they set off across the tarmac in the general direction of Korem, northern Welo. I marvel. Mr Maxwell is appeased. I pose with him for the television cameras in front of boxes ("Mirror Mercy Mission"). We shake hands a great deal, our expressions conveying suitably sober, merciful sentiments. A reporter with a long hessian-wrapped microphone like an elephant's trunk asks Maxwell what he would say to those who are describing the Mercy Mission as a publicity stunt. For once Mr Maxwell is momentarily speechless.

The Ethiopians are evidently quite pleased with the whole affair. When, later, they provide big stickers to go on the fuselages of the RAF Hercules to identify them as relief supply carriers, not military aircraft, the stickers, in Amharic and English, bear the enormous legend: "MERCY MISSION".

Barder with Robert Maxwell and Col. Habte-Mariam Ayenachu, receiving the Mirror Mercy Flight, Nov 1984

BRIAN BARDER'S DIPLOMATIC DIARY

Saturday 3 November.   With J. to Bole Airport in the bright crisp dawn to welcome the first of the RAF Hercules coming in from RAF Lyneham (Wilts) and Akrotiri (Cyprus) on their 3-month mission (of mercy, naturally) to carry relief supplies in Ethiopia. For the last 4 days we have had 2 splendid squadron leaders attached to the Embassy to prepare for the arrival of the RAF detachment and the 2 aircraft which will run the shuttle, plus the 3 other Hercules which will bring the RAF crews and support staff and all the extensive equipment required to make the operation fully self-sufficient: spare parts (including tyres and wheels and engine parts), tents, beds, compo rations, all the documentation, communications equipment – everything to keep nearly 100 men operational from dawn to dusk, 7 days a week. Even then there will have to be a weekly re-supply plane in from Lyneham with fresh equipment and supplies.

There is perceptible excitement at the airfield. The RAF is the first of several western and now also Eastern European aircraft contributions due to arrive. In addition to J and myself and one of the Squadron Leaders, in the Grosvenor with the flag flying on the wing, we have almost the whole staff of the Embassy out on the tarmac in a motley fleet of British Embassy cars, some to gather the passports from the Hercules and get them stamped with visas by the airport immigration office, whose staff are there already in a state of expectancy: some to organize transport, some to make sure that there are no problems over refueling and parking, some to help the massed British, American and other international press, TV crews, photographers, radio teams, etc., there to witness the arrival in Socialist Ethiopia, military ally of Moscow, of the first of 5 aircraft of the British Royal Air Force, detached for 3 months from their Nato duties .... The Ethiopian airport staff are staggered by all this British activity, with Embassy transport driving up and down the runways and my own car fluttering the Union Jack. "The British are back!"

The dot in the sky slowly expands into the familiar crick-bodied shape of the Hercules. We shade our eyes against the early morning sun. The Sqn Ldr says, "That's her." She is just 2 minutes late onto the runway. The press gathers round as the forward door opens, the steps flop down, and the detachment commander, Wg Cmdr Barry Nunn, steps out onto the tarmac and salutes. We shake hands while the cameras click and buzz and the boom microphones are thrust into our faces (happily the din of the engines drowns out shouted words of greeting). Later when the first 3 aircraft are in and parked on their apron, we hold a short welcoming ceremony with the Deputy Commissioner of the Relief and Rehabilitation Commission (my old travelling companion of the trip to Asmara and Massawa last year to receive and hand over a much earlier consignment of food aid from Britain, Col. Habte-Mariam Ayenachu) in which the Colonel and I welcome the RAF, and I boast without shame that the detachment has begun to arrive less than one week after the first offer of help from the RAF was made to the Ethiopian Government. It's a good moment.

Within a couple of hours the aircraft are unloaded, the Ops Tent is up, the third Hercules has left to return to Lyneham, and there is agreement from the Ethiopian Airlift Co-ordinator that the detachment commander and the crews will leave that afternoon to reconnoitre the landing strips at Assab, Mekele and Axum where they will be picking up grain at the port and delivering it to the worst-hit famine areas. The first shuttles will begin at dawn tomorrow. No messing about!

Sunday 4 November.   Barry Nunn, the RAF detachment commander, rings up in the evening to say there's been a little spot of bother. I have visions of both the Hercules crashing …. But no: everything's perfectly all right; just that one of the aircraft, on its 3rd and last shuttle of grain into Axum in the late afternoon, burst a tyre on landing, on the rough, stony, gravel strip. Too late to send in the second Hercules to pick up the crew: and Axum in the middle of guerrilla country. The crew radioed to Nunn in Addis: what should they do – leave the aircraft on the strip and spend the night in the little local clinic, and hope that the guerrillas would leave them alone: or risk a take-off on the sharp stones on 3 tyres, knowing that if a second tyre burst under the extra pressure, the aircraft would keel over, the wing-tip would touch the ground and the Hercules would cart-wheel spectacularly out of control, almost certainly breaking up and bursting into flames? Barry Nunn had taken the immediate decision: lower the tyre pressures and take off. They did, and through sheer skill and professionalism got safely off the lethal runway at Axum and – 75 minutes later – also safely onto the runway at Bole. All this on the first day of operations. Phew.

Thursday 8 November.   Hitch a lift with the RAF to the port of Assab on the Red Sea to have a look at the grain handling arrangements and to see how the new equipment and vehicles Britain was supplying to the port would fit into and beef up the operation: and on by RAF with several tons of bags of grain at mid-day to Mekele, one of the main famine relief centres, run by the RRC (Ethiopian Relief and Rehabilitation Commission), Catholic Relief Services and the International Red Cross (ICRC). As we touch down on the red gravel strip at Assab, the trucks loaded with bags of grain move out from the airport terminal sheds to line up at the rear cargo hatch of the Hercules, and the Ethiopian loaders, wearing only brightly coloured nylon basketball shorts, run across the dusty runway to start loading, in a temperature of about 110⁰. The RAF loadmaster and crew greet the loaders like long-lost companions and help to carry the heavy sacks on their backs from the truck up the ramp into the body of the aircraft. There is a lot of noisy competition for who can carry the most sacks at once. Within 10 minutes 17 tons are loaded, stowed and lashed down. Already the whole turnaround time has been reduced to 15 minutes. In a swirl of red dust the engines start up and the aircraft moves out like a great swollen buffalo onto the runway to take off for Mekele. One of the crews of the East German Ilyushins, also sent to carry relief supplies, but still not operational after several days, watch bemused from the shade of the terminal shed.

Mekele.   Claire Berschinger, Anglo-Swiss ICRC nurse, in a blue dress, her face and arms burned almost black by the sun, waits by the terminal shed with a landrover to meet me and take me into the town. Why is she so familiar-looking? Suddenly realise that she is interviewed in one of the TV programmes shown in the UK which we have on video, describing in the matter-of-fact manner special to these extraordinary people the fluctuations in the daily death rate in the ICRC feeding centre and their need for more grain, more dried skimmed milk, more rehydration fluid packs, more blankets (it is piercingly cold at night in these dry highlands, 9,000 or 10,000 feet up, baked by day and icy by night), more tents or just rolls of plastic sheeting, more edible oil, preferably vitaminised, more flour mills, more vaccines ....

At the Catholic Relief Services main feeding centre Sister Gabriel, British, 88 years old, dismissively recovered last year from a heart attack which kept her from work for only a handful of weeks, upright, patrician, waits to show me round and describe the various sections of the operation. This is the first time I have met the legendary figure. Last year I surreptitiously collected details of her background and career in order to put her up to London for an award (if the honours system means anything it ought to honour the Sister Gabriels, aptly named after an angel), only to be told that she had been an OBE for years....

Sunday 11 November.   Remembrance Day. As usual the Ambassadors of all the countries which took part in the liberation of Ethiopia from fascism in 1941-2 gather at the War Cemetery on the outskirts of Addis for the Remembrance Day service and to lay wreaths: I lay the first, for Britain, and at the very end the senior Ethiopian Armed Forces officer present and I lay a joint wreath in memory of the Ethiopian war dead. This year we have a contingent from the RAF detachment present, lined up alongside the Ethiopian armed forces group and the Ethiopian Army military band; and the RAF detachment commander and I lay the first wreath together. I find this even more moving than in previous years. But the Anglican chaplain (the vicar of the local C of E church, very much a civilian) conducts the service each year out of duty rather than conviction ("Worship of the dead! Necrophilia!").

Tuesday 13 November.   J and I go at last to Korem, the other biggest and most publicised of the feeding centres in the famine areas, in northern Welo. It was to Korem that we were heading in April 1983 when we were stopped at Dese by the local Administrator and told that in view of the security situation it was inadvisable for us to go any further. Two days later Korem was captured by the guerrillas and the expatriates, including the SCF relief workers, taken off into Tigray and Eritrea on a 7-week trek into Sudan before being released a stone or so lighter than when they began.

This time we go by air, not landrover, flying into the tiny strip at Alamata a few kilometres south of Korem and about 2,000 feet lower. We travel in a little twin-engined Beechcraft Queenair chartered by the people of the British west country to carry relief supplies and relief workers to and fro in Ethiopia. By carrying press and TV crews the ingenious Exeter pilot and his co-pilot have managed to raise enough money to finance an indefinite extension of their relief flights and to have enough left over for a hefty donation to SCF. On this trip to Alamata, besides J and me, the Beechcraft is carrying a plump Irish Bishop in a sports shirt and slacks, with his equally civilianised chaplain, and an ITN TV crew led by Joan Thirkettle, with all their equipment. Also the intrepid figure of the Sqn Ldr, John Morley, in a flying suit whose innumerable zipped pockets bulge with packets of sandwiches, flasks of water, maps, charts, and an ingenious instrument for spiking into runways to test their load-bearing capacity.

Once into the Alamata airstrip (clouds of dust and not even a shed for a terminal – indeed no communications or human presence at all apart from a few rather tatty soldiers crouched in the shade of the only bush for miles) we climb out, explain through Belew, my constant travel companion, to the tatty soldiers that John Morley will be doing some tests on the runway, and roar off towards Korem in a cloud of dust in a Toyota Land Cruiser driven by the local SCF nutritionist, Judith Appleton, from Surrey and Ontario. The Bishop and his chaplain come with us; the ITN team stay aboard the Beechcraft as it takes off and heads back south for Kombolcha. John Morley strides out onto the sun-drenched airstrip and begins to assemble his prodder kit. Normally tests like this on an airstrip would take 3 men 3 days. He proposes to complete the job in 5 hours of solid work in the dry, sandy heat (and, of course, does. His readings and calculations show that it is, just, possible to get a Hercules with full load into Alamata, and out again; 2 days later the first RAF flight into Alamata, which is also the first visit by any aircraft bigger than the little twin-engined Beechcraft, takes a load of food and relief supplies in for Korem).

It's a curious sensation to drive through the little town of Korem and out to the open land beyond the town to the huge area of the feeding centre, so familiar from television: the corrugated iron sheds containing the starving, sick and dying; the rows of plastic sheeting tepees in which bedraggled groups of emaciated people huddle together in hand-dug pits; the thousands and thousands of motionless people, 8 or 10 deep, squatting or standing around the far perimeter of the centre, watching and waiting until they become hungry or sick enough to be admitted to the privilege of food and treatment. What is more unexpected is the hundreds of cheerful, friendly children who gather round to stare with lively interest at visitors; the little dry brown hands that slip shyly into one's own, with a brown sandy wide-eyed grin peering up beside it. The bright, doggedly optimistic, matter-of-fact relief workers, many of them plainly dog tired, and those packs of lively kids, go much of the way towards offsetting the sense of horror and despair conveyed by the television images and driven home by the sight of so many pathetic hardly-human bundles of skeletal bones and skin, dreadfully reminiscent of Belsen, and the wasted tiny children with huge questioning eyes. The daily death rate is down from about 180 to not much more than 40, so morale has risen, and more food is coming in. But hundreds more half-starved people continue to arrive every day from the parched hillsides hundreds of miles around, demand always outstripping supply and, heartbreakingly, no end in sight. Still, thousands of tonnes of additional food are on the way, the road and air transport capacities have quadrupled within weeks, and even the pitifully destitute know that they have not been written off completely.

The Irish Bishop has found an Ethiopian Orthodox Church priest, a haggard half-starved fellow with a wooden staff. Told that this sports-shirted jolly figure is a Bishop, the haggard priest clearly thinks something badly wrong with the interpretation.

Above left: Barder with Col. Habte-Mariam Ayenachu, Deputy Commissioner for Relief and Rehabilitation, Assab, Ethiopia, 1984.

Above right: Louise at the controls of a C-130 Hercules, Ethiopia 1984.

Below: An RAF squadron in front of a C-130 Hercules, Addis Ababa 1984.

CHAPTER 27

MARCH–JULY 1985: GONDER, WELEGA, ADDIS ABABA, KOREM, KOBO, ASSAB

Thursday 7 March, 1985.   Metema, Gonder region.   For weeks now the RAF relief operation has been delivering grain and flour to Metema, a remote lowland village in west-central Gonder, out by the Sudan border. The grain delivered is stacked along the edge of the short black-earth runway; no-one ever seems to come and take it away. It is not a drought area: why is the grain needed there? We persistently ask, getting different answers each time (it is to enable refugees from famine areas further east to get food and settle down instead of going across the Sudan border and becoming international refugees; it is for a 6- or 7-year-old resettlement centre, helped from time to time by Oxfam and still not able to grow enough food to feed itself; it is for new settlers coming from the drought areas in Tigray and eastern Gonder). I apply to go there to see for myself: the unvarying reply – "No problem!" – but the travel permit fails to materialise. I tell the Relief and Rehabilitation Commission that until I have been to Metema to find out what is happening to the grain and flour that the RAF is taking there, the RAF will not take any more grain or flour – or anything else. This has a fairly rapid effect and a travel permit materialises.

By this time the RAF crews which were earlier flying in and out of Metema have gone home at the end of their 3-week stints in Ethiopia so the crew which carries

PF (my aid officer) and myself and several tons of salt to Metema this time have never been there before. The map is rudimentary, there are no landmarks in the hills, dry river beds look like the one dirt road running west from Gonder Town to Metema, and there are rumours in Addis Ababa that there has been heavy rain recently in the Metema area. If this is so, the black cotton-soil air-strip may well be too soft for the heavy C130 aircraft to land: if the wheels sink in, the aircraft captain tells me reassuringly, the whole aircraft will turn over and explode. I confirm that despite my burning desire to visit Metema, I don't want anyone to take any risks on my behalf. We agree that we will fly up and down until we find the airstrip, then do a low dummy run over it to see whether it "looks wet".

Flying up and down is what we have to do for quite some time, until the flight engineer gives a shout and points to a faint smudge in a distant valley. "That'll be her," the rest of the crew agree. "Black air-strip. Bound to be." It is.

I was prepared to fly low over the strip for the dummy run, but this is ridiculous. The Deputy Pilot (surely not quite the right designation, but it gives the sense), a calm young man who looks about 17, takes over the controls and flies the Hercules at about shoulder height above and slightly to one side of the airstrip while the aircraft captain and I peer out of the flight-deck window at the black surface. It looks to me like the mud beyond the sands at low tide in Weston-Super-Mare. I wonder in what respect wet cotton-soil looks different from dry cotton-soil: the matter suddenly strikes me as quite important. A few people standing beside the airstrip throw themselves on the ground, covering their heads with their arms, as we roar over. "Looks all right, doesn't it, sir?", says the aircraft captain. "Certainly," I say briskly. "OK, then, we'll give it a try." The plane suddenly points itself upwards and banks steeply to go round again for the landing. The air-strip is as dry as a bone (but even so the Hercules wheels plough deep furrows).

PF and I, and BA of my Ethiopian staff, climb out with our notebooks, hats and cameras and watch while the sacks of salt are unloaded and stacked with the rampart of grain and flour alongside the air-strip. The Hercules crew give us a cheery wave, calling out "See you around 4 o'clock this afternoon", taxi out and take off. Although still only about 8 o'clock in the morning, it's already hot and syrupy, patches of sweat appearing at once under arms and on chests.

Early in the afternoon we return to the airstrip to inspect the foundations being laid for a warehouse. We hear the familiar clatter of helicopters and two Russian choppers come over and begin to descend, the rotors blowing up great storms of black dust. They land and a few people jump out with boxes and bags of supplies. A young blond Russian crew member in a flying-suit climbs out and stands on the strip near the helicopter. I go over to him, greet him politely in Russian and ask if I might be permitted to take a photograph of the two helicopters. The young Russian looks as startled as Neil Armstrong might have done if, on alighting on the moon, he was immediately greeted by a small green creature speaking with a Brooklyn accent. "Who are you?", asks the Russian, more in bewilderment than in suspicion. "I am the English Ambassador," I reply, "And I would like to take a picture." He surveys me with an expression of considerable doubt, not altogether surprisingly, since I am clad in by now pretty grimy khaki trousers and a sweat-stained bush jacket, with a limp cotton hat to protect my pate from the sun. Clearly I don't <u>look</u> like an English Ambassador. However the youth returns to the helicopter to consult his boss, who peers suspiciously at me from the flight deck but grants permission for photography. (Only a couple of months later one of the Russian helicopters flying supplies from Gonder to Metema tries some over-ambitious acrobatics at Metema to impress some visiting Ethiopian dignitaries, and crashes into the ground, catching fire and then exploding, causing the deaths of all the 4 crew members then or soon afterwards; I often wonder if my young Russian friend was one of those, fish out of water miles from their homes and families, who met their end in such a lonely and unwelcoming place.)

Back to the airstrip again at 4 p.m. to wait for the Hercules to return and pick us up. The temperature is over 110°F. and we have finished all the cans of beer and soft drinks which we had brought with us. The local people have nothing to drink except water from the local muddy creek, which those who have the equipment for it boil before drinking (most haven't, and don't). At last a dot in the fierce pale blue sky grows into a smear into an aircraft into the Hercules, which lands in a cloud of black dust. We climb aboard as a second consignment of sacks of salt is unloaded onto the side of the airstrip. The sun beats down on the metal skin of the aircraft. Within moments of landing the flight crew are soaked in sweat like ourselves. Mopping at my dust-and-sweat stained face with a limp brown handkerchief, I wonder aloud what they need all this salt for. "I expect," says the load-master, unzipping his flying-suit and fanning himself vigorously, "it's to put down on the roads in the winter."

Sunday 17 March. Asosa Resettlement Camp, Welega Region. This time J. has come on the trip with PF and BA, but the grass runway is too short and bumpy for the RAF Hercules so the RRC has given us the use of their own ancient DC3 (Dakota), rumoured actually to have flown in the Berlin Airlift in 1948. Our faith in the sturdiness of the aircraft was not much reinforced when my canvas seat collapsed under my admittedly substantial weight.

At the old resettlement site at Asosa we inspected the grave-yard of old rusting tractors and other farm machinery, fallen into disuse through lack of money for spare parts, drivers' pay or fuel (a common experience all over Ethiopia). Many of the machines seemed to have been cannibalized, presumably in an imaginative bid to construct just one functioning machine from bits of the others. However when, later, we visited the workshops where people were making simple hand tools, the iron tips for wooden ploughs, etc., we asked where the metal came from, and were told that they stripped it off the old tractors – a kind of reverse technology.

Flying back to Addis in the old DC3 late in the afternoon we encounter fierce but localized thunderstorms with torrential rain and lightning. The Dakota swoops and weaves to avoid the worst of these, flying low to keep under the black clouds, hedge-hopping over the hill-tops. When we land at the airport at Addis it is raining torrents and the runway is under about 2 inches of water. A few weeks later the Ethiopian civil aviation authorities withdraw our Dakota's airworthiness certificate.

Tuesday 16 July to Friday 19 July. Addis Ababa, Korem, Kobo, Assab. Mr Raison, the Minister for Overseas Development, back for a second visit (he came last November) to review the progress of the British famine relief effort, to make a decision on the future of the RAF operation (the Bishops at home are clamouring for another extension beyond the end of September), and to demonstrate continuing British Government concern against the backdrop of more super-colossal concerts organised by Bob Geldof. Timothy Raison is accompanied by a couple of

ODA officials and, this time, by a covey of British journalists brought to cover his visit, some svelte, cool and professional, some pot-bellied, drunken and confused. We have to put them all up in the houses in the compound because the OAU Summit is meeting at Africa Hall in Addis and all the hotels are crammed with the delegations. Mr Raison and the 2 officials stay as usual with us, in the Residence.

The usual breathless programme, which for once goes pretty much according to plan. We hustle the whole party straight out of the London flight on arrival into the RAF Hercules and take off immediately for Alamata; into landrovers and up the dusty road to Korem, where conditions have improved greatly since the earlier traumatic visit (but what are conditions like now out in the countryside? Almost no-one really knows); back into the landrovers and down to Kobo to inspect another Save the Children Fund feeding centre and an agricultural project part-financed by Oxfam. Back to Addis in the Hercules, just time for a quick shower and change out of dusty clothes for a working dinner with a group of agricultural experts to discuss Ethiopian agricultural development policy and European Community aid policy. Next day off at dawn in the Hercules to Assab, to tour the docks in the searing heat off the Red Sea and to watch the grain handling equipment given by Britain actually in use (the journalists scribble away in their notebooks). Back to Addis for meetings and briefings all afternoon and a big buffet supper in the evening to meet the senior relief people. Next morning the visitors go off with the RAF on an air-drop sorties, one of the most moving and exciting experiences available in Ethiopia. Straight from the airport to more meetings with Ministers, members of the Politbureau, etc. Out to the RRC vehicle workshops to meet the Landrover mechanic from the UK, financed by the ODA, and view his landrover repair operation. Back to the Residence for a hasty skim through a mountain of telegrams and messages, a bath, and away to an injera-and-wat dinner at a private restaurant, the occasion organised by the RRC Commissioner and his 3 deputies for Mr Raison. Next morning a working breakfast with Bradford Morse, the former US Congressman and now the UN Secretary-General's Special Relief Co-ordinator for Africa, and Kurt Jansson, the Ethiopia UN Relief Aid Co-ordinator, coming for bacon and eggs at the Residence and talks with Mr Raison. Straight from there to the airport for a final press conference, last talks with the RRC Commissioner and hand-shakes all round as Mr Raison boards the plan for London at mid-day.

Back to the Residence once again for a hasty snack lunch and just the afternoon to make the final preparations for the arrival first thing tomorrow of the Leader of the Opposition and Mrs Kinnock with 3 Labour Party officials and 6 press (plus 2 from the Raison visit who have ignored our frenzied appeals and decided to stay on for the Kinnock visit). Back in the house the staff have already changed the sheets on all the beds in the guest bedrooms, renewed the bottles of Scotch and gin and vodka, replenished the fridge in the dressing-room adjoining the Queen's Bedroom, put new bars of soap in the bathrooms, got fresh toilet rolls out of the store cupboard, and relaid the fires, all urged on by J., still composed but pale. It's like a particularly hilarious episode of Fawlty Towers but with an undertone of genuine panic and not one Manuel but seven.

Saturday 20 July.   Addis Ababa.   The Kinnocks arrive on the flight from London in a torrential downpour. For the first time since we have been in Ethiopia Tommy, the Embassy fixer, indispensable for all airport rituals and the rapid processing of VIP visitors, has disappeared. J. and I lead the Kinnock party in growing panic along miles of corridors in search of a short cut to the VIP lounge. We eventually find ourselves leading them all out of the terminal building into the pouring rain and everyone has to sprint for 100 yards or so to the back door of the VIP lounge, which is locked. No-one has an umbrella. No-one even has a rain-coat. The Leader of the Opposition gets extremely wet. Once inside the VIP lounge, he asks me about the first appointment planned for his initial tentative programme of meetings with African Heads of State and Government here for the OAU Summit: "When am I seeing the President of Angola?" I tell him that since his own flight from London was 2 hours late, and President Dos Santos's Presidential aircraft had left just an hour ago, such a meeting will not after all be possible. Moreover, I say, we have just had, in the past 3 hours, messages from President Kaunda's delegation, Mr Mugabe's delegation, and the Nigerian Head of State's delegation, saying that the appointments made for the meetings with Mr Kinnock would all have to be rearranged because the great men would probably now be leaving Ethiopia earlier than expected, and they would definitely let us know as soon as there was anything more definite, and yes, they would all be leaving today some time and possibly in the next couple of hours but no, they were at the summit meeting at the moment and couldn't see anyone there.

The party expert on Africa accompanying Mr Kinnock takes me on one side to show me a cutting from the previous day's Daily Telegraph in which a devastating "Snub For Kinnock" is predicted. None of the African leaders, it says, whom Mr Kinnock has come to meet is likely to spare the time to see him. The Ethiopians have refused to issue a pass to enable him to enter the grounds of the Ghion Hotel where all the African Presidents are staying (this at least is no longer true as we managed to get a windscreen sticker for this very purpose 24 hours earlier). His journey will prove to have been a waste of time. The Leader of the Opposition is about to be humiliated. The British Embassy is embarrassed, has tried its best, but proved unequal to the task. I tell the party expert on Africa that it is too early to write the trip off as a failure. There are certainly problems, but…

We get a message that Mr Mugabe, the Zimbabwe Prime Minister, might be at the Ghion Hotel. The African expert, Mr Kinnock, Patricia Hewitt (his press secretary) and I rush out to my flag car and drive like maniacs to the Ghion, Berhanu driving down the wrong side of the line of traffic with his hand permanently on the horn. Shall we get there before Mr Mugabe leaves for the morning session of the conference? We do not. We wander among the Presidential bungalows in the pouring rain, trying to find the Zimbabwe suite. Mr Mugabe has left for the conference: why don't we follow him there and see whether he can slip out for a talk with Mr Kinnock in the corridors or a private room? We leap back into the flag car and drive at high speed to Africa Hall. Unfortunately the summit is electing the new Secretary-General and Mr Mugabe can't come out at the moment.

Waves of despair and gloom sweep the visiting party. Luckily none of the journalists has been able to keep up with us or find us so far. We speculate about how many days or weeks it will be before the gales of contemptuous laughter in Britain die down. Mr Kinnock is optimistic: just a few days and it will all be forgotten. Patricia Hewitt is suicidal. We return, damp and cheerless, to the Residence, where various members of the Embassy staff are manning telephones in different rooms with half-drunk cups of coffee beside them. All seem to be talking to various members of African delegations in hotels, embassies and conference centres, in tones of voice ranging from the tragically disappointed to the fiercely indignant.

Hours later and it all suddenly starts to come right. One after another the delegations come up with suggestions for a time and place for a meeting. Commuting at high speed between the airport VIP departure lounge and the Ghion bungalows, we get one after another of the great men. Each conversation is friendly, workmanlike, useful. Emerging from the last appointment (with President Kaunda of Zambia, in the airport lounge), Neil Kinnock visibly relaxes for the first time, smiles a huge smile, and says: "Well, that's it, then: we've done it. Ambassador: you're a genius."

CHAPTER 28

SEP-NOV 1985:
WELO, GONDER, GOJJAM,
ERITREA, TIGRAY, SUDAN

Tuesday 17 September, 1985.   Sekota, Welo region.   Fly in a 6-seater single-engined Cessna belonging to World Vision to have a look at the security situation at Sekota. The Relief & Rehabilitation Commission (RRC), the UN Co-ordinator's Office and World Vision want the RAF to do air-drops of grain to some 90,000 people who have left the relief shelters to try to get a harvest on the land around Sekota from which they originally came. We have hitherto preferred not to send the RAF on air drops of grain in this area because of the possible risk to the aircraft and crews from recent rebel activity hereabouts.

We land on a barely discernible air-strip ("more like a ploughed field," the young American pilot says) which goes from edge to edge of a small plateau high above the surrounding hills and bump down the rocky track in a Toyota Land-Cruiser to visit the little town of Sekota, until a few months ago a rebel stronghold. There are soldiers everywhere. The local RRC man shows us a virtually empty grain ware-house and says no grain has arrived for many weeks. The 3 French medics from Médecins Sans Frontières confirm this but also agree with the local Administrator that there has been no sign of rebel activity for many weeks – important pos-itive evidence. A fair number of the people around in the town certainly look emaciated and sick.

We take off in the Cessna which seems to have difficulty getting up enough speed on the ploughed field to become airborne. I begin to have visions of the lip of the gorge at the end of the air-strip and the 3,000-foot drop into the valley, but we suddenly hit a bump which throws the little aircraft into the air and we zoom safely away. A few concentric circuits, banking steeply, over the surrounding hillsides reveal no sign of insecurity and indeed there are obviously Ethiopian armed forces liberally sprinkled over the landscape. The RAF Detachment Commander and I agree that we can give London a positive assessment of the security situation. No-one has shot at us as we flew low over the area; we hope that no-one will shoot at the RAF Hercules, if and when it does the air drops, either.

Thursday 19 September.   Field trip to Welo, Gonder, Gojjam, Eritrea and Tigray Regions with the UN Relief Co-ordinator (the magnificent Kurt Jansson), the RRC Commissioner (Dawit), the German and Australian Ambassadors and the No. 2 from USAID, various other assorted relief people, a press and TV crew from the RRC and the Chief Foreign Correspondent of 'The Guardian'. We travel in both the Twin Otters of the RRC. After the Cessna, the Twin Otter feels like a Jumbo.

First stop is Sekota once again. The party is pretty shaken, in both sense, by the bumpy landing. All are impressed by the urgency of the need to get food in: I constantly wish I could confirm that we had agreed to do air drops, but of course there has not yet been time for a decision from London (in fact my recommendation is accepted a day or two later and the RAF subsequently drops 350 tonnes of grain on the plateau without incident).

On to Lalibela, my first visit to this most famous of all the spectacular sights of Ethiopia, with its massive churches carved from the living rock, the top of the roof level with the ground. The churches are themselves cross-shaped so that from the air you see huge dark crosses carved into the hills, the shapes outlined by the deep trenches surrounding the churches – from which, indeed, the churches were originally sculpted out of the solid rock.

To enter the church you cross the trench by a rickety wooden bridge and then climb down two steep flights of steps cut into the side of the trench to reach the level of the base of the church. Entering the building, you can scarcely believe that it is carved from a solid block, with its pillars, ornately carved windows, beams and steps.

Friday 20 September.   The field trip visits one of the biggest of the new resettlement areas in western Gojjam Region at Pawi in Metekel Awraja (county). This is hot, humid lowland country, very different from the dry, thin air of the highlands from which most of the settlers have come. The rains are still not quite finished here and for some of the day there is a gentle warm drizzle. The tracks in the settlements which we visit are a sea of mud; the local people have thoughtfully laid branches and bamboo across the sections due to be trodden by the distinguished visiting feet, but even so we all accumulate huge, heavy clods of black mud on our shoes, and have to walk along with a comic bow-legged gait which seems to cheer up the settlers a little. These have been assembled to line our route on both sides, slowly and rhythmically clapping (we politely clap back, Russian-style).

There is a faint but unmissable air of gloom hanging over the settlements, but it is impossible to be sure whether this is because of the drizzle and the mud, or because Ethiopians accustomed to living scattered over the mountains don't take quickly to living in neat rows of identical huts in a settlement, or because of the tedium of being required to clap a visiting group of rather bedraggled visitors apparently from outer space. Certainly the settlers whom we visit in their huts, selected at random, all say with emphasis and conviction that they are incomparably better off here than they were in the drought areas which they left behind and where they are adamant that there could have been no future for them; and indeed here the maize is 8 feet tall, growing in dense stands in the fields around the huts. The visiting Excellencies are presented with harvest festival baskets of ears of maize, sprigs of teff and assorted leaves of vegetables and herbs, an effective way of making a point.

Sunday 17 November to Wednesday 20 November.   Sudan.   This is a return visit of "familiarisation" following the visit to Ethiopia last month by Sir Alec Stirling, my opposite number in Khartoum, the exchange long planned and much delayed. I have a heavy cough and cold, and a congested chest which proves after my return to Addis Ababa and the RAF doctor to have been the start of acute bronchitis, not the ideal state in which to carry out an intensive programme of calls and visit in this hot, dry, dusty place. (The local people say, as the local people always do to first-time visitors anywhere, that this weather is completely untypical: rather cool, actually. It's hot enough for me after the blessedly temperate weather of Addis Ababa.)

After a full programme of calls on the Acting Head of State, the Deputy Prime Minister, the Minister of Defence, the Acting Head of the Foreign Ministry, the Relief Commissioner, the American Ambassador and various other potentates, we drive in the Stirlings' landrover to Omdurman, crossing the river just above the junction of the Blue and White Niles (disappointingly there seems no obvious difference between the colours of the two famous waterways, the Blue Nile carrying down into Sudan and Egypt all that rich Ethiopian soil and all that sadly-needed water). The Mahdi's tomb is fully up to expectation and the Khalifa's house next door, a baked-mud museum, is full of marvelous Gordon memorabilia. It seems a shame that the touchingly simple plaque in the Presidential palace recalling Gordon's death is probably nowhere near where he actually died on Dervish spears.

On Tuesday we fly – this time in an even smaller Cessna, a sort of 5 ½ seater – Kassala, in the far eastern strip of Sudan near the border with Eritrea, just down the road from Tesseney on the Ethiopian side. Soon after we take off from Khartoum, the young pilot asks Lady Stirling, in the co-pilot's seat, if she would like to take over the controls. This seems rather touching. Alison Stirling, although apparently unqualified, flies the plane for some time without mishap, the pilot's hands hovering over the joy-stick, and he makes a faultless landing at Kassala. After a massive welcoming breakfast and briefing session from the Governor of the Province and what must have been his entire provincial staff, we drive across the desert, 5 Toyotas abreast, our dust-cloud high in the air behind us, like a scene in some film about Rommel, to Wad Sharifei, the huge camp for refugees from the famine and fighting in Eritrea. Here 165,000 people live and wonder whether and when they will ever re-cross the border, only a mile or so away, back into their own country. The sights in the clinics and intensive feeding centres of the camp are familiar from many such visits to shelters in Ethiopia – the usual skeletal, huge-eyed children, the expressionless women, the cheerful grubby urchins playing outside in the hot sun. And, of course, the usual sensible practical no-nonsense relief workers, Swiss and American and British and Sudanese (and some from among the Ethiopian refugees themselves), getting on with the job as if they were helping to run a children's outing to Southend. A plump young woman nursing sister from Minneapolis shows me where her face has got painfully sun-burned from lounging by the swimming pool at Port Sudan during her first weekend off for 8 weeks of unremitting labour at Wad Sharifei. A long way from home.

Back in Kassala we have an excellent lunch with a young British couple, both relief workers, who had accompanied us round the camp. They have a nice, cool house, shaded by trees and surrounded by livestock of every description, ducks and geese, an enormous goat (for milk), chickens, dogs, cats, all loudly demonstrating their characteristic calls like something out of a children's instructional television programme. Above the hubbub, I hear something familiar about the way our host, a vet, pronounces the word "actually" – a sort of well-bred "axsherly" – and find myself taken back across three decades to The Whim, the Copper Kettle and the Backs. Where, I ask, had he done his veterinary studies? "Edinburgh," he says (and I could have sworn…) … "— after Cambridge." Gotcher.

After lunch as we sit drinking coffee on the patio outside the little house, our Cessna pilot, an English lad who appears to be about 16 going on 17, puts his hand to his mouth and rushes inside. There are sounds of retching and coughing. The vet hurries inside after him, emerging shortly afterwards with a long face.

"He has a slightly raised temperature, poor chap. He's not terribly well, axsherly. He says it's just a cold, but I think it might axsherly be malaria."

This seems to me to be faintly worrying information.

"Will he be fit to fly the Cessna in half an hour's time?"

The vet says: "Not if it is malaria. It's a 2-hour flight back to Khartoum, and with malaria he could pass out with less than half-an-hour's notice. But of course it might not be malaria."

"When is the next Sudan Air flight to Khartoum?"

"Next week. Of course you could drive back, but even if you left now you wouldn't get back until the early hours of tomorrow morning and it would be a pretty grueling trip."

At this point the boy pilot re-emerges, his face a faint shade of grey, and sits down in his chair as if lowering himself onto drawing-pins. He declines a cup of coffee.

"How do you feel?"

"A bit rough, but I'll be all right. It's just a bad cold, and I haven't had much sleep for the last few nights."

"Think you'll be all right to fly the plane?"

"I think so. Probably, yes. I expect I'll be all right."

None of my fellow-passengers seems at all concerned at this turn of events. Perhaps it happens all the time in Sudan. I try without success to remember any recent stories of light aircraft crashing in the Sudanese desert. The malarial boy pilot may of course only just have arrived in Sudan. Sir Alec makes a helpful suggestion.

"If necessary my wife can always take over the controls."

My expressions of deep misgiving begin to sound as if in poor taste. We leave for the airport. Once we airborne, the pilot invites Lady Stirling to take over. He then enjoys what appears to be a tranquil nap, waking up and taking back the controls just before we land at Khartoum.

PART V:

POLAND,
LATE 1980s

Barder with Lech Wałęnsa

CHAPTER 29

MAY–JULY 1986: WARSAW

About the last thing we expected to find in Poland was a tropical heatwave. For most of our first few days it has been like living in a sauna: much hotter, certainly, than it ever was in Addis Ababa, which actually_is_ in the tropics, though protected from over-heating by altitude.

Soon after us, the new official flag-car arrives: a 4-seater (5 at a perceptible pinch) Jaguar, to replace the old Grosvenor, a stretched Granada which, with the jump-seats, could carry 8 in tolerable comfort and without looking like a telephone kiosk in the Guinness Book of records. But the real plus for the Jaguar is that it has a very efficient air-conditioning system. What a pity that for 8 or 9 months of the year all we shall worry about is the heater!

***

The Residence, designed in 1962, according to legend by a naval architect who had never worked before on anything for terra firma, has no sloping roofs or other upper surfaces, only flat – presumably at sea accumulated water from rain and sea gets tilted off every few minutes. Here, of course, it doesn't, and the water lies in pools more like lakes than puddles, gradually seeping through the various surfaces, destroying electric cables and concrete structures underneath. Some visiting structural engineers from the UK whom we asked to look at the various crumbling rooms and walk-ways were aghast. A lot of work will now have to be done.

***

On 1 August, anniversary of the beginning of the Warsaw Uprising in 1944, we go with our splendid multilingual (including Cockney) Polish driver to the war cemetery where most victims of the uprising are buried and commemorated, and where thousands of Poles light candles and lay flowers. There is a huge, quiet throng of people, all the parking-spaces for miles around filled with cars. The harassed militiaman nearest the main gate of the cemetery sees the flag on the car and waves us to a parking-space on the pavement right in front of the main gates. We thank him warmly; his gesture is only slightly spoiled by the discovery that he is fairly drunk.

Inside the huge cemetery grounds the biggest crowd surrounds the tall black granite memorial to the victims of the Katyn massacre of 20,000 Polish officers, the cream of the Polish army, at the beginning of the war. The reference engraved on the monument to the Hitlerite fascists as the perpetrators has been spray-painted out; all Poles know at whom the finger should have pointed. The crowd here is softly singing patriotic songs, almost every hand stretched out towards the memorial with the V-sign of Solidarność. One of the songs begins: "The Red Herd will be punished one day….." Everyone, even the teenagers, knows the words of this and apparently of all the songs, many of them running to dozens of verses.

The endless rows of crosses, some literally touching each other, are almost unbearable to look at, especially with these hundreds of Poles there to do homage to them and to remember. Nearly all the older men wear war medals on their open-necked shirts or jackets.

***

Walking on a hot, sunny Saturday morning round the New Town and the Old Town, both completely destroyed during the Occupation and lovingly restored immediately after the war, stone by stone, while Poland still starved in the ruins, we are bowled over by the civilised grace of these lovely streets and squares, surely among the most delectable sights of Europe. The general seediness and neglect characteristic of Warsaw have produced the great benefit so far as these old historic streets are concerned that they don't actually look as if they have been restored; they look like genuine originals which have survived well but could do with a little more upkeep. Here and there one comes on a market square that looks like a part of an old German city, elsewhere a street of solid bourgeois buildings that looks French or Belgian; other areas could only, somehow, be Polish. East-West divisions suddenly seem superficial and one just feels rather proud to be European.

Everywhere there are plaques, monuments, busts and statues commemorating Polish heroes and leaders, Kings and Generals, victories and defeats. Here surely more than anywhere else in Europe except possibly Ireland everyone is constantly aware of his or her country's history, stretching back into the middle ages. In England it would no doubt be difficult to find anyone under the age of 40 with a clear idea of what happened at Alamein, or who exactly Hitler was. Is it Roman Catholics who have these long memories, or is it the peoples of countries who have constantly been the victims of bigger and more powerful neighbours?

Every third building in the Old and New Towns is a Catholic church. Inside they vary more than expected (all but one or two restored, of course but all to their pre-war conditions, to the smallest detail). Some are in the familiar tradition of ornate Catholic baroque, with soulful statues of the Virgin and gruesome depictions of the crucifixion in sado-masochistic detail. Others are surprisingly spare, white-walled, high, cool, with a definite air of the reformation about them. All have countless plaques on their walls commemorating those who have died in Poland's endless wars, revolts, occupations, partitions and uprisings. No wonder that the qualities required and apparently possessed by all Poles are irrepressible optimism in the face of irresistible evidence, courage beyond all reason, nationalist fervour which almost triumphs over mistrust of the current system and leadership, and virtual indifference to material well-being – although a surprising number seem to live remarkably comfortably considering that the economy has collapsed and the country is by any normal criterion broke.

***

We now realise that music began and ended with Chopin, despite the fact that if Frederick had been a Pole we should have had to call him "Hoppeen". The house where Chopin was born to his French parents, 50 minutes' drive from Warsaw, is a lovingly tended shrine set in beautiful gardens (like everything else, the house itself was destroyed during the war and has been restored, thick ivy and all). A big Yamaha loudspeaker (mono, evidently) over the French windows to the garden announces the weekly piano recital of the Master's music. Chopin recitals on Sundays seem part of the Polish scene: just down the road from our house in the Kazienki ("Bathroom") Park, not one but two Chopin recitals take place every Sunday at the foot of the huge Chopin memorial statue depicting the great man under giant pianist's fingers which sprout into great bronze branches and foliage arching over the composer's head. The amplified sound of the mazurkas and polonaises drifts across the Residence gardens and into the big open windows as I sit and type.

Still on music: as part of a European music festival the Malcolm Sargent Festival Choir and a choir from Philadelphia came to sing with the Orchestra and chorus of the Warsaw Wielki ('Great', as in Bolshoi) Opera Theatre. I took the German Ambassador and his wife to the first concert featuring the Beethoven Choral Symphony, and the Canadians to the second to hear the Vaughan Williams Sea Symphony. The first was conducted by Robert Satanowski, the great man of Warsaw theatre and music, an imperious maestro of the old school; he came to lunch the day after the first concert and talked enchantingly about tempi and the techniques required to master a massive chorus and orchestra. The second concert was conducted by a visiting American Conductor who did wonders to and for the Vaughan Williams. Both concerts were deliriously received and Satanowski had to repeat most of the last movement of the Choral Symphony as an encore after about 20 minutes of what the Russians call "stormy applause". But when Satanowski and the American repeated the two symphonies in the Royal Festival Hall on the day when Sarah married her Prince, with the same orchestra and choirs, they were panned something rotten in the British press. Ludicrous, of course, to attempt two such massive works in the same evening, and hardly fair to poor V-W, and no doubt they were all tired. But still.

***

Hours of every week still have to be spent on our introductory courtesy calls on the other Ambassadors and their wives, if they have them (most seem to). Each call must last a statutory hour, so with travel time to and from each Residence one is reckoning of 90 minutes or more each. Some are of course useful, enjoyable and worth-while – i.e. those on colleagues who show some interest in and knowledge of Poland, and can offer insights and advice. These include not only the obvious ones from western Europe and north America but also some from whom it is an unexpected benefit: the Moroccan Ambassador, for example, a friend of King Hassan, a fluent Polish speaker and an astute and sympathetic observer of the local scene with many excellent contacts. But most of these calls are most literally a waste of time, and an unwelcome assault on the digestive system. Sweetened orange juice is followed by fantastically strong black coffee with salty sandwiches and other knickknacks plus sweet biscuits and cakes and often hot meat pies, then cakes and other heavy desserts, with sweet pink wine from the hosts' country and then some youngish brandy from the same benighted vineyards, liable to blast off the roof of the mouth. All this at 10 in the morning or 3 in the afternoon can be pretty hard to get down, especially while struggling to express, in French, a lively interest in the agricultural policy triumphs of the People's Democratic Republic of Ruritania. Their Excellencies never take No or Non for an answer.

The worst of many grim experiences so far in this field was at a certain Asian Ambassador's and Ambassadress's Residence where we were insistently pressed to sample not just one but many globules of a delicacy from the hosts' country graphically described as "Sticky Rice", followed by bright green pancakes manufactured from dried cardboard. It took a lot of the sweet pink wine of the country in question ("we have not yet unfortunately succeeded to find an export market for our very fine wine, Your Excellency") to wash that lot down.

Still, we do get a modest Difficult Post Allowance.

***

The one ambition in life of the Residence Footman (i.e. waiter and general factotum) is to be the Residence Gardener. The Residence Gardener has been off sick since long before we arrived in May, with a broken leg – broken only once, so far as we know, but he is seen only on pay-day and crutches. The Footman's wife is the Cook, a stout, beaming (or, sometimes, scowling) peasant lady who cooks huge 4-course lunches for the rest of the Residence staff and serves up whatever is left over, tastefully arranged on large plates, for us. The Ladies' Maid is a chirpy and pretty younger woman whose small son is generally sick and therefore requires her attention. There is said to be another Maid – indeed, J. is positive that she has spotted her once or twice through the swing door into the kitchen – but she has not been in evidence during my occasional visits to the Residence so far. The Butler is a formidable figure who rules the establishment with a rod of iron, as is right and proper. He and the pretty maid speak English. The rest neither speak nor understand a solitary word of English, even after 20 years each working for British families in this residence. If one ventures such a word as "tea", "lunch" or "saucer", it meets a look of profound and quite evidently genuine bafflement. All this certainly adds an element of unpredictability to our otherwise humdrum lives: when we ask for something, we never know what we shall get.

One might have thought such a comparatively large staff quite big enough to cope with fair-sized lunches, dinners, drinks parties, and so on. Not a bit of it. Their conditions of service, established over many years according to the ratchet principle, require them to work only very limited hours each day, so that even the most casual bit of extra entertaining demands the hire of several extra servants, together with special extra bonus payments for our own regular staff. If the going gets too tough for Mrs T. in Britain, perhaps she ought to do a stint in Poland.

None of this is meant to be a lament about the Servant Problem, never one to bring a tear to the eyes of the casual reader, in one's own experience anyway. But it casts a little light here and there, perhaps.

***

Introductory courtesy calls on Polish Ministers, party functionaries, officials, academics, etc., are (happily) much more enlightening and worthwhile than those on the Dear Colleagues, or Chers Collègues, as we fluently call each other, of the Diplomatic Corps. Coffee or tea and a soft drink and biscuits are provided, and welcome, and one is hardly through the door and the preliminary courtesies before being plunged into the most demanding debate on the nature of the modern state, the distinguishing marks of a representative democracy, the effects on modern Poland of national traumas in the fifteenth century, and – for the first grueling weeks – Scotland's prospects in the World Cup. Apart from this last, it has all been rather reminiscent of the Cambridge University Labour Club in the mid-50s, except that the political positions articulated by the senior leaders of this marxist-leninist state have in general been more moderate and middle-of-the-road than those I remember by the Cam three decades ago. But then, as the old hands here say when some new paradox comes to light, "only in Poland …."

***

Visitors from Britain so far whom we have provided with accommodation, food or drink, or a combination of the three, include Tony Benn and the Archdeacon of London (not, perhaps fortunately, at the same time). Both proved in their rather different ways excellent company. Both also proved difficult discussion partners because of the impossibility of questioning their basic underlying premises without risk of seeming discourteous in a manner unbecoming in either a civil servant or a host or hostess. This imposed the faintly irksome obligation of listening without expression, even with every appearance of assent, to a fair old load of rubbish (I am not of course revealing which of the two visitors in question I have in mind). Such is the duty of the diplomat, or anyway one of them.

A feature of these two particular visitors was that one enjoyed generous quantities of gin and tonic, cognac, etc., fat cigars and red meat; the other was teetotal, pipe-smoking only and vegetarian, although without being at all aggressive about it. Now in the stereotypes, politicians eat and drink like pigs/fish, while priests are austerely self-denying in the matter of the pleasures of the flesh. No prizes are offered for sticking the right tail on the right donkey.

*   *   *

In writing these four pages, I have had to look up the spelling – or at any rate check it, since I was in fact right both times – of two words. I must really be getting senile, as long alleged by my spouse. A modest prize – perhaps an invitation to the Ruritanian Ambassador's National Day reception – to the first reader to identify the two words in question.

Right: The British ambassador's residence, Warsaw late 1980s.

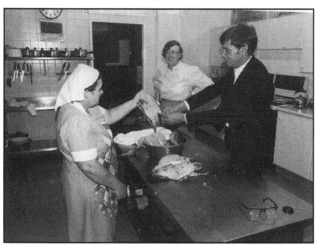

Left: Eugenia, Jane & Kazimierz in the Warsaw residence kitchen.

Left: Father Henryk Jankowski, Lech Wałęsa's priest; Barder; Lech Wałęsa; Nigel Thorpe; Gdansk, late 1980s.

Top: Barder inspecting a guard of honour in Warsaw.

Left: Barder laying a wreath at the Tomb of the Unknown Soldier, Warsaw.

Bottom: Louise, Owen, Jane, Lee, Ian, Virginia; Warsaw, New Year's Eve 1986.

CHAPTER 30

AUG-DEC 1986: MAZURIAN LAKES, KRAKOW, WARSAW, LUBLIN, MAJDANEK

10 August, 1986.   A few days' holiday at the Mazurian lakes, to a hotel geared to foreigners, enjoying something of a local reputation for la dolce vita (Polish-style). Little knowing what to expect, we find something out of an American motel crossed with an up-market Butlins – bars and disco, queues for lunch and dinner, small indoor swimming-pool. Children play shrilly on the defeated grass between the hotel bed-room spurs while their parents sit round small tables drinking beer and playing cards. Most of the guests are Polish, equipped with chic leisure clothes and expensive western cars. Most of the rest are German (GDR and FRG) evidently at home in the German atmosphere of former East Prussia. The hotel staff all speak German but shake their heads impatiently at the sound of English.

Down the hill from the hotel, an agreeable lake, perhaps a mile long and half a mile wide, the rustic view only slightly marred by factory chimneys on the far side projecting dark exclamation marks of smoke into the sky. My morning run round the lake shore followed by a brief swim in the green water of the lake is watched with electrified but on the whole approving attention by elderly Polish and German holiday-making couples out for their early morning constitutionals. They offer encouragement in incomprehensible German.

Touring the lake area in the Escort, we find an agreeable little resort town on another lake, yachts rocking lazily at a small marina, young people in shorts or swimming-trunks and T-shirts strolling the streets and eating ice-creams, cream cakes, hot dogs and bags of chips. We sit at a table outside a small café which dispenses large steaks of lake fish, species unidentified but tasty and substantial; we pay a 100-złoty (33p.) deposit on the paper plate and tin fork, refundable on return of the latter. Unfortunately we have not succeeded in identifying the vendor of the chips, to go with the fish.

At Swieta Lipna, a little village further north, we find a famous and splendid baroque church with the most magnificent organ. Luckily the organist happens to be playing a Bach organ voluntary when we arrive, making the marble pillars shudder. As he plays, gilt angels and cherubs encrusting the organ pipes nod and bow, raising their trumpets and swinging them like an American dance band, and a grave Virgin presiding over the jerkily performing ensemble slowly nods her approval.

Huge blocks of concrete, dynamited into precarious slabs at improbable angles half-buried in the undergrowth, are all that remains of Hitler's Bunker, an hour-and-a-half's drive from the hotel. It is a German-speaking tourist attraction, thronged with a few Polish and numerous East and West German sightseers, agreeably unabashed. From here Hitler, Bormann, Goering, Goebbels and the Generals directed the attack on the Soviet Union; here Count von Stauffenberg made his mad brave attempt on Hitler's life. Now the creeper and foliage do their best to soften the harsh jagged relics of Nazi power. It is an ugly place, best left as it is, a surrealist ruin.

*   *   *   *   *

24 – 27 August.   Krakow.   The Old Market Square is as beautiful as expected, a European jewel, inducing the same sense of European identity as (say) visiting the National Museum in Washington DC and finding there, an ocean from their roots, all those priceless art treasures of our savage old continent's heritage. Many of the more gem-like, smaller and less pretentious buildings are literally crumbling away, poisoned and sapped by the acid smoke from the nearby Nowa Huta steel works (located near Krakow, some say, to dilute that effete old European cultural air with some good, honest proletarian smoke). Sides of whole narrow old streets are blocked by rough timber props supporting sagging walls. Restoration proceeds here and there but the impression is of a race against time which is already recognised as lost.

After these melancholy first impressions, a visit to the magnificent Wawel Castle is a tonic, everything lovingly preserved, indeed in apparently mint condition.

Here in Krakow we set the pattern for what are to become many corresponding visits to Polish cities: calls on such local bigwigs as the First Secretary of the local Party organization; the Voivod or Prefect, appointed by central government as its chief local representative; the Mayor or President of the town, if not the same person as the Voivod; sometimes the local head of PRON, the Patriotic Movement for National Rebirth, as much a turn-off for the majority of Poles as the name implies; the local bishop or Archbishop or – as in Krakow – Cardinal, in this case a charming, austere, multilingual polymath, picking his way fastidiously but unerringly through the religious and political minefields of Polish life; often local newspaper editors and writers, among them in the case of Krakow one of the bravest and most sturdily independent leaders of opinion in Poland, the twinkling donnish Jerzy Turowicz and his delightful wife, who come to dinner with us at what's reputedly the best restaurant in Poland, just off the Krakow Old Market Square.

At the Francuski Hotel, at the far end of the Old Market Square, our bedroom window overlooks a fine C.XVIII church from which there rings out a pure, deeply-felt mezzo-soprano voice soaring over a hushed choir. Magic.

*   *   *   *   *

What a perk to be paid to go to Gdansk, the old sea-port, between the world wars called Danzig – evocative name! The Old Town, painstakingly restored after the war (it was almost completely destroyed by a great fire in 1944), is glorious – more like a Hanseatic town, German or Swedish inspiration rather than Polish, a genuine pleasure to walk (or jog) through, even in the drizzle which fell during most of our time there. The familiar Ship-yard Workers' Monument erected during the

Solidarity period in 1980 in memory of those killed in the 1970 uprising stands like a raised admonitory finger outside the gates of the Lenin Shipyards where Lech Wałensa toiled and made speeches and negotiated and coaxed and threatened in those manic heady days of 1980/81.

Just along the coast is the sea-side resort of Sopot, its charms as a holiday centre rather diminished by the frightful pollution of the sea which makes it dangerous even to paddle, still more to swim. Right on the beach stands a marvelous pre-war hotel, the Grand Hotel, in the style of the 1920s, just as one imagines the Grand Hotel at Cabourg in Proust; now rather run down and needing a lick of paint, but still a lovely period piece, the Gentlemen's loo still boasting immaculate English porcelain. Further along again is the other sea-port and holiday resort of Gdynia, built as a Polish port when Danzig was a Free City, with a nice statue of the Polish-born novelist Joseph Conrad on the sea front.

On the way back to Warsaw we stopped for lunch at a "Zajazd", a roadside restaurant, where we had an excellent and not very expensive lunch. We all (our Polish driver, Jerzy – always "George" – and the two of us) ate the same food and the next two days J. spent in bed with acute food poisoning while George and I were as right as rain.

* * * * *

6 September.   The Terry Fox Run, organised by the Canadians in a pleasant wood by the river just outside Warsaw to raise money for cancer research in memory of the brave Canadian runner. Half of the British Embassy seems to be there in everything from jogging shorts to tracksuits and jeans, plus a fair turn-out of Canadians, an American or two and some Germans. My Head of Chancery, lithe and fit, flashes round the 10-kilometer course in no time, ahead of virtually all the competition. My Assistant Military Attaché and I settle together into a fairly comfortable trot and finish together, miles ahead of the bright young things from my Chancery and Commercial Section, who stagger in much later puffed and speechless. "Appearances can be deceptive!" – portly middle-aged gent in shorts.

* * * * *

28 September.   The 'Wielki' ('Great', or 'Bolshoi') Theatre for Verdi's 'Aida'. The singing is distinctly shaky in places but the production, costumes and sets are sensational. A perfectly plausible Nile flows across the stage, with nubile and scantily-clad nymphets bathing prettily in it. Whole sections of the massive set rise majestically half-way to the flies with the entire chorus wobbling precariously on its various surfaces; other sections descend funereally into what must be an immense pit below stage, carrying much of the cast with them. Monumental buildings revolve, slide out or sink from sight. A massive wall descends from the flies and proves to contain in its forward surface 72 members of the chorus, each inside a gilt mummy-case, stacked in rows 9 long and 8 high, all singing their hearts out. Perhaps they are all working away during the day on some tractor assembly plant, and merely moonlighting as melodious mummies. Alternatively, and more likely, they are full-time opera singers whose nearest approach to manual work is giving an occasional hand with the sets. But enough of these philistine reflections.

*   *   *   *   *

Sunday, 16 November.   The night the Scottish Theatre Company came to supper. After their 3 performances of "Ane Satyre of The Thrie Estaites" at a Warsaw theatre, the opening plays at this year's Warsaw International Drama Festival, and incidentally the first performances ever given outside Scotland of this medieval classic, the whole company, band, directors, managers and a cross-section of the Polish theatrical elite come back to the Residence for a stand-up buffet supper – 167 people all told. As most of the Scottish visitors have had nothing to eat (or drink) all day, they certainly do justice to the fare provided, solid and liquid. Most venerable of the actors is Andrew Cruickshank of Dr Finlay's Casebook fame, and a kind and courteous old gentleman he turns out to be. Once again that odd feeling on meeting someone whom one has never met before but whose face and appearance and manner and style are so wholly familiar from television of the cinema.

The Countess of Strathmore, one of the Governors of the Scottish Theatre Company, a fund-raiser and patron of the Warsaw tour, who is staying with us during the Company's visit to Poland, and ourselves stick it out until the last kilted Scottish actor youth weaves his way out into the courtyard to go back to the hotel, and we collapse into bed at about 3 a.m. To remember the visit by, we have a nice engraved crystal vase and an invitation to Glamis Castle.

* * * * *

30 – 31 December. Warsaw, Lublin, Majdanek and Krakaow: On the Sunday our two daughters and son (understandably resistant these days to being called our "children"), plus two of their friends also visiting us for Christmas, cram themselves into our Escort and drive along the icy roads to Lublin and on to the old Nazi concentration camp at Majdanek, second worst in Poland after Auschwitz. It snows harder and harder and by the time they are at the bleak, windswept camp sites they are tramping round the gruesome huts with their pitiful displays in a blizzard, leaning into the wind to get up and across to the crematoria and the fatal shower block. The snow is too heavy to allow them to return via the pretty riverside town of Kazimierz and they return to the house frozen spiritually as much as physically.

It's hardly any better on the next day when we all seven get up at 4.45 a.m. to catch a 6.20 train to Krakow. The platform at Warsaw Central is bright with gaudily-clothed skiers taking the same train, which goes on beyond Krakow to Zakopane, the mountain ski resort near the Czechoslovakian border. In Krakow it is snowing hard but the temperature is barely at freezing and the accumulated snow is already being trodden into black water and grey slush, in puddles several inches deep. The whole of the Old Market Square is flooded with wet slush. Shoes and boots rapidly fill with icy water. The sleet blows into eyes, mouths and noses, turning spectacles into twin white discs. At the top of the Wawel Castle and Cathedral hill (castle and cathedral closed – it's Monday) the wind blows off the fields of half-frozen snow down below and pistol-whips the exposed face. Soon it starts raining hard, sending great slabs of wet snow crashing onto the pavements from church roofs.

The 7.30 p.m. train back to Warsaw is already full of damp, tired skiers. Having as usual arrived back at Krakow station about an hour and a half too early ("just in case we get lost on the way back") we have been forced to shelter in the only warmish indoor building available in the whole station complex, the ticket office.

O. and I go off to search the food stalls along the platforms for sustenance, returning in triumph with what look at first sight exactly like the familiar triangular Toblerone chocolate bars in yellow-and-red wrappers. But on closer inspection these prove to be quite different, claiming in fact to be neither Toblerone nor even chocolate, although with a tentative suggestion (certainly contrary to the UK Trade Descriptions Act) of a connexion with nougat. The substance inside the packages, brownish-grey and soft, tastes, according to V., like 'warm dirty snow'. Some of us console ourselves by covertly admiring another passenger waiting in the ticket office, a young woman skier in short coat and jeans who has what appear to be the longest legs on record, making the rest of her actually appear fore-shortened.

*   *   *   *   *

31 December.   The British Embassy Country Club, Warsaw: we see the New Year in at the Country Club Dinner Dance (black tie if possible, otherwise bow tie of some kind for men). A lively and expensively amplified Polish dance band plays throughout the cold meat assortment, Chateaubriand steaks and ice cream flambé with the oldest and youngest age groups dancing cheerfully between courses. The waiting time before midnight is usefully occupied by the floor-show. A tall man in a silver suit throws a small woman in diminutive black knickers about and swings her round and round by her feet. A man juggles with burning torches, their flames brushing and agitating the paper streamers and tinsel sello-taped to the wooden ceiling (everyone suddenly notices that there is no fire exit from the crowded room). A tall dark rather beautiful sadistic-looking lady conjuror in a tight blue dress cuts up ropes and reassembles them seamlessly, smiling with cruel triumph as if about to use them for a particularly vicious form of bondage. Two men, one inexplicably wearing a moustache and a green dress, emit piercing whistles from their mouths, gesticulating unintelligibly to enthusiastic applause. At last, amid traditional celebratory rituals and to the accompaniment of semi-sweet Bulgarian champagne, it is 1987.

CHAPTER 31

SEP 1987: WARSAW

Letter to Owen, 27 September 1987

Your letters are as good as ever. Don't stop. I might yet publish them and get rich quick. The post-cards create a bit of a stir when people notice them on my desk or in the Residence, picture up, with Herself or Fergie and Prince Thing staring out. We can see people thinking: "Funny, wouldn't have thought that was their cup of tea ...."

[...]

It's Sunday evening, and I've finished the first easy-flowing VM on the rocks, and the mignons morceaux are beginning to run out (more commissioned from George and Jane Sutton, due in tomorrow week). David Ratford, the Under-Secretary in the FCO responsible for Europe (my God, who'd be responsible for Europe?) and an old friend from Moscow days – remember Karin and Louise? – who arrived on Friday evening has gone off to watch the Mass for the Fatherland (it being the last Sunday of the month) at St Stanisław Kostka Church, the Solidarity Church in Zoliborz, with Ralph Griffiths and will then be going back to Ralph and Pam's for dinner before returning late to the Residence.

We got back an hour or so ago from a day out with D.R. in the Jaguar, George dumbly mutinous at having to turn out on a Sunday – but we went to Zelazowa Wola, Chopin's birth-place, and to various places in the Campinos Forest, and to Chopin's family church where he was baptised, and were received at the Chopin shrine like visiting royalty, so decided to do it in style (after all, D. R. is an official visitor, no?). A very young pianist indeed, looking about 17, played an hour of Chopin on a tinny Yamaha boudoir grand with immense zest and panache, blowing on his fingers between polonaises to stop them freezing solid (it's got steadily colder through the day). It was good stuff.

We've been doing a lot of concerts lately, all over your Mama's dead body, in the course of the Warsaw Autumn (contemporary music) festival, mostly with sundry recent house-guests. It's involved a fair share of shrieks and bangs and discordant squeals, with large mezzo-sopranos wailing to "Ah", but also some exciting and vigorous things between whiles. After one of them, given by an English group called the Lontano Ensemble (conducted by a tiny Cuban American lady with enormous horn-rimmed spectacles), John Booth from the British Council, M's favourite chap in Warsaw apart from Jan Kluk the Computer, gave a drinks party in a room below the concert hall, at which the first guest to arrive was none other than Lutosławski in person, grand old man of Polish music and much revered. We talked a bit to him and he was very nice indeed but what does one say when Beethoven is introduced to one – or rather, say, Rismky Korsakov or Delius? ("Gosh, wow, it's **really great** to meet you, I mean that fantastic music, well we don't understand it but I mean you're so **famous**, right?" seems not quite appropriate.) Last night at a concert given by the BBC Scottish Symphony Orchestra they played a piece by Lutosławski who was in the audience and went up on the platform afterwards to thunder and lightning of applause; he looked terribly pleased. So did the Scottish S.O.'s conductor, Maksymiuk, a Pole who is rarely in Poland now but still a great favourite with Polish audiences when he appears. Even the Hallé Orchestra the other night (not performing in the Warsaw Autumn but playing proper music, thank goodness) was conducted by its own principal conductor who's also Polish and who had conducted only once previously in Poland for the last 20 years. More audience rapture.

This begins to sound as though it's been just one unrelieved round of concerts and indeed I think M. feels it has been. In fact we had a pretty solid 5 or 6 days with the Speaker and his party, immediately followed by the head of Overseas Estates Dept. from the FCO who stayed with us for another 4 days, immediately followed by D.R. who will be immediately followed by the Suttons who will be immediately followed by the British Ambassadors from E. Berlin and Budapest and their wives who will be immediately followed by the Suttons (back again from the Grand Tour) who will be immediately followed by Lord Bonham-Carter (already sending us lists of people to invite to our dinner for him) who will be immediately followed by the Head of the (British) Diplomatic Service, my Permanent Under-Secretary, and his wife.

The strain of all this is already telling on Kazimierz who keeps Irenka, Malgosia and Eh-oo-GAYNya in floods of tears all day while sharing out the lucrative extra duties between himself and Perfect Basia. Kazimierz and Mrs W. aren't speaking to each other. M. is exhausted by endless mediation and constantly having to shout at Kazimierz not to shout at Irenka. I come back from the latest round of official talks with the current house-guest to find the whole household red-eyed and mad with despair. It's all great fun really. When I go for a moment or two every 5 or 6 days into the Embassy I can't see over my IN tray and it takes an hour to wade through all the invitations to National Day receptions, dinners, lunches, etc.

CHAPTER 32

JAN 1988:
WARSAW

(From New Year round-robin letter)

24 January 1988.   c/o FCO (Warsaw), King Charles Street, LONDON SW1A 2AH.

There never seems to be time to write proper – or even improper – messages to go with the Christmas cards. And anyway it's quite nice to write back after getting the latest news from other people's Christmas card messages.

1987 was our first complete year in Poland – if one can call it that after 2 ½ months at home in the spring. And now it looks as if it will be our last, with another move coming up, much earlier than we'd expected. Lips are still tiresomely sealed to protect the details. We have mixed feelings. Certainly we shall miss the Poles with their high spirits, so argumentative and lively, fizzing with conspiracies and denunciations. But the extreme Polocentrism we might miss a little less, the central European tunnel vision and self-absorption. It must be a function of having had a tragic doomy history and knowing that one is condemned to a tragic doomy future.

Another feature that we shall look back on with qualified retrospective rapture is the never-ending stream of official visitors, mostly staying with us, interesting and agreeable individually, but inevitably limiting the scope for private life. I have especially warm memories of the visits by the Speaker of the House of Commons and his wife, and by Bob Burchfield, the Editor of the Oxford English Dictionary – and some others, too; it's been very worth-while to meet and get to know these and several others. But a complete week-end to ourselves has become a treasured rarity.

The flow of official visitors has also made it difficult to squeeze in time for visits by our own family and friends, which we value beyond price – indeed, without them life like this overseas would be insupportable. So we have treasured all these visits by old friends who have braved the rigours of Polish visa procedures, currency forms and restrictions, and the astonishing fantasy world of Polish car hire, to spend time with us in Warsaw and see a bit of Poland.

Above all we have been unusually lucky in having had several visits by all the children, alone or in varying combinations and sometimes with friends of theirs too. It's been striking how each of them has found something quite different about their time in Poland to savour and remember. In the depths of the last frightful winter, in temperatures of around -20C and in driving snow and sleet, they all (with 2 friends) took our Escort down to Majdanek, the grim former Nazi concentration camp on the outskirts of Lublin, and toured that terrible place in the blizzard. At least one of them didn't sleep for weeks afterwards. Another, after also visiting Auschwitz and Birkenau, has become interested to the verge of obsession in the whole gruesome history of the camps, the human extermination industry – "Holocaust" has become a cliché term concealing rather than flood-lighting the reality.

It's hard to spend any length of time here without becoming a bit preoccupied with the camps – those resonant names, Auschwitz, Birkenau, Majdanek, Sobibor, Treblinka – and what was done in them by our fellow-Europeans, people of the same culture as ours, our contemporaries, compatriots of Mozart, Beethoven and Goethe. It seems inescapable that if those people committed, in whatever circumstances, such nightmarish acts, turning horrors into routine, then each of us must be capable of them too. I don't know how to come to terms with that.

Some of those who have been to stay with us have refused to subject themselves to visiting any of the camps, on the grounds either that they would not expect to be able to stomach the experience, or else that they see the conversion of such places into tourist attractions as a monstrous perversion, a masochistic self-indulgence. Such views clearly deserve respect. But it would be an even greater blasphemy, I think, to let these things be forgotten, or gentrified into something nasty that happened in history, like burning witches: nothing to do with us. Living in Poland where the worst of it actually happened, only a few years ago, in daily contact with the people who were among its main victims, one sees it as a central fact about our century, which we have to face in order to grasp something fundamental about the human condition. And visiting the camps seems an indispensable part of that.

Apologies for these gloomy thoughts, inappropriate to a newsy round-up for the New Year. It must be the mild, grey winter: the first snow is only now falling, incredibly late by Polish standards. Despite the hassle of the long months of snow – the changing from boots to shoes and back again, the scarves and gloves and hats, the dirty slush, scraping the windscreen, frozen windscreen washers, slippery pavements – it actually comes as a sort of relief when the snow at last arrives, like a delayed sneeze. And it certainly helps you to appreciate spring.

The adult progeny keep busy: Virginia an Inter-active Video producer, taking film crews off to exotic locations to make computerized user-directable training and information programmes; Louise at Novello, the music publishers, as Editorial Assistant on the Musical Times, the oldest music magazine in the world; and Owen, having completed a hectic year as Steward (President) of the New College JCR, in his last year at Oxford and on the run-up to Finals. They're all, though I say it as shouldn't, extremely good company.

We'll let you know where we're going next, and when, as soon as we can. Meanwhile do keep in touch.

Top: Invitation to the Queen's Garden Party at
Buckingham Palace, July 1988.

Bottom: Virginia, Brian, Louise & Jane, ready for the
Queen's Garden Party, July 1988.

PART VI:

NIGERIA,
LATE 1980S

CHAPTER 33

NEW YEAR'S DAY 1989: LAGOS

(From New Year round-robin letter)

1 January 1989.   Lagos, Nigeria

This is the sort of letter that should have gone out with our Christmas cards. This year – or rather last year – the process of settling in at Lagos, interrupted by the need to return to London to complete various bits of unfinished business for 7 weeks after only 9 weeks in Nigeria, seems to have soaked up all our spare time and it's only now, in the long New Year week-end, that I've got around to booting up and getting something down.

Nigeria after Poland was a sharp contrast, verging on culture-shock. We had mixed feelings about leaving Warsaw before Mrs Thatcher's visit, instead of leaving just after it as originally envisaged (the visit was postponed to avoid a clash with the Reagan-Gorbachev Moscow summit): and, ironically enough, we came to Lagos only a few months after Mrs Thatcher's visit in January to Nigeria, missing out on the experience, for better or worse, here too. Partly as a result of that visit, Britain's relations with Nigeria, often turbulent, are currently on a bit of a high – not necessarily the best moment for a new High Commissioner to set up shop, since there's only one way things can go from a peak, and guess who will carry the can soon after the start of the great descent? But for the time being all is sweetness and light, and that certainly smoothes the way for making all the necessary initial contacts.

One major difference (apart from the more obvious ones) between this and our other recent posts is the special role played here by any British High Commissioner, simply because he is the British High Commissioner – treated almost everywhere as the senior diplomat, even if he's in fact the most recently arrived and hence the most junior of the whole diplomatic corps. It's hard, often, to believe that British colonial rule ended almost 30 years ago, long before the majority of Nigerians now alive were born. Nigerians have a special feeling, though an ambiguous one, about Britain – a mixture of familiarity, affection, exasperation, and impossibly high expectations which modulate imperceptibly into bitter disappointment. This is not a recipe for a quiet or easy life, but it certainly seems to make for an interesting one. "Never had a dull moment" my various predecessors all say, with the merest hint of menace.

The minus factors are all the obvious ones: a trying and unhealthy climate, an economy in recession and decline with most public services unreliable or defunct, poor local medical services and facilities, corruption tainting every area of life, and extensive violence on all sides – attacks by gangs of armed robbers on houses at night, hi-jacking of cars in broad daylight or darkness alike (with or without the murder of the occupants), incredibly gruesome road accidents a daily occurrence, all apparent indicators of a society in a process of disintegration.

The other, happier side of the coin is warm (and how!) and generally sunny days and mellow nights, palm trees waving idly over glittering swimming-pools beyond shady patios, the bracing nip of roaring air-conditioners, magnificent beaches, a colourful, volatile, exuberant people, quick to laughter; teeming open-air markets, a spicy, lively, irresponsible press; good fruit, Pimms always in season. We could certainly do a lot worse.

We spent a flavoury Christmas with our old friends Emeka and Bunmi Anyaoku at Emeka's family home in Obosi, near Onitsha in eastern Nigeria, exchanging Ibo greetings with local bigwigs and smallwigs, ranging from the Anyaoku family retainers to the local Ruler and his court, and the Foreign Minister and his wife who motored over from their home village for lunch (accompanied by a modest retinue of about 40 people), followed by a splendid Masquerade which combined Petrushka with harlequinade and a dash of Nijinsky. It all seemed a planet away from Melrose Road, SW18.

Virginia, still a flourishing Inter-Active Video programme producer, spent Christmas with us at Lagos and Obosi, soaking up sun to see her through the rest of the British winter. Louise has moved from her old job as Editorial Assistant on "Musical Times" to being a sub-editor on "Radio Times" and is now therefore a BBC-person (the move not at all connected with her having got engaged to the Editor of "Musical Times", Eric Wen, with the wedding due in June). Despite a lot of hectic extra-mural activity throughout his 3 years at Oxford, Owen came down from New College with a First in Politics, Philosophy and Economics and is now working for the Treasury as an economist – a situation which forces me to reconsider my long-standing view that a necessary condition for a durable improvement in the British economy is dynamiting the Treasury and sowing Great George Street with salt.

Next week we are off on tour in the north, making our initial calls on Emirs and Sultans, Military Governors and businessmen, ancient British nuns and beardless VSOs. It should give us a flavor of another Nigeria altogether. We shall return (Range Rovers, Nigeria Airways and armed robbers permitting) in time for a visit by the Duke of Edinburgh and another by H M S Bristol, a conference of British Community Liaison Officers from all over Nigeria, various Foreign Office luminaries on familiarization visits, and the preparations for the State Visit in May by President and Mrs Babangida to London (at which those jogging in St James's Park may, if they're quick, spot us both languidly doing the royal wave from Landau No. 8 in the procession along the Mall)….. Of this, as they say, more anon.

CHAPTER 34

MARCH–NOV 1989: WESTERN & EASTERN STATES, LAGOS

25 March 1989.   J. and I had a rather grueling tour of the western States (Oyo, Ogun and western Lagos State) which involved a lot of calls on extremely self-important Traditional Rulers in their corrugated-iron 'palaces', exchanging tatty (or otherwise) presents and trying to remember their fantastic titles. Luckily "Your Royal Highness" seems universally acceptable, whatever the sonorous and polysyllabic title. Several laid on elaborate displays of dancing, acrobatics, fire-eating, speeches, etc., in our honour, making it difficult to confine the call in question to the 45 minutes laid down in the programme. One wild-eyed man in pantomime costume came right up to J. as we sat in our ancient arm-chairs under the buting-clad awning on each side of the Royal Highness, and cut off the end of his tongue with a rusty knife. J. went green. Actually I think it was a trick, but it seemed like the real thing at the time.

One slightly disconcerting feature of these tours is that the local and national press and television seem to regard my every move and call, and every polite if asinine remark, as tremendously newsworthy. There were photographs in the national dailies for days after we were back in Lagos of me shaking hands and grinning madly at some local dignitary in Abeokuta or Badagry. My diplomatic colleagues are all a bit bemused at seeing me day after day featured in the media doing nothing very much.

Later: just broke off for egg-and-bacon lunch. Sat outside on the patio afterwards with J. with a cup of coffee. Fantastically hot: soon driven back inside. Now is the hottest time, between the Sahara dust of the harmattan which cools the sun's glare and the rains which start any time now, making it even more humid but marginally less like a furnace. Now back upstairs in the air-conditioning of the tiny study, with Herself on the BBC World Service ruminating about Africa before setting off on her tour, to include a couple of hours of talks and lunch at the airport with the President and his senior Ministers. The UK side is to comprise Mr and Mrs T., Charles Powell and me. It was not all that easy to convince the Nigerians that this represented a wholly serious effort on Britain's part: not even the Foreign Secretary?

2 April 1989

- our 31st wedding anniversary ….

Phew. Just coming up for air after not one but two visits to Lagos by Mrs T – mercifully both only stop-overs, but the first (last Tuesday, 28th) pretty concentrated. She was on the ground for only 90 minutes but it must have involved a good 90 man-hours of preparation for a working lunch given by President Babangida at the airport, with private talks before and afterwards and a mini-press conference, plus inspection of guard of honour, 19-gun salute, bouquets presented by bashful moppets, and British press swarming blasphemously all over the place from the RAF VC 10 demanding International Direct Dialling, Scotch, type-writers, gin, computer terminals with Modems, vodka, a private room each, brandy, shorthand secretaries, beer and AIDS-free girls. These last (the press, not the AIDS-free girls) gave us much more aggro than Mrs T, Denis, her Private Secretary Charles Powell and the well-known activist and press secretary Bernard Ingham combined.

Then on Friday we heard that they were all coming back to re-fuel again en route between Windhoek (Namibia) and Heathrow, arriving at 0040 on Sunday morning and leaving at 3.10…. Happily the guidance was that most of them would want to sleep through the stop and didn't want to be disturbed or to have to disembark to be greeted by big-wigs. This proved almost as difficult to arrange as the high-profile greetings and meetings on Tuesday had been. Nigerian Protocol and bigwiggery were deeply suspicious of the suggestion that no-one needed to go out to meet Herself, who indeed would be asleep. Perhaps the First Lady, Mrs Babangida, should be there? The Military Governor of Lagos State? (What did the trick in the end was my firm undertaking not to go out to the airport myself.) All went smoothly and the bigwigs stayed away.

The "working lunch" on Tuesday was quite an interesting occasion, with only 4 on the British side (Mrs T., Denis T., Charles Powell, and me) and 6 Nigerians – the President and Foreign Minister, 2 other Ministers, the Secretary to the Government and the Governor of Lagos State. As you can imagine, merry jests flew to and fro with a will. Since the President and one of the Ministers are Muslims, nothing stronger than orange juice was provided (not that I would have risked spirituous liquor even if available), suggesting ribald commentaries in "Dear Bill". Denis, whom I'd never met before, turned out very good value, friendly and funny. We all parted with extensive lookings forward to seeing each other again in London in May at the State Visit.

All this, plus the State Visit preparations, plus quite a lot of touring and official visiting outside Lagos of Emirs, Obas, Princes, Alaafins and Oonis, State Governors, Editors and tycoons, has left precious little time for writing letters or even paying bills, reading newspapers or having the odd dip in our lusciously luke-warm pool. Hence this long silence. Things have been made even worse by both my No. 2 and my No. 3 being away. The bright young men have been having their head, rather a worry for grey old me trying to rein them in.

Now the State Visit looms up ahead with all its ceremonial terrors – an endless vista of hasty changes of costume, from morning dress to lounge suit to white tie and tails and back to morning dress with hardly a pause for pyjamas in between. Jane and I stay at the Carlton Hotel, right by Buckingham Palace, throughout the Visit itself (9 – 12 May), although I think I shall need a place in the Palace itself to change in on several occasions. I fear that our jeering children, armed with incriminating cameras, will be lining the Mall for the carriage procession on the first day from Victoria Station to the Palace to record for all time the humiliating spectacle of us in open carriages, self in fancy dress, black top hat and all, limply doing the Royal Wave. Jane gets back for all this jollification on 23 April, I on the 29th, for last-minute kitting-out, briefings, rehearsals, memorizing of lines, dieting, fasting and prayer. After it's all over either I shall be compulsorily retired from the Service, or else we shall stay on for a few weeks' leave, until about 10 July – a prolonged convalescence.

Accompanying President and Mrs Babangida of Nigeria during their state visit, May 1989

The visit of the Duke of Edinburgh in February was, compared with all these other activities, a piece of mildly alarming cake, although hard enough on the nerves at the time. Not the least of its terrors was being aboard the HS-146 of the Queen's Flight while the Duke, only a year off 70, piloted it with immense assurance into obscure air-fields through dense Harmattan dust, presumably in happy ignorance of the fact that none of the landing aids in Nigerian airports actually works. Taking off with HRH at the controls was a fairly adventurous experience, too. The RAF crew seemed quite relaxed about it all, no doubt from fatalism born of long experience, and I generally managed to get the finger-nails out of the palms of my hands without too much agony after each hop. In fact, of course, one has to admit that he flew the thing with conscientious care and no doubt justifiable confidence.

Jane survived our big dinner for the Duke with flying colours and a signed photograph, despite some pretty frosty exchanges across our dining-room table between the royal Personage and a fairly senior and extremely obstinate diplomat who hadn't heard about tactical retreats. When I got up to make a few welcoming remarks and disclaimed any intention of making a formal speech, our guest of honour invited me, fairly loudly, in that case to sit down and shut up, but being increasingly deaf these days I was lucky enough not to hear this advice and ploughed remorselessly on. He didn't seem to mind. I suppose even listening to me was less irritating to him than continuing to argue with the obstinate diplomat.

26 August 1989.   I'm writing this partly as a way of putting off the evil hour when I must get down to helping J. fill in endless and complicated forms for the Inspectors about every aspect of our expenditure since we arrived in Lagos more than a year ago. I find this difficult because I don't know the answers to any of the questions. It's also an exceptionally boring way of spending a precious weekend, the first for ages in which we have had no drinks parties, dinners, lunches, weddings or funerals that we have to go to. Luckily it's raining cats and dogs so we needn't feel guilty for not having gone to the beach / golf course /yacht club / High Commission club / slums along the creek. Instead we have been putting off getting down to the chore of form-filling for the inspectors by going along to the staff compound where the Residence staff live to see how the cook, Bartholemew, is getting on after smashing his leg in a motor-bike accident a few weeks ago and having an 18-inch steel pin inserted in his thigh in a squalid hospital in Cotonou; and inspecting the 5-week-old baby of my driver, Casmir.

J. and I spent all of last week and most of the last 2 week-ends touring eastern Nigeria, including much of the area that was Biafra – lots of formal calls, speeches, exchanges of gifts, and deeply unappetising meals, but also plenty of friendly and often impressive people to meet. Much of the time we were escorted by police cars with flashing lights and howling sirens, government protocol cars with protocol officials leaning out of the windows trying to bash passers-by with truncheons, press cars and assorted hangers-on – 12 vehicles in the convoy on at least one occasion. At the University of Nigeria at Nsukka we called on Chinua Achebe, the novelist ('Things Fall Apart' and a splendid recent book, 'Anthills of the Savannah') and had a long talk – and quite a lot of beer – with him. I have created rather a stir by being reported, quite wrongly, in the press as having told the Onitsha Chamber of Commerce that British investors wouldn't invest in Nigeria because of 'political instability'. I handed over hundreds of books to a poly and listened to the whinges of expatriate Brits, applauded crouching traditional dancers and broke the kola-nut with a sinister multi-millionaire politician while clad (both of us) in a sort of decorative Ibo silk-lined mini-dress covered in pictures of the heads of cocker-spaniels (J. was taken off by 3 strong-armed [women], stripped and dressed up in a stunningly vulgar but actually rather sexy number with puffed tulle shoulders and an extremely tight bodice with a long tight skirt in which she couldn't either walk or sit). What we do for our country. Anyway, it was better than working 11-hour days in Lagos.

30 September 1989. Interesting, what you say about your reluctance to tackle work that looks difficult or tedious, and the resulting mountainous backlog. I have just the same hang-up. I have partly overcome it by remembering advice given to me by my first ever Assistant Secretary, the Head of West African Department in the Colonial Office, during my first week in that establishment in 1957. "Brian," he said – he looked a bit like Captain Mainwaring in Dad's Army – "remember that if you put to one side a task that you fear will be difficult or boring or likely to demand more time than you can spare at the moment, it will grow and grow in your mind, and become a more and more terrifying bugbear, until in the end you will be too frightened of it to tackle it at all. Whereas if you get on with it straightaway, you'll usually find that it's perfectly manageable after all." Verb. sap., I've found, on the whole, apart from the last bit. (Tom Williamson, he was called. He dropped down dead at the age of about 48 or 50, apparently from the strain of swimming every morning, winter and summer, in Highgate Pond. He also advised me, on that very first occasion, never to try to be funny in writing on an official file, a temptation I have successfully failed to resist.)

J. is right, as always, about our Visa Section. It does a very good, fair and speedy job. The huge proportion of fraudulent applications, especially now that Nigeria is in deep recession, and the vast number of supporting documents that prove to be forged, make careful scrutiny unavoidable, the honest as usual the victims of the crooked. This is not racist, just factual. How the queues waiting outside the building during the peak season behave is not something we can do anything much about, since we already have a massive building with a lot of space in which people can wait once they get inside in air-conditioned comfort, but there is a limit to how many can get inside at one time, and there are fire regulations limiting numbers too. We try to disseminate information about the procedures and the forms, etc., but the touts and con-men still prey on the queues, selling promised favours and wheezes which they can't deliver. Our rate of rejection of visa applications is about a quarter that of the Americans. The Americans give no right of appeal against a rejection; we do, in every case (but very few exercise it because most know that they have been rumbled). But I don't suppose your colleague, our critic, Juliana, will believe any of this.

We had a dinner party last night to celebrate the 70th birthday of a very special and distinguished Nigerian, the first to qualify as a Chartered Accountant, and a man widely known as completely incorruptible (rare, alas). The other guests, chosen by A.W. (the guest of honour) included a former Nigerian Ambassador in Washington who had been in the embryo diplomatic mission in London before independence and had come to have a squalid dinner with J. and me in Putney in our bed-sitter when we were first married; and it turned out that 4 of the 14 of us round the table had attended the Nigerian Constitutional Conference in Lancaster House in 1958. I suppose what all this proves is that we were all incredibly old.

Louise's Birthday, 1989.   Nigerian politics are as unpredictable as ever. As part of the programme for the return to civilian rule (to be completed in October 1992), the military government last May removed the ban on forming political parties, and set down guide-lines for deciding in October which two (maximum) of the new parties would be registered and thus permitted to contest the local, State and finally national elections due to be held between now and October 1992. Frantic political activity ensued, with a mass of groups and associations splitting, merging, coalescing and subdividing, with millionaire businessmen and straw figures acting as front men for the disqualified (and discredited) politicians of the last civilian regime bumping, boring – especially boring – and manoeuvring bald-headed for the ascendancy. Party offices, flags, logos and slogans, programmes and manifestos (all wholly indistinguishable from one another), national office-holders and obscure committees, proliferated like weeds. By the date for applications to be registered (only two to be chosen), 13 parties had emerged. The National Electoral Commission chose 6 of these as coming nearest to obeying the guidelines, while accusing all of rampant cheating, and handed the 6 over to the Armed Forces Ruling Council to make its decision on which 11 of the 13 should be thrown off the sleigh to the wolves. Not a matter to be taken lightly, especially for those who had spent millions of Naira to buy a ticket to power and (especially) fortune!

The President lived up to his nickname – Maradona – and confounded everyone by declaring that none of the 6, still less of the 13, came up to his required scratch. All were disbanded, with the stress on the 'banned', with instant effect. The military government would set up the two parties itself, one "a little bit to the left, the other a little bit to the right of centre". They would be called the Democrats and the – yes – Republicans (good stuff, eh?). A Committee would write their party programmes and any variations would have to be approved by the military government. Members would have to join at local level and the leaders would have to seek election from the bottom tier – no fat cats starting their own parties from the top down.

Well, a deafening howl of rage and frustration went up from the thwarted pols, and from their bank managers, but the general public seemed rather pleased by the whole thing, and indeed it deserves to succeed, even if it does smack a little (or a lot) of managed democracy. When J. and I were up in the north a few weeks ago (Kaduna, Kano and Daura) we talked to some of the party leaders of the now-defunct 13, still burning and smouldering. In general the professional politicians are not impressive, quite openly in it for power and influence (that rather than money – indeed it seems a costly rather than a profitable business for all but a handful at the very top), few of them giving any indication of interest in public service, reform, helping the disadvantaged, etc. However we both suspect that the same old gang will manipulate and spend themselves up through whatever system the military can devise and pop out at the top as the new leaders, however contemptuously they might be regarded by the generality of people.

BRIAN BARDER'S DIPLOMATIC DIARY

The trip to Daura up in the far north, on the border with the Republic of Niger, was mainly to attend the annual Durbar to mark the Prophet's Birthday. All the local chiefs and subordinate rulers come along to pay homage to the Emir of Daura in a big day of processions, horse-riding in elaborate costumes (worn by the horses too), entertainments, dancing, etc. All these characters are heavily armed (guns, spears, heavy swords, machetes) and do a lot of pretty impressive macho shouting to demonstrate to the Emir and his court that they are extremely tough warriors. The only snag to the day was having to drive back to Kano in the dark, an undesirable thing to do but in this case unavoidable if we were to attend the Durbar at all: the road is infested with armed robbers after dark, as well as bad and unlit, most of the vehicles on it have no lights, and after only a few minutes the windscreen becomes thickly encrusted with smashed insects, making the chances of running into some unlit vehicle in front quite a reality. Fortunately all was well. Dodgy, but safer than local flying, I suppose.

Now we are in the thick of planning the next trip, starting at the crack of dawn on Sunday 19 Nov: in one of Shell (Nigeria)'s Dorniers to Obudu, a cattle ranch on the edge of the Mambilla Plateau in Cross River State; up to Yola for formal calls on the Governor, traditional ruler, etc.; across to Makurdi for more formal calls and to see the VSOs doing their thing locally; then by road through Enugu to Benin City, for 2 days of calls there; and back to Lagos on the Saturday. It will be wearing, with lots of mustard-keen people coming along and building dawn starts into each day's programme, but should be fun.

The British High Commissioner's residence in Lagos, late 1980s.

Barder presenting his credentials to President Babangida, 1988.

HOME ... NEWS AT HOME ... NEWS AT HOME

Alhaji Abubakar Alhaji (right) discussing with the British High Commissioner, Mr. Brain L. Barder during the visit. Photo: ADEBOLA IDOWU.

"Brain" Barder in "New Nigerian", 3 Sep 1988.

Barder with Emeka Anyaoku, Obosi, Christmas 1988.

Top: Jane with children in Nigeria.

Bottom: Barder and Denis Thatcher, Lagos Airport, March 1989.

Top: Barder and Margaret Thatcher, Lagos Airport, March 1989.
Bottom: Ambassador's residence, Lagos, Christmas 1989.

CHAPTER 35

NOV 1989:
GONGOLA, BENUE, BENDEL
STATES, LAGOS

Lagos, 28 November 1989.   We had a good but pretty grueling tour of Gongola, Benue and Bendel States last week, preceded by 24 hours at a cattle ranch resort up in the hills by the Cameroon border, at about the same altitude as Nairobi's – i.e., compared with Lagos, cool, dry and delightful. We walked across the grassy hills in the sun, with the 2 Range Rovers (ours and Shell's) crawling along behind us to take us back when we had had enough. Thereafter it was all calls on Governors and traditional rulers, speeches and dinners and receptions. We called on a multi-millionaire in Benin City with a gigantic Cadillac and a white Rolls outside the front door, a small Lamborghini (also white) temporarily stored in the vast dining-room, champagne in all rooms and grapes flown in especially for our lunch there from Selfridge's (what's wrong with Fortnum's, I nearly asked?), gold cutlery and prawns the size of baby lobsters. You'd have loved it. We visited threatened rain-forest (too degraded to rescue in my not-very-expert opinion) and an ecologically hyper-responsible timber business. We called on Nigeria's only female Vice-Chancellor at her Nissen-hut university and received 25 specific requests for British aid, including an international student centre and a medical students hostel, not to mention the suggestion that British universities should teach grammar as part of their Eng. Lit. courses for the sake of Nigerians who don't speaka da lingo so good. We watched a lot of Cultural Displays (means tribal dancing, invariably – I'm sad to say – demurely clad). I explained in numerous press, radio and TV interviews why sanctions against S. Africa are a bad idea but all they ever printed or transmitted was hopelessly garbled misinterpretations of what I also said about the gargantuan aid programme bestowed on Nigeria by the warm-hearted British tax-payer. I forgot to tell the multi-millionaire about our aid programme, now I think about it.

Our Range Rover, flying rather a large Union Jack, broke down conspicuously on the main roundabout in the middle of Benin City at midday on a Friday and had to be pushed by a sweating policeman and protocol officers to the side of the road. A mechanic then had to come out from Lagos to repair the Range Rover but the Land Rover he came in kept on breaking down too. Not an especially sexy advertisement for our tough, go-anywhere British vehicles.

Time for a chaste vodka martini before lunch, then off to a multi-national football tournament which we have to attend part of because Jane has recklessly agreed to present the trophies.

CHAPTER 36

APRIL-AUG 1990:
LAGOS, KANO, JOS,
KADUNA, ABUJA

Lagos. April 1990

Life in Lagos doesn't somehow lend itself to narrative journals of the kind I've been sending round to friends for a few years from previous posts. There's too much sameness. When you've extracted all the humour, farcical potentiality and colour from (say) a courtesy call on some traditional ruler in his ramshackle corrugated-iron palace ("Your Excellency, it is a great honour and pleasure ... my people are suffering from ... because of our historic connexions we look to Britain ... just a modest residential school complete with staff ... before We wish Your Excellency Godspeed, hope We may seek your immediate intervention to settle a small problem over Our niece's visa ..."), it doesn't leave a lot more to say after the next identikit tour. There's a tranquillising sameness about the scenery: when you've seen one bit of the coastal mangrove swamp, you've seen it all, ditto the central savannah and ditto the northern arid belt along the Sahara. We're glad to have seen them, but only moderately excited about the prospect of going on seeing it indefinitely.

We have a brief tour coming up with the usual round of official visits in Akure, capital of Ondo State (western, Yoruba, cocoa), and when we have done that we shall have visited and done our official calls in all 21 of the State capitals and the Federal Capital Territory of Abuja – so we'll be ready for this year's leave starting, we hope, on 4 May and lasting until 11 July. We shall go and stay with Gerry and Betty Ratzin in Paris for a few days in mid-May and then go and stay in the Ockendens' house at Cadenet near Aix for a week or two – Owen and his girl-friend stayed there last year and said it was delectable, and it should provide excellent opportunities for wrecking my diet. Apart from that we shall be in London as usual, and hopeful that you might put in an appearance …

We've just emerged blinking into the far side of a 4-day visit to Nigeria by the Prince & Princess of Wales – now known familiarly to all of us in the High Commission as 'TRH'. The 2 – 3 months of single-minded slog by most of my quite large staff kept everyone fully occupied on preparing for and planning the royal visit to the exclusion of just about everything else. Now we have the tricky task of explaining to the trade experts in London why we haven't made any progress for 4 months in drawing up our Commercial Strategy and setting ourselves Objectives, Personal Job Targets, Performance Indicators, Bonus Criterion Markers, and all the rest of the trendy jargon which has taken over the FCO like an epidemic. We could say: "Sorry, we haven't had time because of the royal visit," I suppose, which would be true, but it doesn't sound like fluent Management-Speak.

Anyway, They came, accompanied by the Royal Yacht and an escorting frigate, two aircraft of the Queen's Flight and a cast of thousands. It was exceedingly hot, even for Nigeria, and HerRH was terrified of giving the escorting British press rat-pack the story of the month by fainting on camera, but by tungsten-hard will-power contrived not to. We all flew about together in the royal Bae 146, Jane and me sharing the royal compartment with TRH, the Nigerian Minister of Culture and the nice lady Permanent Secretary of the MEA. I can now reveal, as they say, that HerRH is a quick-change artist of considerable talent, in addition to her other accomplishments. It was lucky, I suppose, that we'd been blooded last year by being In Attendance at the State Visit by President and Mrs Babangida, when 4 days' solid exposure to B. Palace, its courtiers and a nightly banquet in white tie and tails made us feel that nothing in this line of country would ever again cause us more than an anxious twinge of apprehension. So we're great hob-nobbers with the royals, these days. All slightly out of character, you might say, and you might be right, but nice in some ways to look back on.

left to right: Jane Barder;
Diana, Princess of Wales;
Mrs Babangida;
Lagos, March 1990

Politically, Nigerian-British relations have been on a faintly unreal high almost ever since we arrived (July 1988), sustained by a substantial British aid programme and a lot of high-level visiting in both directions. All this has hugely increased the High Commission's work-load compared with the relatively quiescent few years preceding our arrival. Needless to say, the management at home has responded to this by cutting our staff and our budget, while wringing its hands and thanking us all profusely for doing such a grand job. The Treasury has apparently relapsed into one of its demented campaigns to cut public spending and as the diplomats famously have no constituency and no sympathisers, we are naturally the fall guys. Perhaps the truth is that it doesn't really make that much difference anyway. But it does make for rather long hours. Meanwhile we are the Nigerian Government's blue-eyed boys, an unfamiliar role for the Brits here, and I can't so much as go for a hair-cut (or at any rate a beard trim, since cutting my hair these days is a complete non-event) without getting my picture in 8 Nigerian newspapers the next day, often with pictures of Jane and Mrs Thatcher thrown in for good measure. Fame at last.

The rather vague expectation seems to be that I'll be moved ("Now then, move along, please") some time earlyish next year to my last job before retirement, although where that might turn out to be is not yet in even the Divine consciousness, so far as I can make out, never mind the human. I expect, without too much confidence, that someone will tell me in due course. When that happens, I'll let you know. If, alternatively, I am eventually told by some embarrassed functionary that "most unfortunately ... nothing terribly suitable at the right time ... absolutely no reflection ... extraordinarily good job ... frightfully grateful ... remarkably favourable terms, actually" – we shall crack the last bottle of bubbly and sleep the sleep of the just. The prospect is far from unpleasing and it's nice to know that whatever happens, in less than 5 years and in one bound, Jack will be Free.

Lagos – July 1990.   We have a ceremony at the Residence at which I formally present the insignia of his Honorary CBE to a very prominent and distinguished Nigerian businessman with strong British connexions, Chief S. The guests invited to witness the formalities and to celebrate them in champagne include a good selection of the local captains of industry, Nigerian and British; members of Chief S.'s family and his friends; and two rather senior traditional rulers, a northern Emir and a western Yoruba Alake among whose subjects the honorand, Chief S., is numbered. The Emir and the Alake arrive with the usual substantial entourages, ranging from pretty wild-looking tribesmen who have to be plied with chicken, rice and Coca-Cola at the back of the house, to smart ADCs, Prime Ministers and buglers who line the walls of the reception, not drinking, but certainly adding a touch of class to the proceedings. The Emir's Chief Bugler blows a few random fanfares from time to time, presumably when moved by pride or boredom, bringing speeches and cocktail conversation to a momentary halt. The two Rulers sit side by side on a large settee bestowing gracious nods on those of their subjects who come or are brought over to them to pay their respects. The Alake's Chamberlain explains to me in a discreet murmur that Their Royal Highnesses will of course remain seated for the presentation, speeches and toasts. The whole thing is generally judged a considerable success.

Kano, Jos, Kaduna and Abuja – August 1990.   Delivering a dryish lecture after dinner at a dubious local hotel on the economic theories of Adam Smith and their present-day relevance to a bemused mass meeting of the Rotary Clubs of Kano may not be everybody's cup of warm Sprite, but it makes a change and provoked surprisingly sharp questions, including one from a local Nigerian farmer about Britain's current fad topic, Mad Cow Disease. Having just that moment given up the unequal struggle with my own piece of Kano Cow, I was disinclined to slag off our own home beef industry in reply. Our British steaks, medium rare, may come from crazy beasts, but at least they generally yield to dedicated chewing.

We had a warm but embarrassed welcome in Jos from our generous host, the leading British businessman, head of the local power supply company (the only such enterprise in the Nigerian private sector). He was embarrassed on two counts: our arrival coincided with his first power cut in several years; and the comfortable guest-house in his compound where he had planned to accommodate 3 of our party had just been the object of the attention of a group of armed robbers who had stripped it right down to the plaster – refrigerators, television set, cutlery and crockery, beds, tables and chairs, curtains and carpets, the lot. However he had secured instead the VIP lodge of the main Jos hostelry, the nostalgically-named Hill Station Hotel, redolent of the days when the British Colonial Service officers and their wives moved up to the relative cool of the Jos Plateau during the hotter months from the steamy mangrove swamps and the baking savannah. The Hill Station VIP Lodge looked after our out-housed party almost as well as our mortified hosts, and we were exceedingly well fed and watered – a welcome relief after the Kano Rotary steaks.

As usual this visit had its comical moments. We thought we had an appointment with the traditional ruler in Jos, who enjoys the title of His Royal Highness The Gbong Gwom (the first 2 Gs – in Highness and Gbong – are silent as in Gnu). So we turned up at his crumbling cement bungalow ("His Royal Highness the G G's Palace") and were asked to wait a moment in big leaking armchairs. Jane asked whether they had received the message that she and Mrs. G. would like to make a separate courtesy call on His Highness's two wives. Consternation, hurried consultations, messengers sent off at a brisk sprint, return, whispers. "Come this way." The ladies led off across grubby yards into a dim room. Two bewildered ladies produced, neither speaking a word of English. Exchange of courtesies through equally bewildered courtier, whose attempts to explain who Jane is are evidently unsuccessful. Jane and Ms. G. return to our waiting-room. We ask if the Highness is soon likely to be ready to receive us. After more consultations we are told that unfortunately His <u>Royal</u> Highness is out to lunch. Back at the Managing Director's house we are told that the Gbong Gwom's senior wife (of 2) died the previous day. So who were the two bewildered ladies? Alas; we shall never know.

Kaduna: lunch with C. and L. W., head of our Kaduna office and his wife, at the Jacaranda Out (a jokily-named establishment run by the former proprietors of the Jacaranda Inn). Enjoy the views over the rolling northern plains, the Chinese garden, the little water-fall and the linked ponds. Some of these are inhabited by still smallish but authentically homicidal-looking crocodiles, kept as a sort of exotic decoration, and prevented from escaping only by rough stone walls a few feet high and topped by a concrete overhang. It seems to me that as they grow bigger the crocs will make short work of these defences, scaling the battlements, waddling briskly into the open-air dining area and making the guests who happen to be enjoying their repasts at the time into tasty hors-d'oeuvres.

Abuja is to be Nigeria's new capital, although there is not much evidence of this so far apart from a splendid British-managed Hilton Hotel and an immense, gilded, Saudi-financed mosque. The Ministry of External Affairs has just recently been given a 3-week deadline to transfer here from Lagos, and is currently trying to get established in uncompleted buildings originally ear-marked for the offices and staff housing of the Ministry of Education (the educators, still in Lagos, have been temporarily reprieved). Senior diplomats of the Foreign Ministry are to be seen everywhere, desolate, shell-shocked or in a mood of grim defiance, searching for someone to order the installation of a roof over their flats or houses or of power and water supplies to the Ministry's new offices. Clearly it is going to be months before they are ready to resume normal business with the Embassies and High Commissions – all of them 10 hours' drive away in Lagos. Meanwhile perhaps we should all go on extended leave.

CHAPTER 37

AUG 1990:
LAGOS

(A letter written by Jane Barder)

22 August 1990. FCO (Lagos).

Dear James,

We are both delighted to receive your letters with news of Addis. We all think frequently, and with nostalgia, of the Residence, the compound, and Ethiopia in general. Derek Day told Brian before we went to Addis that we would never again live in such a beautiful Residence. So far he has been right. For us, as far as Residences are concerned, it has been downhill all the way. In Warsaw we had a grandiose black marble cube, built by MOW in the '60s, with no regard to the climate or the architectural style of Warsaw. All the clockwork electrics which powered central heating, water, blinds and curtains were seizing up after 25 years. OED told us that they didn't have enough money to do anything about it. Our successors must have been even more pressing than us, because I gather that during their tenure they closed the Residence down and moved into a hotel while essential work was carried out. Here we live in a suburban house which the then High Commissioner moved into as a temporary measure in 1975 when the Nigerians confiscated our Residence. Various ad hoc additions have been built on at various times. It is still a small house with more or less useful extensions which have swallowed up most of the garden. Each QBP since 1986 we have bored people with the glories of the covered courtyard in Addis Ababa.

I must say, however, that fond as we were of the Addis Residence staff and well though we wish them, our staff here, contrary to most people's perception of African staff, are the best we have had. We tolerated Dafaru while finding his constant complaining about all the others a great trial. Abdullah was everybody's favourite and was a sweetie, but he was getting terribly deaf and irascible. Kurri was, of course, a constant worry. She did go through a very bad patch while we were there. I hope that she is now on an even keel. She was our first suspect for your ghost. Our daughter used to lock her door against Kurri at night. Beyene was butterfly brained – intelligent, but his train of thought was something else, we used to think. Teferi was a thug. Bekele was marvelous, in the Berhanu mould. While we were there life was dominated by demarcation disputes, with constant reference to the pillars in the hall. "Never since Sir Lascelles, or Sir Busk, or Sir somebody else", they would say, pointing to the name carved in gold, "has it been my job to clean the patch of floor beyond such and such of carpet". After we had been there some weeks, I realized that nobody ever swept the terrace. I enquired about this and was told by Dafaru that that was Mohammed's job. We had no Mohammed working for us. I then discovered that Mohammed had been a gardener who had been a casualty of an Inspection about 18 months before we arrived. I then had to have great negotiations to get Kurri and Beyene to sweep the terrace as part of their joint duties in cleaning the bedroom corridor. For us it was our first 3rd world posting and therefore our first experience of dealing with staff. We were thrown in at the deep end but I think it was a useful start.

Our Polish staff, like the Addis staff, had been there forever. They were, like them, well trained and excellent. Like them, however, they were very demarcation conscious. Over the years, in common with all Residence staffs in Warsaw, they had achieved very feather-bedded conditions for themselves. I think that diplomats had generally felt sorry for Poles, quite rightly. The result was that (not only in the British Embassy), their hours of work did not, on the whole, coincide with the hours when they were actually needed. We used to think that the $ cash registers rang with the door bell.

Here, the staff are West African, multi-national and multi-lingual (a bit like the ECOWAS force). We have Nigerians, Togolese, Beninese, and Ghanaians. They have no quarrels. They will all cheerfully cover for anyone who is sick. Any one of them will clean anything that has been overlooked and discovered at a crucial time, whether it is a shirt, making a canape, or scrubbing a floor. They are delightful. I wish it would rub off on their various governments.

I was interested by your references to C.B. and C.S. C.B. had been very much part of the family while Robert and Jean Tesh were there. I was told that one of them had been baptized by C.B., and both of them were confirmed during their time in Addis Ababa. He was very put out to learn that not only were we not church goers, but also that we were quite indifferent to religion. Neither of us care what people believe in as long as they don't frighten the horses. Nevertheless, we tried to make it clear to him that we treated his position with a great deal of respect. We would support him in any way we could, even attending church on special days, if he thought that was necessary. We made sure that he was invited to our first dinner party, and also that he was included for any other special functions. He seemed, however, to choose to interpret anything we did or said as being anti, either him or the church. I don't think that Christian charity was one of his virtues. The thing I found most surprising about him was that he seemed to have no idea of the meaning of confidence. He was an obvious person to approach about pastoral problems, affecting individuals or even charity enterprises. I would get his assurance that what I was consulting about was in some kind of confidence, and, as an inadequately, by today's standards, trained social worker, I still observe those confidences. Time after time, right until we left, I found that having asked for his help for one of his flock, he had told them, and others, exactly what I had talked to him about.

It is not breaking any confidence, I think, because it must be on file somewhere, to mention that in about 1985 he applied for the job of Anglican Priest in Rome. He did not give Brian's name as a reference. I suppose he thought that as part of this anti-church attitude Brian would ditch his chances. However, the Bishop of Gibraltar, or whoever deals with that part of the world, and the Ambassador in Rome wrote to Brian to ask him both for a reference and to ask why he had not been given as a reference in the first place. Brian wrote a very good reference for him. He was asked to keep the enquiry in confidence so we never mentioned this to C. He obviously did not get the job, but it used to annoy me when I was told how devoted he was to his mission in Ethiopia, knowing that he was trying to move elsewhere.

C.S., we thought, was a different kettle of fish. He struck us as much brighter than C.B. Funnily enough it was partly because of an intervention by C.B. that negotiations to get Esme's house for the Embassy, at a time when we needed an extra house because of expansion during the famine crisis, broke down. Even I, I suppose, can't think that he already had his eye on it for his curate!

I am writing this letter, while downstairs Brian is giving a lunch to try and secure Nigeria's vote for Manchester to house the 1996 Olympics. It reminds me of a much larger party we had to give in Addis for Birmingham's bid, when the African Olympic Committee was meeting in Addis. Everyone had their delegations in. Birmingham had sent us a video, but it was interrupted by advertisements. It was over the Christmas period and all our children were there for their last Christmas in Addis, plus assorted boyfriends and girlfriends. They edited out the advertisements down at the club, and managed to get the video on some kind of a loop. Birmingham, led by Denis Howell, turned up in full force. So did – my main memory – a huge Dutch Judo Gold Medallist. The young went on, with the RAF who were in their closing days, to Castelli's and persuaded the huge Dutchman to dance on a table, while they sang some English song (it was before the days of 'Ere we go, I think). They then went on to a party at the Hilton. It didn't get the Olympics for Birmingham, but they have always remembered it. The other event they always remember is our New Year's Party, I think in 1984/1985. We decided that this was going to be the best party of our lives. We thought our children would probably never again take pity on their old parents by coming out to spend Christmas wherever they might be (they have in fact been very good and we have never been entirely without family for Christmas). We used all the Residence – Disco dancing on the terrace with a bar in the morning room, Golden Oldies in the Durbar Hall, with a bar in the courtyard, Brideshead Revisited all night in the study with a bar in the drawing room, breakfast from 2.30 in the dining room.

We shall never have a party like it. It was the middle of the famine. We had all the relief workers from all over Ethiopia, and collected* a lot of money in the Hall. We felt we should have an in-house letting down of hair and, for a few hours, forget tragedy.

It was a marvelous house for a party. Enjoy it.

Best wishes,

Jane

* "Tell a lie" – we didn't collect money at New Year's Eve – decided to live in a time warp. We did collect money – for that year only – at the carol party we used to give for the British Community on Christmas Eve: we divided it between local Oxfam and local SCF.

PART VII:

Looking Back,
Christmas 1992

CHAPTER 38

DEC 1992:
CANBERRA

(From a Christmas round-robin letter by Jane Barder)

10 December 1992.   c/o FCO (Canberra), King Charles Street, LONDON
SW1A 2AH

Christmas has crept up on us again and, as usual, I (J.) am unprepared to write
the cards. When a rainy day is a disappointment because we are hoping for summer, it is difficult to make the psychological leap to thoughts of Christmas. We
should be used to it. I have just worked out that we have experienced 12 summer Christmases during our overseas postings. We had 9 winter Christmases in
New York, Moscow, Canada and Warsaw. In the last 29 years we have been at
home for 8 Christmases. One of those marked a new stage in our lives. In 1990,
after 7 consecutive Christmas Days abroad, we managed to be at home for our
granddaughter's first Christmas. Lily Wen, aged 7 weeks, won't remember it, but
we shall add it to our Christmas memories. She spent her second Christmas in
Australia with us.

We shall also remember Christmas trees on Park Avenue and Christmas decorations on Fifth Avenue in New York; Father Frost and the Snow Maiden and glass
tree decorations in Moscow; the arrest of John Stonehouse and the blowing away

of Darwin by Cyclone Tracy in Australia on Christmas Eve, 1974; the hideous discomfort of buying and transporting a Christmas tree from Canadian Tyre in a Canadian blizzard in 1977; Feed The World and the RAF in Addis Ababa in 1984; our maid queuing for 6 hours for Christmas tree lights in Warsaw (had we known where she was we would have told her to abandon the quest), and Kazimierz delightedly performing his annual feat of getting 9 Christmas puddings alight at the same time for the Warsaw Embassy staff party; Christmas shopping in Lagos to the tune of "I'm Dreaming of a White Christmas".

I remember too bursting into unexpected tears of homesickness last year when I found myself in a Christmas decoration department in a store on the Queensland Gold Coast. It was a reminder that even after all these happy years there is an underlay of yearning for home.

We are beginning to count the months until Brian's retirement in June, 1994. We have no qualms at all about this now that we are on the last posting. I know that to all outward appearances we have led very sheltered lives and no doubt look as if we shall get a nasty shock when we return to live in the UK rather than just visiting for leave. We, on the other hand, have now experienced a good many other imperfect systems and, as Churchill said about democracy, believe that our system might be very faulty but that it is better than any alternative.

At least we'll be able to complain about it, which will be a great relief. Abroad it would be undiplomatic to complain about the host country, and we are paid to praise the UK, not to criticize it. We shall revert to student-type activism, which will be very appropriate since we shall be living on a student-type income. Economic recovery led by public sector pay restraint won't do much for Brian's pension. Still, Christmas and 18 months to retirement are not the time to go into that, and we know we shall be vastly better off than most pensioners, some wage-earners and above all the unemployed.

This is my first attempt at a round-robin Christmas message and somehow it hasn't turned out to be the usual digest of a year's happenings, although it probably does express our current preoccupations. I'll finish on a more traditional note.

Virginia still lives in Tooting and is still very much in demand as a free-lance interactive media consultant. She will start getting paid all that she is worth once the recession is over, but meanwhile she seems to be doing all right.

Eric, Lily and Louise moved to New York in January, back to Wandsworth in July and will be moving into a house in north Oxford in December, if they get back from 3 weeks in New York in time. Lily has crossed the Atlantic more times than Princess Beatrice [who she? –B.]. She (Lily) was in Wandsworth for her second birthday.

Eleanor works all hours as a barrister, which is just as well because otherwise she might complain about Owen working all hours (he is Assistant Private Secretary to the Chancellor of the Exchequer). He is too loyal a public servant to tell us whether Mr Lamont follows his advice and we are frightened to ask. We're sure he is doing his best.

Brian's speeches about the GATT are skillfully drafted and a joy to hear …. It has been a difficult 6 months to represent the British Presidency

END

BRIAN IN HIS RETIREMENT

Brian and Jane
visiting Berhanu
and his family
during a return
visit to Ethiopia
in 2009.

Brian with Jane, his children and his grandchildren, NYC Nov 2016.

ACKNOWLEDGEMENTS

Had Brian lived to see his diary published, we know he would have been chuffed. He was thrilled at the idea and possibility of his dusty old papers seeing the light of day.

Sincere thanks to all his lifelong friends who challenged, amused, engaged and quarreled with him, and who were very much in his thoughts until his death. They are the people for whom he wrote this diary: many of them are in it, or became his friends while he was writing it.

We -- Virginia, Louise, Owen, Lily and Flo -- miss our Dad and Grandad so much, and we thank him for leaving us this precious document of his life. Thanks to our many friends who encouraged us to put this diary into print; to Jonathan Steele for his poignant obituary; to Tom Hull who proofread the diary with such care and enthusiasm; to Adrian Merrick for her lovely cover design; to Brian Kannard for his publishing guidance; and to Richard Jopson and Rachel Stadlen for their invaluable eyes, words and wisdom.

Finally, on Brian's behalf, we want to thank our mother, Jane Barder, the love of his life, without whom he wouldn't have been the man, husband, father, grandfather, friend or diplomat that he was. And we're sure he would have thanked us for putting this simple truth in his diary.